CW00688227

IT'S THE WORLD'S BIRTHDAY TODAY

IT'S THE WORLD'S BIRTHDAY TODAY

FLAKE

Translated by Marshall Yarbrough

RARE BIRD
LOS ANGELES, CALIF.

THIS IS A GENUINE RARE BIRD BOOK

Rare Bird Books
453 South Spring Street, Suite 302
Los Angeles, CA 90013
rarebirdbooks.com

FIRST HARDCOVER EDITION

Set in Minion
Printed in the United States

10 9 8 7 6 5 4 3 2 1

Library of Congress Cataloging-in-Publication Data

Names: Flake, 1966– author. | Yarbrough, Marshall, translator.
Title: It's the world's birthday today / written by Christin 'Flake' Lorenz;
translated by Marshall Yarbrough.
Other titles: Heute hat die Welt Geburtstag. English
Description: Los Angeles : Rare Bird Books, 2020.
Identifiers: LCCN 2020013247 | ISBN 9781644280638 (hardback)
Subjects: LCSH: Flake, 1966– | Rammstein (Musical group) |
Rock musicians—Germany—Biography.
Classification: LCC ML420.F554 A3 2020 | DDC 782.42166092 [B]—dc23

LC record available at https://lccn.loc.gov/2020013247

Ich habe endlich keine Träume mehr
Ich habe endlich keine Freunde mehr
Hab endlich keine Emotionen mehr
Ich habe keine Angst vorm Sterben mehr

"Alles Grau," Isolation Berlin

At last, I don't have dreams anymore
At last, I don't have friends anymore
No emotions at all anymore
I'm not afraid of dying anymore

"Everything's Gray," Isolation Berlin

I wrote this book on tour, in my downtime on the bus or at the concert. Any resemblance to actual persons or events is the result of my lack of imagination and is not intentional.

I'VE LOST ALL SENSE of what time it is. Our flight left this morning, and the clock on my phone automatically resets whenever the plane even gets close to a new time zone. Inch by inch the bus makes its way through the city center. Budapest seems to be pretty big. We're stuck in rush-hour traffic. Today is Friday; everybody wants to get out of the city as fast as they can. But fast is not an option here.

I look out the window. My view extends about two feet—to a big, dirty delivery truck in the next lane. Even it moves faster than us. Our driver has no patience for this situation; whenever he spots the tiniest opening, he floors it, and I get thrown back into my seat, which doesn't smell very good. Immediately he has to brake again, and I lurch forward. When the truck passes us, it opens up the view of a gray wall. So we do seem, ever so slowly, to be approaching the outskirts. I would have preferred to sit up front, but the driver has all his stuff laid out on the seat next to him, and he gave me a weird look when I tried to open the passenger door. Like I'd tried to climb into bed with him.

In the back, I feel so cast off, like I'm luggage. Like I don't have any say. Plus I enjoy talking to the drivers—a lot of times they're our only real point of contact with the country we happen to be in. Right now I'd like to ask him about the music that's blaring out of the speakers.

I found out about a new band in a shuttle bus one time. Or at least the band was new to me. Their music sounded very urgent and kept jumping between different loops, almost like a record skipping. I was totally fascinated, and I asked the driver who the band was. We were in Barcelona, and I couldn't really understand what the driver was saying. That wasn't his fault: I speak neither Spanish nor passable English. And so he just pulled the CD out of the CD player and gave it to me. Or at least that's what I assumed was happening. When I got back to Berlin, I proudly played the CD for my daughter. I wanted to show her that even at my age, I was still with it, still had my finger on the pulse. I tried to explain to her that I liked this music so much because it sounded as if a broken record were randomly determining the melody. All it took was a glance at the CD player display for my daughter to figure out that the CD was actually just skipping. The look she gave me is indescribable.

I do still like listening to that CD, though. It's meditative, in a way, and plus you really can't predict when it's going to skip. It doesn't feel like I'm listening to a piece of recorded music; rather, it's like I'm an active participant in the listening experience. I always hear something new.

The song that was just playing, which I also really liked, has finished. Now comes the news—also in Hungarian, of course—which means it's too late to ask about the last song. I don't know how else I could start a conversation with the driver, he makes such a tight-lipped impression. Not that there's anything to talk about at the moment. When I got in, all he wanted to know was if anyone else was going to ride with us. Assuming I understood him correctly. And I couldn't even answer this simple question, because now that we all sleep in separate hotel rooms, I never know where the others are.

I'd hoped we would all ride to the venue together, but when I came down, I was the only one of us standing there, and so the driver drove off with just me. The others probably know how pointless it is to leave at this time of day. Assuming it really is what time I think it is.

I've also had it happen that the clock hasn't reset itself after we've flown back from a concert somewhere far away—at any rate, I can't rely on the clock on my phone anymore. And you can't even trust the TV, since the networks all broadcast from different countries. If it's three o'clock in England, it'll be much later here.

In Australia, there are even time differences of a half hour. Sometimes a city will be split between two different time zones, with the dividing line running right through the middle. There you can't even make it to the dentist on time. It might be like that in America, too. In Hartford or someplace.

It was in Hartford that we once climbed up a railroad bridge on a dare. If I'd spent less time sitting around the house as a kid and more time playing with the other kids, I wouldn't have had to do this kind of thing at a much older age when the fear is that much greater. Naturally a train came, and right when we'd reached the middle of the bridge. We had to press right up against the edge; there wasn't any railing, and when we looked between the crossties we could see straight down to the water. The train was infinitely long, which was probably why it moved so slowly, and it felt like an eternity until it was all over, especially since I spent the whole time staring at a run-over dachshund or raccoon that looked like a cut-open teddy bear. On this bridge, I had the opportunity to experience how elastic time can be, how much it can stretch out. Unfortunately, it usually tends to stretch out in unpleasant situations.

Like here on the bus, where it feels as though we've been driving forever. I'm not entirely without blame in this, since I insisted we book a hotel in the city center—that way all the sights are right there. Though the sights don't really interest me much. That may sound strange, but back in Berlin I don't ever go to TV Tower or the Brandenburg Gate. Meanwhile, most of the venues we play are located outside of town so that the fans, whether they're our fans or the fans of the local soccer team, don't mess up the city's image. This works pretty well, and I can tell we're getting close to the venue because I can see quite a few fans on the sidewalk to the left and right of us. They've parked their cars on the side of the road and are now walking in little groups. On foot, they're faster than the bus.

I used to walk to the concert myself sometimes—it's not like I could get lost, I just followed the fans—but at the larger venues I sometimes had trouble getting backstage. The phones at these venues don't always work, and the security personnel aren't counting on somebody in the band just showing up at their doorstep. In Berlin, I once tried to take a taxi to the concert—that way I could drink a beer on the way and wouldn't have to leave my car somewhere. When we got to the venue, I asked the cab driver to take me to the stage entrance. I was a bit pressed for time, since I'd had a bunch of stuff I was trying to get done that afternoon and didn't leave until the last minute. When we play where we live, we basically have twice as much to do. I tend to forget that we have a concert. Anyway, I was trying to go to the artists' entrance.

"The end of the line's back there, big man!" said the driver, pointing toward the line of people snaking around the venue. All I could do was tell him

I was in the band. "No way, buddy!" He started laughing at me. "Rammstein's playing here tonight, you're not fooling anybody with a trick like that." When I carefully tried to explain to him that I was playing *with* Rammstein, he answered with brutal logic: "If you," and here he had to laugh again, "were playing tonight, then you wouldn't be sitting here in my cab." And with that he dropped me at the end of the line. That's why now I just take the bus that the organizers provide for us.

Out the window, an ugly industrial area comes into view. That means I'll be there soon. I peer out the dirty windows for a closer look. There are our big nightliners, the buses the crew sleeps on. Not right now, of course, but at night, when they're driving to the next concert. A short distance away, I can see something that looks like a convention center or a sports arena. A parking lot stretches out in front. Everything is gray. And this is supposed to be rock 'n' roll?

—

Rock 'n' roll isn't what it used to be, I would say, and hasn't been for a long time. Of course, it's an open question whether I'm qualified to speak on the subject simply because I play music. Come to think of it, I'm pretty clueless when it comes to most things. And rock 'n' roll—what is it, anyway? Wasn't it that peppy music our parents used to listen to? Or was it our grandparents? Weren't they the ones who saw that Bill Haley guy play at the Deutschlandhalle shortly after the war? Or was it the Waldbühne? For us kids from East Germany, it was all the same, neither venue meant much to us, and even later, as teenagers, we didn't know much more than the Cultural Center—we called it the *Kulti*—and the House of Young Talent. Of course, some of the talent that played there was already pushing seventy, but they were playing blues, so it was all right.

It might sound hard to believe, but when I was young there weren't any old rock musicians, since rock 'n' roll was itself so young. Back then, Mick Jagger was twenty years younger than I am now. Just think about that. I was also of the firm opinion that once you turned thirty you weren't allowed to play rock music anymore. And no jazz before thirty. Nowadays, too, you have to be at least forty before they let you be chancellor.

I was talking about rock music. By my day, they'd already dropped the 'n' *roll* part. Not even the kids who got held back a grade said that anymore. They were talking about *hard rock*, which I of course heard as *hart rock*. I mean, who writes *hart* with a soft *d*? And the rock 'n' roll bands I knew played their songs more like museum pieces; when they played classics like "Sweet Little Sixteen," they were really trying to bring back that special feeling from back then, that particular lifestyle. A big part of this lifestyle of course was a leather jacket or a motorcycle. And jeans. When I was a kid, I actually heard an old lady complaining about these lousy *Jenshosen*. Like me, she had a hard time with the English words. As a rocker, you also had to hang around in little gangs. Obviously that was only something for really tough guys. Are heavy metal fans rockers? AC/DC is always singing about rock 'n' roll. And what about rockabilly fans? Do they also get to call themselves rockers? There were so many ways to mess up. Especially when punk came onto the scene. The unlucky ones never got to call themselves punks; they were immediately branded plastics.

Can you be a punk and still live with your parents? In my opinion, yes; after all, I didn't move out till I was twenty-three. If you were a punk, it also helped to have good connections in the West or at least a lot of money, because how else were you going to get combat boots? And a leather jacket? In the East you couldn't just go out and buy leather pants, you had to have them custom made. That meant it took about a year till you had the pants, and they really weren't cheap. A lot of punks I knew came from well-to-do families and could afford it. They got good grades and were very interested in current affairs. If they weren't in a band, they painted or wrote poems. Sometimes they did all three. All they had in common with their proletarian role models in England was their love of punk music and the fact that they could deal with being yelled at or beat up on the street. The career prospects weren't exactly overwhelming if you looked like a punk, but most of us were quite satisfied with our jobs at the post office, the senior center, or the cemetery. I never met anyone who really meant it when he painted *No Future* on his jacket. At most, they saw no future for themselves in East Germany, but a bright future in the West. Sometimes their exit visa was approved before their leather pants were finished; then I would ask if I could have them.

But it was rock 'n' roll we were talking about. Johnny Cash once said he could look out the bus window and know exactly where he was, give or take a few miles. I believe it. What he meant was that he traveled around America so much that he knew almost every stretch of road. He played an incredibly large number of concerts in his life. It wasn't unusual back then to play three hundred concerts a year. Or for bands to be on tour for years at a time. Now they're always breaking up at the first sign of trouble. Sometimes before I even knew they existed. But even I, who have been playing music for a few years myself, know at most a few roads in East Germany. The Hermsdorfer Kreuz and so on. Or the Schkeuditzer Kreuz, where the big Höffner furniture store is. Now, though, when we fly to our concerts, all I see is a few clouds. With them it's hard to get your bearings—by the next day they've already disappeared. I guess real rock 'n' roll happens on the street.

And then the women. The Stones had women standing in line outside their hotel rooms, patiently waiting their turn. That's impossible to imagine. Standing in line! Even from a purely technological standpoint, something like that could never happen today. These days, in hotels, you have to put your room key in a slot in the elevator, otherwise it won't budge. How are the women supposed to get up there? I consider myself lucky if I make it to the room myself.

If the stories are to be believed, musicians used to have sex before, during, and after the concert. And they radiated it, too. Every guitar solo was basically foreplay. Their shirts were always open down to their belly button. Nowadays you've got monogamous, politically engaged vegans up on stage, and as if that weren't bad enough, they're even sober. They've conscientiously prepared for the concert with yoga breathing exercises. And done stretches to warm up their muscles.

That's probably not all true. I probably just have a certain perspective on things because I've gotten so old. I suppose that too great a distance has opened up between my own meager life and rock 'n' roll. Assuming they were ever close in the first place. And that's doubtful, objectively speaking. Nor has anybody other than me ever noticed that for years I've thought of myself as a punk. Right! It's not because of my age. I'm a punk, not a rock 'n' roller. That's why I don't know what rock 'n' roll is, or how a rock 'n' roller is supposed to act. I don't know how a punk is supposed to act either, but I just feel better when I tell myself that I'm a punk.

I

I PULL AT THE zipper of my jacket with all my might, but it just won't budge. Probably because I sweat so much on stage—everything gets soaking wet and starts to rust in the dresser. I thought zippers were made of stainless steel and didn't rust, but this one here is totally stiff and won't move an inch.

"Got any guests?" a voice shouts in my ear. It sounds a little like Kermit the Frog, only much, much louder. I jump up and knock my elbow against the little table in front of the couch. The pain is like a lightning bolt coursing through my entire body. I'm so startled I slide off the couch.

"Got any guests?" Tom, our band assistant, looks at me, blank-faced. He's not tall, but very muscular, especially his face. And he wears giant horn-rimmed glasses, behind which you can barely see his eyes. Tom is nearsighted, which might be why he gets so close to the person he's talking to. Right now, he's working on getting the guest list finished. Because he has no interest in the alternative—hectically trying to radio the box office with the names that we shout at him at the last minute, right before the concert starts—he prefers to track everyone in the band down early in the afternoon to see if we want to put anyone on the list.

"Got any guests?" As I still haven't been able to answer him, he shouts it a third time. Actually he's not shouting; he just talks loudly. This is his normal on-the-job volume. Really he's totally calm and relaxed.

To stop him from yelling a fourth time, I quickly shake my head, and just to be on the safe side I say quite clearly: "No, thanks, I don't have any guests today."

Tom nods, satisfied; he figured that was the case. But better safe than sorry. This is something he's learned in years of dealing with musicians. But who am I supposed to know here in Budapest? It's true sometimes people I know who happen to be in the area will call me and ask to come to the concert, but that's really the exception, and whenever it does happen, I let Tom know right away. Just so I don't forget, and the people aren't standing desperate outside the venue later that night. I know that awful feeling when you set out to go to a show, full of eager expectation, and then don't get in. The guests can't reach me at that point, since I can't hear my phone so close to the concert. And so they stand sadly outside, watching all the people streaming into the hall and wondering where they went wrong in their lives. Counting on me was definitely one of the mistakes.

Tom storms out of the dressing room to go looking for the other guys in the band, and I turn back to my jacket. If I can't get the zipper to open, I won't be able to wear it tonight. See, the sparkle jacket, as I call it, because it sparkles like a disco ball when the light hits it, fits my body very tightly. It was lovingly tapered—or, no, I mean of course tailored—especially for me from sequined fabric, but since I sweat so much, it gets a bit tighter after every concert. Or I get a little fatter after every concert. One shouldn't always try and lay the blame elsewhere. This jacket is, of course, an essential part of the show. It's not like any one of us can just wear anything he feels like—people should be able to tell that we're a band. Besides, some clothing makes you invisible on stage. And I stand way in the back. I don't want to know what the band would say if I were to walk out on stage without my sparkle jacket—or, well, maybe they would even be happy, since my sparkle suit definitely makes me stand out, which doesn't sit well with everybody. We all want to be equals, after all. But it's kind of part of my character on stage that I look different than, for example, the guitarists. And nobody would buy it if I stepped out there all serious and mean-looking—the credibility of the whole band would suffer for it. The funnier I look, the meaner the others seem. It's like a police interrogation, where you've got the good cop and the bad cop.

I reach down to grab a soda from the blue plastic tub under the table. When I was a toolmaker, we would put rusty screws in soda to get them smooth again. I have to root deep down into the ice. All I can find is diet soda, but who cares. I pour it on the zipper. Most of it lands directly on the white tablecloth. For some strange reason, Tom is adamant about there being white tablecloths on the tables, even if most of the time they don't even last till the start of the concert. *What do we need white tablecloths for?* I think, and pull it off the table. The bowl of nuts comes off with it. I'm allergic to nuts. But since they're usually on the table, probably for the same reason as the white tablecloths, I'm always absentmindedly stuffing a whole bunch of them into my mouth. When my throat starts to itch and I can no longer breathe, I remember that I'm really allergic. I should ask them not to put any nuts in the dressing room, but ordering something is easier than canceling something, just like a wedding goes a lot quicker than a divorce. And in general nuts are very healthy, if you don't count the hydrogen cyanide.

Rather than leave them lying there on the floor, I gather up all the nuts and, since I can't find the bowl, I do actually end up stuffing them in my mouth. I'd completely forgotten how gross old nuts taste. It makes me think of fish oil, and I've never even tasted fish oil. I go looking for a bottle of water to get the taste out of my mouth. Again, I have to dig through the ice. At least I'm washing my hands—even if it is diet soda, it sure sticks to your fingers. Man, this water is cold. My fingers go numb. I'd much rather have a bottle of water that hasn't been sitting in ice for hours. But there's no warm water here, at least not bottled water, and so I put a few bottles out on the table for later so they can at least thaw. Is this what people mean when they talk about rock stars and their irrational demands?

The thing with the warm water is definitely a First World problem, but if I come off stage all hot and then drink ice-cold water, I get stomachaches, or I catch cold basically from the inside out and then I'm sick for days. Being sick on tour is a whole other story. Some code of honor dictates that only in the case of death can you justify canceling a tour date. At least that's what all the veteran musicians I've met have told me. And so I keep ending up on stage with a raging fever, feverishly looking forward to the end of the set. Then all the fire on stage makes me even hotter. It's almost like a treatment. I know the English word "treatment" because that's what the Ayurveda people say. I just really shouldn't breathe in the smoke—all the various toxins it contains have no place in the human body, whether you're sick or not. Usually after the concert I'm feeling a little better. Thanks to all the excitement, I've tuned out the aches and the general sickly feeling; it's only the next day that I really start to feel bad. Then I'm standing there at the airport, shivering, and have to suffer through long rides in the shiver—or I guess I mean shuttle—to the hotel or the venue. I long ever so intensely for a bed, somewhere where I can just lie down. These are dark hours. And so, who could hold it against me that I'm thinking of my health in advance and would rather not drink ice-cold water?

I stare blankly at the water bottles on the table. They slowly start to bead up with condensation; the first drops trickle hesitantly down the side. I wait for the soda to finally take effect. And when I think of the soda, it occurs to me that I could also drink some coffee—it too is supposed to wake you up. When was the last time I was actually awake? Even after drinking coffee, I have no problem falling asleep, but since I can fall asleep immediately, anywhere, I don't attach too much significance to that. The ability to fall asleep quickly is important if you want to be a musician. Someone who often goes to bed late should be able to make up the lost sleep in the daytime before climbing back up on stage.

I know a guitarist who falls asleep as soon as he sits down in the tour bus. He once told me of the trouble he has getting out of bed. If he stands up too quickly, he said, he gets lightheaded and his vision goes dark, then he falls back on the bed. But if he sits up slowly in bed, he smells his feet, and then he feels so ill that he again has to lie down. Compared to that, I've got it relatively easy. I'm just tired. And now I feel like having some coffee, so I head into the next room, because I assume I'll be able to find some coffee there. You see, Paul—one of our guitarists, whose dressing room this is—likes to drink a freshly brewed cup of coffee before the concert. Paul really makes the best of life with the band. He has the gift of being able to enjoy to the fullest all the trappings of success. He gets a huge kick out of talking shop with other bands we used to only know from the radio. It makes him happy to be recognized and greeted at festivals. He likes to go out to dinner at fancy restaurants and drink fine wine. Once he even bought himself a brand-new car! I envy this, but can't really pull it off myself. And Paul of all people can. Paul, who for years didn't even have a guitar case, but just wrapped his guitar in a plastic bag and carried it around like that. Paul, who as a young man seemed to subsist entirely on crackers. Who walked around in shoes that he'd found in a dumpster and immediately put on. Who even in our Feeling B days jumped off the stage as soon as the concert was over and spent the rest of the night dancing with the crowd. And now he's in a cozy little room that looks like it was clipped out of a catalog for cozy living.

The homey atmosphere immediately envelops me. Standing lamps give off a warm light, and I hear soft music. Oliver, our bassist, is lying on the sofa in workout clothes and trying to fall back asleep—Tom just asked him if he had any guests. I don't think Olli is bringing anyone tonight. But of course I don't know. Unfortunately, I know as good as nothing about him. Or at least I have no idea what goes on inside his head or what he thinks of this whole circus. It's supposed to be a trademark of bassists that they just stand there and play their parts without saying much, but that doesn't necessarily have to hold true for him. I've heard that he actually wanted to be a guitar player, and it was only because there was already a guitarist in his band that he picked up a bass. Bassists are known for stoically playing the same line for hours and hours, but Olli is much too impatient for that. I think that's a good thing, since it means he's always thinking up new ideas that none of us would ever come up with. Whether these ideas are actually realized is another story.

I shovel two spoonfuls of coffee into a cup and go to turn on the electric kettle, but the water is already hot. The dressing room looks so nice and tidy, I feel bad for spilling some of the coffee grounds. And now I've spilled some milk too—I have such a hard time opening these cartons. What you really need is a pair of scissors.

I walk quietly back to my dressing room. To make sure I don't get lost, the band assistant's assistant has stuck a laminated sheet with my and Till's names on the door. In the hallway are the other signs indicating which way to the stage, the catering room, and the production office. They get taken off and packed up every night after the concert. I never go to the production office— at most when I have guests and forget to tell Tom. And that actually can't happen. All the signs are in English, and at first we had to learn all the terms.

The first time I saw a sign for the "wardrobe," I assumed that some wiseass was trying to make a pun on *war*, since sometimes after a bad show we'll all yell at each other a little bit in the dressing room, and sometimes something gets knocked over. But other bands have "wardrobes" too, even Coldplay, and those guys are just about the quietest and most conscientious musicians you can imagine. In any case, I'm looking for my dressing room— sorry, wardrobe—and when I find it, I go inside. It wasn't that hard to find it; I mean, I was coming from the next room. Now I'm sitting on the couch again and pulling at the zipper. It still won't budge. Has the soda not had enough time to take effect?

My eyes wander over to the clock. In every dressing room, there's a discount-store clock on the wall. We pack them up with us after every concert, and the next day Tom hangs them up so they're nice and visible. One time our clock stopped because the battery was dead. That shows you how long we're on tour. Unless someone stole the battery. Needed it for a video game or something. That day we almost didn't make it out on stage on time. Well, okay, I'm being a little dramatic; most of the time we do manage to start on time. In this respect we're no punks, we're as orderly as German bureaucrats—assuming they're actually as orderly as I think.

—

THERE WAS YET ANOTHER new band. I just couldn't keep up anymore. Almost all the musicians I knew played in several bands at once, and each band played a completely different style of music.

I was hardly the exception; in fact, every time a new band was formed, I tried to play in it. On a given night, it could happen that we played in multiple bands that all shared the same bill. The band you'd started most recently was the most exciting one. If my bandmates got something else going with new people, I was of course happy for the new band, but at the same time I was also a little jealous. Why hadn't they asked me if I wanted to play with them?

When Paul joined Die Firma, I liked the music so much that I would ride with the band to their concerts as often as I could, even though I wasn't even playing with them. I just liked to hear them play. I was a male groupie. It works without sex, too. The main thing was that there was an open seat in the bus. Or in some other car. In this band, the whole approach to the music was different. Whatever had once been important to us, now nobody was interested. Nobody wanted to hear me goofily plinking the keys. If I wanted in, I either had to play something really edgy or play with emotion, which was even harder for me. The groupie thing worked both ways, too. When I started a band with two other people, Paul tagged along to a few concerts. Later on, when I left, he was still playing in the band.

And now there was another new band, and Paul hadn't told me anything about it. I only got wind of it because there was a piece of paper taped to the door. It said something about band practice, and below the writing was a ballpoint pen drawing of a plane crash. I took the paper off the door and read it again closely. Then I put it on the kitchen table—Paul and I were roommates. Now I had to find out who Paul was playing with. Maybe he was getting picked up. Aha, by Schneider. He was our drummer in Feeling B, too. I hadn't seen him in a long time.

If I'd been honest with myself at the time, I'd have had to admit that Feeling B wasn't really together anymore. We hadn't written any new songs in a long time and we only played for our old fans every now and then when we needed money. Of course, I didn't want to accept this, and I was slightly worried when I saw that Paul and Schneider were looking into starting a new band.

Apparently there were two more people involved, from Schwerin, a city a few hours northwest of Berlin. And they wanted to make new, really hard music. At that time we were listening to a lot of Pantera and Ministry in the car. That was because we took Schneider's car to our shows, and being the driver, he naturally got to pick the music. It was a style of music that I couldn't really get into at first. But the bits of sound that kept repeating, what you could also call samples—those I liked. I'd bought a sampler at some point for Feeling B so I'd have something to contribute to all the modern music we were playing, since with my toy Casio from the eighties I really didn't need to bother showing up. I did anyway, of course. But back then a sampler was, in my opinion anyway, a very modern piece of equipment. The kind of thing the really hip bands were using.

And so eventually the day came when I finally felt invited to band practice. I was totally intimidated. There in the semi-darkness stood five mean men. I recognized the guitarist next to me. That was Richard, a cool guy from Schwerin, whom I'd seen play in a bunch of bands. First, he was good-looking, and second, he had an incredibly good guitar sound. He had started this new band with Schneider and Olli. Then they added Paul. He, too, was completely different. I hadn't experienced such a serious and focused rehearsal in years. Actually never, to tell the truth. To my surprise, Till was supposed to be the singer in the band, an old friend from outside Schwerin whom we'd always liked visiting. Actually, he was the drummer in a cool band called First Arsch. Paul had played with them too. I thought Till was an incredible drummer, even though—or maybe because—he didn't seem like a real drummer. I think he was a little like me. He'd seen all these different bands sprouting up and realized how much women liked musicians, so he just wanted to get in on it. In doing so, he perfectly embodied the idea of punk music.

I guess he chose drums because they best suited his personality. He didn't have a refined technique, but he played with passion and incredible strength. It was a joy to watch. Whenever this band played an encore, Till would get up and start singing. The song had a special charm because of that, and you could hear what a good voice Till had. Really it was the band's best song.

And now the guys wanted to start a band with him as the singer. What am I saying, wanted—they had already done it, I just hadn't heard anything about it. I could never quite suppress the thought that they'd intentionally not said anything to me. And there was some truth to that. But now I was standing there with them in the basement and trying to make a good impression. They didn't want to hear what I thought of the songs. But if they had asked me, I would immediately have answered that I was totally blown away. The songs were simply perfect. I had never heard guitar riffs like that, let alone tried to think up anything like them myself—they were dead on. Even I, who was already somewhat older than the audience that would later respond so intensely to the music, was over the moon. And Till's voice touched my heart; at that moment, I didn't care what he was singing about. The first songs were partly in English, not that I noticed.

When kids are growing up, a lot of times it's some small coincidence that determines what kind of music they're going to listen to and what direction their life is going to take after that. And this music was made for that, for people to jump on board and carry it with them throughout their lives. For me it was like falling in love for the second time.

When I played in Feeling B, I was young and growing up myself, and I felt infinitely happy and fulfilled. Every day I would walk to practice full of excitement, no matter what we ended up doing. Mostly we just sat around and got drunk. I had to tell everybody about my band, and even then it was already clear to me that I didn't want to do anything else with my life. That is, both as a musician and as a person. I enjoyed every inch of the long, bad roads that took us to concerts, and when we arrived in the afternoon in some forlorn town in the middle of nowhere, I inhaled, deeply and happily, the beer-filled air of the town auditorium. I didn't need anybody else in my life. I just needed the band. I never once had to wonder if I was doing the right thing or if I was happy. And then, years later, when I wasn't even counting on it, life was like that again. I was happy with everything that was happening to me.

The crazy thing was that now this feeling was much stronger than it had been in the other bands. I liked the music so much that I wanted to hear it again and again. With one song—we called it "Der Matrose," which means *the sailor*, like it was a living being—it never occurred to me that I wasn't playing on it, because when we practiced I heard every note so intensely it was as if I was playing them all myself. I didn't really understand why the guitarists wanted to keep tweaking every song and trying to improve things. For me there was nothing to improve; the songs had everything they needed. Whether a note was played this way or that way or the song was played faster or slower didn't change the result one bit in my eyes, or rather my ears. The songs were good, simple as that, and the experience of playing them was much different than it was with the kind of songs that had a lot of thinking put into them. They were like puppy dogs, they just took off running. I could barely keep up. I couldn't figure the music out or really understand it, but that wasn't necessarily a bad thing. It's true that with this music I was out of my depth, but I was forced to come up with something that would go with it. A lot of the time it was something that was completely dissimilar—I couldn't play what someone else would have played in my place, since I didn't know what that would be. This kind of music, with this guitar sound plus a keyboard, wasn't so popular at that time. I just played the first thing that popped into my head. I didn't give it a lot of thought, I just tried to play loud enough that I could actually hear myself. That wasn't easy, so I waited until one song where there was a short pause, and I filled it up real quick with a few notes. Then everybody gave me a scorching look. Once again I'd managed to do exactly the wrong thing.

Another thing that would set this band apart from the others I'd played in was its discipline. Also, in the beginning, the fact that no one tried to put themselves front and center—a principle that, for musicians, is almost impossible to adhere to. And so I didn't play in the pauses anymore, but instead in the spots where everyone wasn't hammering away with all their might. You were supposed to be able to hear the singing, after all. And then I found a sound that was very loud and distorted and not at all recognizable as a keyboard sound. It sounded more like a dying dinosaur. I played that dinosaur on every song because it was audible even amidst the loudest cacophony. Even if it wasn't exactly what the band expected from me, it was still better than nothing, and luckily they didn't know anybody else who played keyboard and had both the time and the interest in playing.

In our group of friends, joining a band didn't have any conditions attached to it, and most of the time it was never formally stated whether somebody was in the band or not. If you came to practice regularly, you were in, so long as you weren't explicitly asked not to come. But that never actually happened, since normally you yourself would know if you were welcome or not. A musician should have at least that much of a sense for these things.

In any case, I kept coming back to the basement after that first practice, so I didn't have to think about whether I was a member of the band now or not. Besides, it wasn't yet clear if this was actually going to be a band and if this lineup would even last. I mean, at this time we hadn't played a single show yet. For me, playing a show in front of strangers is more or less the starting point for a band. But in the meantime, I was able to get to know those members whom I still didn't know very well.

Finally, here were some new people whom I could make music with, even if I was a little afraid of them. These were guys who expected real commitment from me. For them it wasn't enough that I was the goofy, awkward Flake whom everybody indulged. My musical limits were quickly made apparent to me, and I'd have to wake up if I wanted to keep playing in the band and not be left behind with my stale memories of East Germany.

There really were times when it was enough for me to stand up on stage with my Casio in whichever band, like for example die anderen—the name means *the others* and would later be the namesake for a whole group of bands in the GDR known as *die anderen bands* or *the other bands*—to feel like I was doing something really cool and was myself a really cool guy. These days were now over; there would be no more handouts. Now, though, I got to be there for these awesomely loud and powerful practice sessions, and I quickly came to feel that I was part of something big, not suspecting in the least all that was in store for us. It was like being in a cult—once you were in, there was no turning back.

Pretty soon we had to leave our first practice space and move into the basement of the Kulturbrauerei in the Prenzlauer Berg neighborhood of Berlin. Though back then it wasn't the Kulturbrauerei, it was just an old empty brewery on Knaackstraße. Here we got in the habit of practicing every day. Everybody except for me had just broken up with his girlfriend and as a result had no interest in sitting at home alone. Plus we realized how fun it was to make music together in an intensive way. As I said, we hadn't played a single show yet and still weren't sure where the journey would take us, but we could sense that we'd opened the door to an unknown world, and it looked very alluring.

Even then, I was already proud of our band. We came off as really mean; none of us had any interest in pleasing anyone. We didn't want to be like the other bands—didn't want to look like them, and above all, didn't want to play by the usual rules. They were all so small-minded in their thinking. Weren't we in the West now, where supposedly everything was possible and you didn't have to kowtow or lie to anyone? We wanted to do it ourselves. We didn't need any help, not even a favor. There were six of us; we had all we needed.

I proudly told my family about my new band, and my brother was really curious about us. At the time he was playing in a band that covered international hits with the lyrics phonetically altered. "Like a Virgin" by Madonna became "*Wie ein Würstchen*"—*like a little sausage*. On "Heroes" by David Bowie, he sang, "*Hallo, ist hier ein Stuhl frei? Nein, da sitzt Bärbel Bohley. Na, dann nehm ich ein Rührei*"—*Hello, is this seat taken? No, Bärbel Bohley is sitting there. All right, I'll have some scrambled eggs*—you get the idea. So more like comedy, but very entertaining. Anyway, his band was playing in Leipzig, and he invited us to open for them. Since no one knew we were coming, and because my brother had already played there a few times, the audience at Club Nato in Leipzig was mainly genial college students and intellectuals who just wanted to have a good time. Much to their surprise, there we were on stage.

I really would've liked to have been in the crowd for our set. We looked really serious and started playing without saying a word beforehand. The same slow riff, over and over. It must have been really menacing—we didn't do any kind of dramatics, just went ahead and played our songs without paying the audience any mind. After each song ended, no one clapped—it would have been inappropriate somehow. The people just stood there and stared at us. They were probably wondering what our problem was. Till didn't make the slightest attempt to say anything between songs or do anything else to lighten the mood. Of course, we were keyed up ourselves—we wouldn't have known how to ease the tension even if we'd wanted to. Sometimes Richard even forgot to breathe while he was playing.

After our set was over, a few people did start clapping hesitantly, especially when they saw that the band they had actually come to see would be playing soon. The night was really fun after that. One guy came up to me and told me he thought our band was really cool, and what he liked best was that one of our guitarists looked like Karl-Heinz Rummenigge, the soccer player. Another said we should call ourselves AIDS, that would suit us better.

Since we'd driven down to Leipzig in my sweet station wagon, that meant I also got to drive the band back to Berlin after the show. Everybody climbed into the car, euphoric and loaded down with a massive supply of alcohol, but fifteen minutes later I was the only one still awake. I had a lot of trouble keeping the car on the road; the power steering was broken and the lane was improperly marked. I didn't have the money for repairs. Nevertheless, I could sense this huge feeling of happiness. It had been fun to surprise those people.

In the last phase of Feeling B, we had mainly played in front of people who knew us. True, they were our fans, they were happy to see us and gave off a real good vibe, but it was a very special feeling to play in front of people who had never seen us before. There's really nothing like it.

—

I COULD SMOKE A cigarette right about now. Actually I want to quit. Or to only smoke just one cigarette at sunset with my friends and take my time and really enjoy it. For me of course that's completely unrealistic. Either I'm a smoker or I'm not. Smoking is prohibited in here anyway. The no smoking signs are visible everywhere—it doesn't matter what country I happen to be in, the symbol of a cigarette with a line through it is understood all over the world.

In the United States, I was once in a café where they had "no smoking" written on the wall in Braille. Or at least I think it said no smoking; above it was the corresponding symbol, but that doesn't necessarily mean anything. It's just, how are the blind people supposed to find the spot where the sign is? They'd have to feel along the entire wall. And that's unhygienic. But at least they weren't being discriminated against. If the thing you're being excluded from is a prohibition, it's still discrimination.

We were once in Austin, Texas, in a Western bar. Everything looked almost exactly like it did in the movies, with the old wooden furniture and the real horse paraphernalia by the door and everything all nice and rundown. The customers were drinking beer right out of the bottle, and Johnny Cash songs were playing on the stereo. But something was missing. You had to go outside to smoke. This bothered me, even though I wasn't smoking at the time. A cowboy who goes outside to smoke is a cowboy who's scared of Indians. Here in the backstage area, there are always security personnel patrolling the corridors. They say they'll kick us out immediately if they catch one of us smoking, even if it means canceling the concert. We don't really believe them, but none of us wants to let it get that far.

My eyes slowly wander over to the clock. It's working again. Or it's still working. There are still three hours left till the concert. So much time! Really time is the most valuable thing a person has. Your whole life consists of nothing but time. Everyone gets the same amount—so long as you're alive, the day is just as long for you as it is for everybody else. And when you're dead, you're not there anymore to take advantage of the time, so you don't need it anymore. Of course for some people in some parts of the world it gets dark earlier, but time itself is the same; you can just turn on a light. You can't buy time, either. At most you can arrange things so you don't have to work for a while and can do something else with your time. A woman once told me she worked in order to make money to pay the babysitter who looked after her kid so that she could go to work. Brilliant. The time is the same, but the woman felt connected to society again, and that's very important for people.

With all my free time, I should feel very rich, but the time isn't all that free when I know I still have to perform later. When I was still working, free time seemed much freer to me. Back then I was happy for every half hour that I didn't have to do anything. That's a long time ago, though, and it was also just three years of my life, all told. And of course it wasn't real work either, just an apprenticeship.

I guess I can go and see if anything's happening with my zipper. It still won't budge. Strange, it always worked before. Could it be the soda?

In the East, of course, we had Club Cola, which was probably a bit more potent. One of my fellow apprentices once put a sausage from the cafeteria in a jar and filled it with Club Cola. The next day, the sausage was basically dissolved. "That's what it does to your stomach lining," said the boss. So the soda should be able to deal with my zipper in no time.

I look at the clock. Well, I managed to kill four more minutes. Man, is it cold in here! Now I really am going to go outside and smoke a cigarette. I just need my backstage pass so I can get back in. The crew hang their passes around their necks or clip them to their pants with a lanyard, but I don't want to wear my pass that visibly because I'm afraid if I do it might look like I'm associated with the band when I'm out in the city somewhere. People could think I'm trying to put on airs and act important by showing everybody that I'm with the Rammstein crew. Like I'm trying to improve my chances with the ladies. You wouldn't believe the ideas some people come up with.

I rummage through my bag. I always carry a handy tote bag with me with all my stuff in it. In the East, there were these cool mesh shopping bags. You could see at a glance all the things somebody had bought. The smaller items fell through the holes, so you had to stick them in your pockets. But only very old men still have these bags. And right now I've got a gray bag from the Thalia bookstore. So it looks like I've just bought a book. There's still a sandwich in here from yesterday. I took it with me after the concert last night to eat it in the comfort of my hotel room and then forgot about it. I didn't mean to forget about it. This sandwich has now traveled more than a thousand kilometers—and it looks like it. I feel bad throwing it away, though, so I put it back in the bag.

And here's my tour packet. It's called an itinerary, another English word, but I can't pronounce it and always say *eternity*. Which is sometimes what the tour feels like.

On the first pages are listed all the companies that are working with us on the tour, with their addresses and telephone numbers and everything. So that means the travel agency, management, the security firm, the insurance company, and of course the companies that do the lighting and sound. That means I could call and ask how many speakers we have. Now I really want to—as a kid, I never got to make prank calls, for the simple reason that we didn't have a telephone, and I would have felt bad using all my money on payphones. I was just happy if I got through to the people I actually wanted to talk to. Mostly I wanted to know when the next band practice or the next party was.

On the next page are the band members. I look for my name. Aha, it says "keyboard" next to it, so far so good. And I'm listed second. That's really good. There was a poll on the internet where they asked people who their favorite Rammstein member was. I came in sixth place. Out of six people that's not so good, but of course somebody's got to be last, and it's probably better that it be me, because I act like I don't care.

I turn to the next page. Here come all the crew members, listed by job. It's crazy how many jobs there are. I read through their names and try to picture the faces that go with them. Some of them I've known for years, but others are new. I don't really know the riggers well yet. Those are the people who get to the venue first and attach all the hooks to the ceiling for the trusses and motors on stage. Not the thing for me—I'm afraid of heights.

As a kid, when I went to go visit my aunt in her high-rise on the Fischerinsel in Berlin, I could step out from the stairwell onto a small balcony and look up and down the side of the building. I got so dizzy that for the rest of my life I never needed to go on any carousels or roller coasters. Then, when my parents took me climbing in Saxon Switzerland, my father tied a rope around me and secured the other end to a pine tree so I wouldn't fall. Before that, I'd been so excited that I failed to spot a crevice and would have plunged to my death if I hadn't grabbed hold of a stake in the ground with one hand like a monkey. So I can't be a rigger, I guess. Maybe a lighting technician. Some of them are with us for the first time too, looks like. They're from the Netherlands; I can tell from the email addresses. There's an ".nl" at the end.

I keep paging through my tour packet. Now here come the sound technicians, system assistants, the guy responsible for the curtain, the stage crew, the account man, the bus drivers, the truckers, and of course the audio technicians in charge of the backline. We interact with them directly every day because among other things they tune our instruments and look after us during the concert. So we know them pretty well. We worked with them to get everything ready before the tour started. You could say we're actually friends with them, but that's true for a lot of people in the crew. Some of them I've known for a really long time. Some I was friends with even before Rammstein got started. A few of them used to make music themselves. I even used to play with a couple of them. But now they seem more content somehow. It's hard, you know, playing punk your whole life. I mean playing punk music, not acting like you're a punk, although that's definitely hard too. For some musicians it also seems to be hard to spend so many hours of their lives not making music and not getting to be a rock star during that time. Because even if you're playing a show, that's only two hours out of a whole day. The rest of the time you're insignificant. Some musicians just can't deal with it—they drink themselves to death or commit suicide. But really, there's only so much time in the day in which to play music.

I read once that you spend two years of your life sitting on the toilet. You spend a whole third of your life asleep. The most you can do then is dream of music. In some of my dreams, I'm recording music on a tape recorder, which is how I used to spend every second of my free time. If I'd somehow managed to borrow a new instrument or, even better, a new effects pedal, I made a goal of recording at least three songs with it. Since I put so much pressure on myself and wanted to record so many songs, I never took the time to actually play the songs well enough that they would sound good. I still loved these recordings, though. Little by little I lost all the cassettes. I left them in car stereos or lent them to people I knew and didn't get them back. And now in my dreams I rediscover some of these tapes. I listen to them and get really excited. Of course, even in the dream I know that it's all just a dream. And so I try and come up with some trick that will allow me to take these recordings back with me into the real world. After all, I manage to slip back into reality myself, so why not the tapes, too? What can I say—it's never worked, and the old recordings fade more and more into oblivion. Incidentally, the money I find in dreams also stays there. But then, what do I need the money for?

Here I sit, idly flipping through my tour packet. The next pages list all the concerts. First come the ones we've already got behind us. Bologna, London, Paris, Rome, and Erkner. Not Erkner, that's just an ancient joke about someone from Berlin who wants to seem worldly and mentions Paris, Rome, and Erkner in the same breath. Erkner is just a few miles southeast of Berlin. Anyway, between the concerts, there's always a day off here and there. That's called a travel day, and we get to relax and slowly make our way to the next city. We once did a whole tour without a single day off. We called that the Ochsenknecht Tour, in part because an *Ochsenknecht* is someone who does hard labor and that's what we felt like, but mainly because our bus driver looked like Uwe Ochsenknecht the actor. His sons later became actors too, but we weren't thinking about them, nobody knew who they were yet. I don't know when tours started to get names, or why. I think they used to be named after the band's most recent album, so the fans knew which songs they were going to play.

I can see here that it's the same with us. Our tour packet says MIG 2013. The MiG is a famous Soviet fighter plane. It's called that because its inventor was Mikhail Iosifovich Gurevich. Lots of inventions are named after their inventors, like the Geiger counter. It doesn't count Geigers; rather, it was invented by a Mr. Geiger. As a kid, I was really fascinated by the MiG 21. Once on vacation, I got to climb inside one. I was sitting right on the turbine. The whole plane was just a single turbine. Oh, man, you could call the tour that— Tourbine. There's no limit to the names bands come up with. I'm thinking maybe you could have the Skull Fractour, or just Tortour.

It's just a coincidence that this tour shares a name with the plane. MIG is simply our abbreviation for *Made in Germany*. That's what they used to put on things that were made in Germany, because it promised a certain level of quality. And that was the name of our last album, which, strictly speaking, is just a collection of old songs. The record company put a clause in some contract ensuring that they got to put out a best-of record. We were at least able to stop them from calling the record a *Best of*, because I mean, who would presume to know what the best is? Not to mention that when a band puts out a best-of record, it always looks like the end. A little like getting a prize for your life's work. Most of the time the people getting the prize die soon afterward. So we figured if we called it *Made in Germany*, hopefully it wouldn't give the impression that we want to stop. We don't. I mean, we're on tour right now because we want to play.

Ah, here's today's concert. Budapest. Here's the event organizer, along with his telephone number. Maybe I'll give him a call. I can ask him what would really happen if they caught me smoking in here. But I don't have the nerve right now. I take a look at the next page. There it says where we're playing tomorrow. In Zagreb. Till said he was going to sing a sack rap there. Zagreb, sack rap—get it? I'm looking forward to it already. And our hotel there is really old and beautiful. We were there last year, too. Or does it just seem like it, when actually it was many years ago?

Often when I return to a city, I feel like I was just there yesterday. Everything is familiar, and often the hotel employees and the shopkeepers are still the same. I could give an exact description of the hotel in Zagreb from memory. You never have any trouble finding it, because it's part of the train station, and in order to get to the train station, you just have to find the tracks and follow them. Worst-case scenario, you get to the next train station. Then you can take a train back. But at any rate, you really can't get lost.

In that respect, I should be grateful that we're not in the US. There it was still morning sometimes when we got to the arena, before anything was set up yet. If I tried to go for a walk, there were times when I didn't even manage to leave the property—the whole area was fenced in. At the gates were fierce-looking guards who wouldn't let me through. When I finally did manage to get out, I understood why they had been so dismissive. There was just one street, and it led to a highway. There was no sidewalk, nobody needed it. My only option was to walk between a fence and the highway for as long as I could until I was arrested.

A few times I was able to see, off in the distance, the tall buildings of the cities where, in my opinion, we should have been playing. If I tried to walk in this direction, the buildings always moved farther and farther away. It was a kind of optical illusion, a little like a mirage. Once, though, I did manage to get to the city center. Though I'm not so sure about that. Sometimes what they call *downtown* is just four skyscrapers without any visible windows, businesses, or any other sign of human life. I only thought I was in the city. It was like I had walked through Erkner and then told everybody I'd been in Berlin. The worst, though, was having to find my way back to the venue. It was really short and squat and couldn't be seen from the city.

I started following people who looked like fans and who then led me through ugly neighborhoods with single-family homes. At some point the people I thought were fans disappeared inside a doorway because that's where they lived, and I realized that I was the only white person far and wide. The people who lived there started laughing when they saw me hurrying past. I had just gotten my hair dyed red, and I didn't realize that this was apparently a sign I was into dudes. Four guys in a convertible playing loud music followed me until they got bored. I never understood what they were yelling at me. But finally I wound up back in the dressing room and began speaking excitedly of my adventure—only to find that no one was the least bit interested.

Why did I get to the venue so early today? How dumb am I? We got in pretty late, and I decided to do without taking a nap, because sometimes I can't really wake up afterward. Then I'm even more tired than before and I'm wandering around like a zombie. I do have a trick where I act like it's early in the morning and a new day is starting. I take a shower, brush my teeth, and put on some clean clothes. It doesn't help every time, though; I'm still tired. All I actually want to do is keep sleeping. That's why I took the shuttle here right away. And also because today—luckily I just remembered this—I wanted to try and get my things in some kind of order. Especially my sparkle jacket.

I try the zipper again. Still nothing. I could cut out the zipper completely and try to close the jacket with snaps. Zippers are pretty dangerous when speed is a priority. Bad things have happened on that front with the pants I wear on stage, since I don't wear any briefs underneath. If Till wants to pop me on stage—to use the vulgar term—naturally I don't have time to pull off my undies. I'd better ask Tom if he has an idea. And so I go looking for Tom's office.

On his door is a sign that says *Sackhäusler*. There's no other, more proper designation for his office. During the concert, Tom stands under the drum kit in the so-called Sackhaus, or ballsack, which, grammatically speaking, makes him the Sackhäusler, or ballsack inhabitant. Paulo, Tom's assistant, is also a Sackhäusler, though he doesn't stand in the Sackhaus, he just shares this office with Tom. Which makes things more complicated. At any rate, Tom isn't here. I take a little look around. In the early afternoon, Tom is often the only one here, so he accepts the gifts from the organizers, fans, or people who want to sponsor us, and then he thinks about whether he should maybe pass them on to us or if it would just be a waste. We don't actually need anything, of course. And if we don't ask for the things, he takes it to mean that we don't actually want them either. I don't see anything interesting, so I'm on my way.

There are a lot of signs on the walls, but not a single one that tells me how to get out of the building or where else I can smoke a cigarette. I try my luck down a few hallways. Then I hear shouts. I follow the noise and end up in an arena where women are playing ice hockey. I myself can't see that it's women playing, but I can tell from the look on the face of one of our crew members. He's leaning in the doorway and can't look away. I ask him what's going on, and learn that the European championship in women's ice hockey is being played here. It's Slovakia against Sweden. Or the Czech Republic against Croatia—I can't really make out what he says. It's jam-packed in here. You can't see much of the women, since they're all wearing pads. It doesn't surprise me that there's a sporting event taking place—we often play in venues where multiple events are happening at the same time.

It's especially entertaining when we play at a convention center. Before our concert in Erfurt, I was able to go see hundreds of rabbits. I almost bought one, since I was bored and I had enough money with me. The rabbits or hares that they had—no idea what the difference is—were as big as German shepherds. It happens more often than you'd think that I end up buying something out of boredom. It was easier in East Germany—there just wasn't anything to buy. If the opportunity ever did come along, then you bought whichever thing you saw, since somebody was bound to be happy to have it. Luckily, with the hares, I was able to stop myself.

Not so the next time, in Dortmund. There was a hunting convention being held in the building next door, so of course Till and I went. We stood there completely fascinated by equipment whose purpose we couldn't figure out. I was amazed at the huge number of hunters and hunting enthusiasts. But then again, it had also seemed strange to me that there were so many rabbit breeders. There are many parallel worlds of whose existence we don't have the slightest clue. We bought two freshly stuffed golden pheasants, which we apparently got a great deal on. They spent the rest of the tour on our beds in the bus so they wouldn't get messed up. Either I slept with my legs drawn up, or I slept at the hotel.

Another time, we played at a venue with an annex where a gun show was being held. After the concert, we walked among thousands of machine guns and checked out the most utopian of all rocket launchers. You could have armed a small country with all the guns lying around. And there are just as many guns— actually many, many more—in American homes. A bored security guard was standing by the door; otherwise, nobody was watching us or the guns.

And in Oklahoma City, we played at a racetrack. The dressing room was a horse stall. There was fresh straw for us on the floor. Or for the horses that would be racing there the next day. Musicians sometimes think the whole world revolves around them, but venues usually have a different event every day, and sometimes these events are even better attended than the concerts. I, at any rate, found it very cozy in the stall, even if we weren't allowed to smoke in there.

We've also played off and on in stadiums where the Olympics had once been held. In Moscow, the giant Olympic rings are still hanging from the ceiling. They've been pulled up and placed flat against the ceiling so they won't block anyone's view. Whenever I looked up at them, I was a little afraid they would fall. It didn't look like much of anything had been done to the stadium since the Olympic Games. But we've also played in brand-new stadiums. And so every now and then we get to catch a game.

At the moment, though, I don't have the patience to follow the game. Besides, it doesn't matter to me who wins. Most of the time I root for the loser, since I figure the team that's winning doesn't need my support anymore, and sometimes they're acting kind of arrogant. So I much prefer a weaker team that's really putting up a fight. And if they end up in the lead, then I'm happy for them and don't find them arrogant. But here I can't even begin to figure out who's in the lead and which is the better team. I can't even figure out when a goal is scored.

I keep making my way around the venue. In a hallway, a security guard asks me for my pass. I don't have it with me; it's probably back at the hotel. And I checked specifically for it in my bag, but I must have forgotten it. I also don't know if he wants to see the pass for the concert or for the hockey game—not that it matters, since I don't have a pass for the game either. The man doesn't have any reason to believe that I'm in the band, and doesn't really know what to do with me. I ask him how I get out of here, and he's happy to tell me. Normally the people he deals with want in, not out.

—

THE WAY THINGS WERE looking, we were now a real band. We had about seven full songs and were working merrily away on parts of a few more. Little by little we were finally starting to focus solely on music again, instead of building toys for some government make-work program. We had to make money somehow, after all, and the best way to do that was with homespun make-work schemes.

In East Germany, too, most musicians had worked some kind of bogus job. Less because they needed the money than because, as an amateur musician, you had to prove you had some kind of trade, otherwise they made trouble for you, trouble that could end with you landing in jail. Or with your performance license being revoked, which meant the people at the venue could also be held culpable if they let you play.

For that reason, a friend of mine worked in the coat check at the library, and I liked to go there with him, since a job like that is simply more fun with two people. We took a tape recorder with us and would listen to the recordings we'd made. People were always asking us about the music, and it made me really proud that such educated people seemed to be so impressed by it. We also chain-smoked the whole time. All the coats must have smelled horribly of smoke, but no one complained about it. I was only there for fun anyway. I made enough money with Feeling B, and my job as a secretary existed only on paper.

But in the early days of Rammstein, things weren't going so well with Feeling B anymore, and I had a make-work job that I would lose sooner or later because I never even pretended that the thing interested me. I was all the more excited about the new band, and although we had only played a few small shows in the East, which people had only come to because they knew about our old bands, all of a sudden we thought we were a really big deal.

Before I'd started playing in the band, the others had sent a cassette with four songs on it off to some contest for rock bands that was judged by a panel. The band was chosen as the winner—nobody knows why, maybe it was the only tape that got sent in—and so we got to spend a day in a real studio recording these songs again, only professionally. The engineer was the same guy who'd recorded the first album by the band Ideal. We were all filled with admiration and would never have thought to disagree with him. Those were the first recordings with the band that I played on—though it could be that we had recorded the songs before then, when we were practicing in Till's garage.

Now we told all our old friends and drinking buddies about our new ideas and our new band to see how they would react. None of us in the band had an objective opinion anymore, obviously; we thought everything we did was unbelievably good. Naturally we also tried to get our music played at the bars we went to. Each of us always took a cassette with him whenever he left the house. The key thing was to have a good relationship with the waiters and bartenders, since we weren't the only band who wanted to get their music played. At that time, there were a whole bunch of people around us who made music. Really almost everyone. We would see them at the practice space— hardly any band could afford their own, so everybody practiced at different times in the basements of Prenzlauer Berg.

We also moved into an old bottle warehouse on Greifswalder Straße because there we could really make a racket. No one lived in the building, and the businesses that had set up shop there weren't bothered by our noise. The sewage pipes ran under the steel plates on the floor, and especially when it rained there was a really horrible shit smell. Actually, it didn't necessarily have to be shit—as I learned when I tried to help my daughter with her homework, sewage runs through a separate sewer line, and the rainwater from the courtyard or the water from the roof gutters would have smelled just as foul. Or maybe it was just shit and it had gotten mixed in with the runoff. We put in a fan that made a really aggravating buzzing sound but didn't seem to have any other effect.

But there was another upside to the space, which was that there were full crates of beer lying around everywhere that the owners had never picked up. They were past the expiration date, but I quickly learned that this date only guarantees the best quality and isn't meant to imply that the product isn't drinkable anymore. It's more of a suggestion.

At any rate, we could drink the beer, and it didn't taste that bad. I had pretty severe diarrhea the whole time, but there could have been any number of reasons for that. Thanks to this free beer, I also hit upon the bright idea of drinking alcohol early in the day. It's almost a criminal waste if you only start drinking at night and then go to bed. You don't get anything out of it. We built walls out of all the crates to make the place a bit cozier. On one of the beer-crate walls we hung a poster from the theater in Schwerin. It had a painting of a little alleyway. The acoustics in the space hadn't improved as we had hoped, but at least it looked discriminating and artistic. Then Till offered up the nice leather couches from his apartment and brought them down to the practice space. We assumed, and rightly, that we would be spending the next weeks or years in this space. And now it was really great in there.

A lot of times we wouldn't go out to lunch, but instead would just sit there on the couches stuffing food in our faces. Whoever was least interested in practicing would run over to the Indian place and bring back something for everyone. It really wasn't all that bad in the West. We could buy something really delicious to eat almost 'round the clock.

First to arrive after the wall fell were the Chinese takeout places. Dull-eyed, we devoured the giant noodle portions until our faces went numb from glutamate. Then came the Greek, Mexican, and Vietnamese restaurants.

Once I even had African food. The bones were still in the meat. I went to an Australian place once too. The food wasn't bad, but next to my table there was a young man with dreadlocks blowing incessantly into a didgeridoo. When I let fall a few negative remarks, it turned out that his girlfriend was sitting at the table next to mine. But Indian food in particular brought about a massive improvement in our lives. So simple and so good. There were times when we would eat the same dish for lunch every day for weeks at a time. For us East Germans, there were even plantains. I liked eating them, but after the wall fell, I was pretty careful not to be seen too often with anything that even looked like a banana; we had enough problems with stereotyping as it was. The plantain dish was number twenty-three. Bafflingly enough, it was also twenty-three in other Indian restaurants. Is it the same worldwide? That would make ordering nice and easy for us musicians. Just always number twenty-three. In America, I noticed that the dishes at the Indian restaurants had the same names as they did in Berlin. At first I thought the waiters were giving me the German menu. Though of course "chicken" isn't German. Anyway, chicken tikka masala is always chicken tikka masala. In Berlin, in Stockholm, and in New York. Or am I talking nonsense? Either way, I was past forty before it occurred to me that pizza Napoli always means the same thing. Something with olives and tomato sauce. I'd thought it was just a made-up name. I didn't even know that Napoli meant Naples. And pizza funghi is something to do with mushrooms, it comes from the Latin. It also says something about fungi on the foot cream you get from the doctor.

It really is a good thing, though, to get to go all around the world with the band. The food alone is a reason for playing in other countries. But even back home in Berlin, we had, like I said, a lot of good things to eat.

Right next door to us for a short time there was a Russian woman who served goulash and other meat dishes. "A man needs his meat!" she told us. From that moment on, we called her the meat lady. After eating her food, we couldn't get off the couch. Even if a man does need his meat, he also gets tired afterward. It's like after sex: the man tends to fall asleep, and then the woman just sits there looking disappointed.

Across the street from us, two twins who, as chance would have it, had been in a class with Schneider when they were all apprentices had opened up a shawarma shop. The food clearly wasn't in high demand, which meant that sometimes there were just a few really dry, crusty strips of meat hanging off the spit. No way were we going to eat that, but we did find a good use for it. Back then we had trouble starting practice on time, since often one or several of us would get there way too late. So then we made a rule that the last one to arrive had to bring a bottle of wine, but that didn't work at all—how's the latecomer supposed to know he's the last one? For all he knows there might be somebody who's even later than he is. Plus no one minded having to buy a bottle of wine, because it meant there was at least one bottle on hand for drinking. It got to the point where we even liked coming late.

And so we thought up a new punishment for the latecomer. The last one to arrive had to eat a shawarma sandwich from the twins' place. And really, none of us wanted to do that. The threat of this punishment alone was enough to ensure that from then on we all made it to the basement relatively on time. It really wasn't all that bad down there. Like I said, it smelled a little of rot, it was pretty cold in the winter, and sometimes the lock on the heavy iron door got stuck so that after practice we had to pull on it for half an hour before we could breathe fresh air again—but other than that, it wasn't bad.

The space next to ours might have been even worse. It was called the Tropfsteinhöhle—the cave, basically—which for sure didn't mean that the space was nice and bright and dry. Whenever we passed by it, we would hear this vague droning sound. The Inchtabokatables practiced there, the band that Olli had left to play bass with us. The Inchtis, as we called them, since no one wanted to say their full name, were already much more successful than us. They weren't playing one-off shows anymore, they were going on tours with multiple dates back to back. They got picked up in a nightliner, a giant bus with a lot of beds built inside. We once got to take a quick look inside the bus when it was standing in the courtyard outside the practice space, and we thought it was all very luxurious. We couldn't believe that a rock band we knew got to ride in such a cool bus. We thought that kind of thing was only for bands like the Stones. The mere thought of being driven to the next town you were playing in the night after a concert seemed amazing to us.

Around then, we started taking the Inchtis' old, small bus to our shows, since they didn't need it any more. Once, in Rostock, we managed to lose the keys, and after the show we were standing around the bus like idiots. Just then the Inchtis drove past us in their nightliner, blind to our predicament. There weren't cell phones yet, otherwise we could have just called them and gotten the other set of keys. At some point, the tow truck came and towed us away while we just sat there in our bus, or rather the Inchtis' bus, not saying anything.

For a few other shows, we rented a bus from Robben & Wientjes. We'd have to stand in line forever on Saturday morning until they'd taken care of all the college students moving to new apartments, and returning the bus late Sunday night was even worse. They would search every inch of it for potential scratches or damages. We'd stand there, hungover, wanting only to get home and to the toilet as quickly as we could.

But what were we supposed to do? No tour meant no tour bus, and without a record contract there would be no tour, and without playing good shows and having a good demo tape that would really stand out from the masses of tapes submitted, there would be no record contract. And so all we could do was practice. Every day of the week. And on the weekends, too.

We spent our days in the practice space. We went there automatically; not for a moment did we stop and think about why we were doing it. You could say that we spent all our free time practicing. I sat back against the wall next to the drum kit. One of Schneider's cymbals was about ten centimeters from my right ear. Whenever he hit it something inside my head cracked and I couldn't hear anything for several seconds. And I mean just in general we were very, very loud. The speakers we used were from the theater in the Palace of the Republic. They were given to us for helping to clear out the massive amount of equipment left in the building after the wall fell. So these speakers were built to provide sound for an entire theater.

When our producer came to our practice space to hear our songs for the first time, he immediately put earplugs in his ears, and he always had them in whenever he came to hear us after that. I didn't understand it. I thought he was coming for the express purpose of hearing us play—why would he do something like that? At this point, though, I've been wearing earplugs in the practice space myself for years, and I'm a little mad that I didn't start doing it much earlier. Your ears don't heal once they're damaged. But when you're young, you don't think about things like that. The reason you go to the practice space in the first place is so that you can be really loud. It would never have occurred to any of us to call it work. We'd decided of our own free will to keep going to the practice space, and we didn't get a penny for it. When I think of work I think of something I have to do. Or something that I do to pay for my living expenses. But we could never have known if we'd ever make money with music. Simply having the opportunity to play music together every day, without any limit placed on it, was all we needed to be happy. I would even have paid money to be able to do what we did. Though that's exaggerating a little, if not lying outright. Who knows if we would have sat so cheerily together in the practice space if there hadn't been this feeling among us that something really great was starting to form, something that would last and that we might be able to live off someday. I don't think any of us wanted to have to take a job to make ends meet ever again. But we were less and less afraid that we'd have to go back to the employment office. It was the practices that made us feel this way, especially when we saw these little ideas we had turn into actual songs. And of course, the feeling also came from the shows we'd play on the weekends.

We tried to play as many shows as we possibly could. And we put an extreme amount of effort into it, since of course we wanted to win people over. We paid really close attention to their reactions to certain parts. We had to prove ourselves every time—if people didn't like us one night, then nobody would come to our next show. At the beginning, they mostly came because they went to their town cultural center every weekend. It didn't matter what band happened to be playing there, just so long as something, anything, was going on. Music tends to be overrated—most of the kids just wanted to meet a girl, and the only way to do that was to head to the town social on Saturday night. I don't mean that in a bad way; the truth is, these were some of our best shows. People were happy to finally hear someone playing a different kind of music. And, of course, a few people came because the posters mentioned Feeling B, Die Firma, or the Inchtabokatables. These bands were relatively popular in the East, especially among young people. Meanwhile, the established East German bands grew less and less relevant. But luckily none of us had ever played in any of them, simply because, musically speaking, we wouldn't have been at all capable of doing so. With Rammstein, in the beginning, we played exclusively in the East, in the clubs where we had already appeared frequently with Feeling B or Die Firma.

Our manager from Feeling B took care of booking shows for our new project. It was all pretty casual. He still knew most of the booking agents at the clubs personally. And so we were slowly able to get used to playing in front of people. Even though we'd already played a bunch of shows with our old bands, the nervousness would grab hold of me every time. It was a feeling I'd never had with the other bands, the punk bands—since with punk music, failure is actually built into it from the start.

It was probably hardest for Till, since he didn't have an instrument to hide behind and had to sing with his real voice, which of course is something very personal. Luckily he had a fairly perfect command of the art of not letting his nervousness show. He would put on his welding goggles, that way no one could look him in the eye and he could look out at the audience through the darkened lenses. No one told Till that with the goggles on he looked like a big friendly insect. He'd wear them at every show. He still probably would have worn them if he had known, because it was his way of shielding himself, and it worked really well. At least in the beginning.

And then at some point the goggles were just gone. It was almost impossible to think of everything when you were hopelessly drunk and trying to get all your stuff together after a show. We had other worries than trying to remember this or that piece of clothing, which meant something always got left behind. I was a little sad when I lost the hat I'd bought for a monumental fifty dollars in Tallahassee in 1993—it was raining so hard there that the water was running down my shirt; I didn't care how much the hat cost. And then it was gone. It's hard to find good headgear. Once I found a kind of folkloric Peruvian knit hat with two braided ear flaps in the park. It was really practical, since when it was cold I could tie the two earflaps under my chin. The band didn't think it was that funny. One night the hat flew out the window of the dressing room, in flames.

After our shows, we were lucky just to round up all the band members— and of course I, myself, was sometimes the one the others had to go looking for. If I was in a bad mood—and the smallest trigger was enough to set me off, like seeing a skinhead in the audience or missing a note on the keyboard—I always wanted to go home immediately. It didn't matter how far away home was.

In Dresden one night, I got on the train to Berlin and waited for the conductor. When he stepped into the car, all the people in my compartment jumped up and crawled under their seats. I thought about crawling under there too to save myself the cost of the ticket, but the conductor was already in the compartment. The people stayed under the seats for the rest of the trip. I also rode back from Rostock one night. In doing so, I missed being there when the band tore apart their room in the sailors' hostel. The next morning, the management had to order a giant dumpster. Hey, it's one way to invest your money. A very amusing way.

Every time this happened, as I sat there on the train and slowly felt the drunkenness wearing off and the hangover setting in, I would regret my hastiness and wish I had stayed with the band. I have no idea where this childish temper of mine comes from. Once it takes hold of me, I can't help myself.

One time I headed off to the train station after the final concert of a tour because the bus driver had said something stupid to me. The tour manager came after me in a car and drove up alongside me as I walked, trying to get me to change my mind, but I was too proud and too dumb to get in. Then when I got to the train station, it was closed, and I had to wait with the local homeless people on the street until it opened again. Which isn't to say that my train came at that point. I had to listen to stories for hours while constantly trying to avoid getting grabbed.

Another time, I slept in my clothes on the floor at a fan's place, then planted myself on the side of the road trying to hitchhike from Dresden to Berlin. I had on a brown suit that was too small and that I'd found a while back in the apartment where we were supposed to sleep after a concert. The person whose apartment it was had died shortly before. I'd spilled a ton of mustard and beer on the suit the night before my hitchhiking escapade, and even in the state I was in, I could tell what a murderous stench of alcohol I was exuding. And if that wasn't bad enough, the friendly driver who picked me up was a teacher, and every time I said something he corrected my grammar. Of course, I was only talking gibberish anyway. It was all very embarrassing, but I just wanted to get home.

So at any rate, the beginning of our time as a band was also the time when we had the most exciting concerts. Whenever we traveled to West Germany, it still felt to us like a trip to another country. It wasn't that the people there weren't welcoming, it was just that almost nobody came to see us, since we were so little known. In Hamburg, where we played the Logo, we counted eight paying attendees. But we wanted to win them over, and that in itself was fun. Maybe that's why we liked to go abroad so much after our first successes in Germany. Simply for the chance to play in front of people who didn't know us again.

Driving to our early shows was pure joy. In the morning, we got into some car or other and drove off with our few possessions. I still didn't have a case for my sampler, so I would set it on its end between the two front seats in the bus and sit down on top of it. That way at least I had a place to sit. We stopped at every rest stop, even though the food there in the early nineties was improbably bad, actually it was unconscionable, and this was apparent even to us, who, being from the East, were used to a high degree of unpleasantness on this front. Does anyone still remember what a Heiße Hexe hamburger tasted like? Plus all of a sudden the food was absurdly expensive. We couldn't believe it; we thought it was shameless, and naturally we weren't about to pay the new prices. So we stole whatever we could get at the rest stops. Sunglasses, newspapers, shoes, gas cans, cookies and chocolate, bottles of liquor, etc.— travel supplies, basically. Beer was the only thing that wasn't worth it. Also, before we left Berlin, we always stopped at the music store. I could say this was our way of protesting the West taking over, but the truth is we just didn't have enough money for the expensive western instruments. Plus we loved the adventure, if you can call stealing adventure. The guys from Schwerin could still walk into the music stores in Berlin because no one knew them there. I stood around in the shops for hours staring at the instruments and waiting for one of the frustrated musicians who worked there to condescend to explain something to me. Till did it a little differently. He just grabbed whatever it was we needed, put it under his arm, and ran to our waiting bus. During this time, a lot got stolen from the businesses in the East. Little by little they hired security personnel who were meant to put a stop to it. They tried to get in our way, but they lacked the necessary resolve. During these operations, I was probably the most nervous of any of us.

In those days, everything about our lives seemed incredibly exciting to me. And of course the concerts most of all. It started with the preparations. Which songs were we going to play? Maybe we'd even play that new one— nobody knew what should happen after the second chorus, but it had an amazingly brutal riff. And did we want to bring the vegetable crate again so they could lock me up after the first song? Because I was so dangerous that I had to be put behind bars? Of course nobody bought that. As a surprise, we covered the crate with paper and then just lit it on fire. It looked really good, plus it really stank, because the paper kept burning on stage after it had peeled off the crate. And then you could see me. Though sometimes the curtain also caught fire. In one song, Till was supposed to put a gas mask on, for the simple reason that we had one on hand.

It was even nice when we fought about what we should wear. At the beginning, each of us wore what he thought looked good on stage, but really we wanted to figure out a uniform so we'd seem a little meaner. It should be apparent at first glance that we were a unit. To that end, we conducted several amusing experiments. At some point we even tried white tank tops. I've hated them ever since I was a kid. I always had to wear them back then, and I looked so horrible in them. This kind of shirt was worn by mean landlords, retirees working in their garden, and my father. Now I was happy that I was finally an adult and could decide for myself what to wear. Never say never, I guess. For the show, I wore a white tank top. But only for the first song—then I played the rest of the set with my shirt off. We all did it that way, and it looked good, too. But once the band saw that Metallica had had the same idea with the white tank tops, that put an end to it.

Another time we put on black East German navy jumpsuits. These were black coveralls that were originally designed for house-to-house fighting. No sooner did we all have the same thing on than we realized that the outfits looked good on some of us and not so good on others. I would say that on two of us the jumpsuits looked really good. And so each of us started to bring his own individual note back into it by ripping parts of the uniform or rolling the sleeves up, which made the whole thing look even sillier. We didn't have much time to do all this, since we had to get in the bus to drive to Freiburg for a concert.

When we got out of the car in this new city wearing our new clothes, we didn't think we looked so good anymore, and the people on the street looked at us like we were crazy. It wasn't the look people give rock stars. That didn't bother us, since we didn't feel like rock stars either. We felt like a band that was about to start some real trouble. That afternoon at the cultural center where we were supposed to play, a teenage dance troupe was having a very serious rehearsal. Till amused himself by frightening the young girls with obscene remarks.

They then served us a meal of cold bockwurst. I don't have to tell you what these sausages made us think of. And so Till stuck one in his fly. During the show, he took it back out as if it were his penis. I don't know if they'd planned it, but Olli took the sausage in his mouth. No one but us could see that it was just bockwurst. I couldn't really see it myself and preferred to look away. Finally, out of sheer exuberance, Till smashed a spotlight that hung directly in front of his face.

The people at the venue got horribly worked up about it and didn't want to pay us. We took it calmly. Or I did, anyway. The rest of the band grabbed a rug that sat rolled up in the stairwell and put it in the bus. Once that was done, we ran back inside, stood around in a group and hoped that one of the women there would come talk to us. The chances of a woman coming up to you when you're in a group of men are close to zero. Then off we went to the college dorm. Who could think of sleeping at that point? A lot of times we all slept in one room. If one of us had managed to take a woman home, the others got to share in his pleasure, at least acoustically. Or maybe even in actuality. Everyone in the band had experienced his bandmates having sex.

If, before or after the show, it looked in the least like there'd be a party, we got amped up and started clowning around. We juggled with full beer glasses. We danced to all kinds of music, no matter who was around or if anyone actually saw us or danced with us. We stood in groups of three or four around a pretty girl and excitedly but vainly attempted to pick her up. During the day, we invited people we met on the street to our shows. If they were girls. Or knew any. We had huge eating contests in small-town restaurants, trying to see who could eat the most dumplings. Later on, there would always be time to get mad about our fat bellies. Which of course we didn't do; we just drank ungodly quantities of liquor afterward. We slid off the road on some black ice in our rented bus and only survived thanks to Schneider's quick thinking. Backstage we practiced shooting ourselves in the bare back with a paintball gun at a distance of three meters. It hurt and then wasn't at all visible to the crowd. We tried everything out on ourselves. We didn't have anybody working for us. We didn't pay for any insurance. We had no hotels, no limousines, no shuttle buses. We didn't need a tour manager. We didn't give interviews and didn't go to any photo sessions. We didn't have any meetings. There were no appointments with the accountant, the manager, or the PR department. In short, we did absolutely nothing that wasn't fun. We were exactly what we wanted to be. We were the ideal band. We set off into the world together, like in a fairy tale. Nothing we did after that could replace the frenzied excitement of the early days. No sold-out stadium or private jet could change that. This early form of energy can't be bought, and sadly it can't be preserved, either.

By the way, we sold the stolen rug in Berlin and used the proceeds to buy out our manager. He could barely keep up with how quickly we were evolving. We could barely do so ourselves. And so we wanted to split with him. On a human level, it wasn't right. But then, who says that musicians have to be good people? For the direction the band was moving in, it was definitely the right decision. Assuming there's such a thing as right or wrong in a case like this.

No one can say what things would have been like if we had kept him on. By this point, we're good friends again. Actually, we remained good friends the whole time, it's just that sometimes it's hard to separate the personal from the professional.

FINALLY I SEE DAYLIGHT. MAN, is it nice outside. And so warm. I light up a cigarette and stroll around outside the venue. I really don't want to smoke anymore, but I find out again and again how hard it is to quit. Twenty years ago, I once stopped without even trying. Someone I knew, not knowing what else to give me for Christmas, gave me Allen Carr's *Easy Way to Stop Smoking*. I read the book a few weeks later and the next day immediately quit smoking. In the book, it says that if human beings were meant to smoke, they'd have chimneys. That sounded so ridiculous that it immediately got through to me. After that I went almost ten years without smoking. Unfortunately for me, the book only worked the first time. At least I don't smoke that much anymore. That's what I tell myself, anyway. It's astounding how much you can lie to yourself when it comes to addiction. You're too willing to believe yourself. Who wants to know the truth, anyway? And I barely ever smoke; actually, I'm a nonsmoker, if you don't count the mysteriously empty packs I keep finding in the morning.

Our trucks are back here too. They're painted an ugly greenish-brown, since we rented them from some trucking company and that's what their fleet looks like. Almost like the trucks in the GDR. Back then I knew only two logos: DEUTRANS and AUTOTRANS. There were also sedans with "Service" written on them. No one knew what that was supposed to mean. But besides those three, none of the cars had anything written on them. East Germans valued their vehicles too highly for that. That's why we were so amazed when we drove through West Germany for the first time in 1989. On every truck there was something different. Our favorite was a shit-brown truck with Braunschädel GmbH written on it in orange script—Brownskull, Inc. The word immediately found its way into our vocabulary. We used it to refer to brown liquor like brandy and whiskey. We liked Anton Aschenbrenner too— Anton Ashburner. Mordhorst wasn't bad either, or GLUNZ. They would have made really wonderful band names, but they were already the names of freight companies, who I'm sure wouldn't have found it so funny.

A few years ago, our band trucks still said "Rock 'n' Roll Trucking." I was always happy when I saw them driving into the city where we were about to play. They looked like what I imagined a real band's trucks might look like. Somebody told me once that Emerson, Lake, and Palmer had three trucks with one of their names on each of them. That really impressed me. I wondered if they always drove in the right order. At first we only had a little delivery truck, and we would never have had the idea of writing our name on it. In the front seat sat the three we called the *Digedags*, after the cartoon characters in *Mosaik* magazine—kind of like an East German Three Amigos. There was the sound guy, the lighting guy, and the third guy for the stage and effects, all endowed with MacGyver-like talent.

When, twenty years later, we rented a plane for the whole summer festival season, we did finally have our band name pasted onto the rental jet. Other than us, maybe four pilots saw it—there aren't that many people walking around at 36,000 feet, and on the runway the plane was parked somewhere behind the fuel truck. The gesture cost us 1,500 Euro, and of course after that we never did it again. Maybe that's what I mean when I say that rock 'n' roll is going downhill. No one's interested in these acts of brilliant, pointless waste. No more driving your Bentley into the pool. There's not even a pool to drive it into anymore. In any case, rock 'n' roll isn't the first thing you think of when you see our trucks.

I take a closer look at them. They've been unloaded, all except for the power truck, which has a diesel generator built into it. It's already running, and the electricity flows into the venue through a cable as thick as your arm. We bring our own power with us. It used to be that sometimes the whole neighborhood would lose power when we started playing. We lost power too, of course. Now that kind of thing doesn't happen anymore, but the tradeoff is that it stinks of diesel exhaust behind the venue. I find that the exhaust from diesel engines smells worse than gasoline exhaust. In my mind's eye, or rather my mind's nose, I picture the bus stations in the GDR. Or the trucks that used to unload vegetables outside our building and for whatever reason never turned their engines off. I think I'll move off a few steps.

Here it stinks even worse. Turns out it's not the power truck that smells so bad but rather the exhaust from the—watch out, here comes a long word—*Merchandisingverkaufsstand*. That's the merch booth. Huh, it's a lot shorter in English. At the merch booth, you can buy our T-shirts plus the complete line of band accessories, as it were. Incidentally, the word *accessories*, which is *Zubehör* in German, is *Tillbehör* in Swedish, which we thought was really funny on account of Till. In Sweden, a cell phone is called a *Ficktelefon*, which to a German sounds like *fuck telephone* and which we thought was even funnier, also on account of Till. *Willkommen* is *Tillkomma*—the fun really never stops.

In any case, when we go on tour we bring an ungodly amount of clothing with us, all with Rammstein on it somewhere. We bring it in order to sell it. It was 1983 when I saw something like that for the first time. The singer in the band I was in had a T-shirt with the Stones' tongue-and-lips logo that he'd apparently stolen from a merch table at a concert in the US. He just ran away with it. I guess they figured it wasn't worth chasing after him on account of one T-shirt. For me that was unimaginable—I would never have let somebody take a T-shirt like that from me. Of course, the people at the merch table had a whole lot of T-shirts, so one wasn't all that important. For me, on the other hand, such a T-shirt would be worth a lot. For me it was like owning a piece of the Rolling Stones. Imagine my shock, then, when our singer took this holy relic and cut the sleeves off like it was no big deal.

But I wasn't any better myself. In sixth grade I traded a record by the band Prinzip for a plastic ABBA bag with a photo of the band on it, which I then used as a gym bag. Of course an LP was worth a lot more to me than a bag, but as a principled blues fan I really couldn't get into the band Prinzip. One song was called "Die Supernummer," which could mean *the super track*, and I was expecting as much, but it was just a song about the singer's girlfriend's phone number, and she never picked up, if I'm remembering correctly. And so I walked around carrying my nasty gym clothes in the ABBA bag. Even though ads and other things from the West were prohibited at our school, nobody said anything. ABBA stood outside of any system of value. Unfortunately, the handle broke off way too soon. And it just goes to show I wasn't a real fan, because I threw the bag away.

What made me start talking about this again? Oh, right, the T-shirts. At this point you can buy T-shirts at our concerts, too. Lots of different kinds.

There were only ten copies of our first T-shirt. It was put together by the guy who would later be our lighting technician; I think he made a draft design that he took to the copy shop around the corner. The draft consisted of a big R. To make it look really cool and distinct, he chose an Old Germanic rune that was meant to be an R. Stupidly enough, though, it looked a bit like a swastika, and because of that was thrown away. Our next R was taken from the old East German matchboxes. They came from the town of Riesa, which of course also starts with an R, but this didn't look as good. We kept looking. We just needed a good symbol, for the T-shirts and for our stickers too.

In the GDR days, all the bands had a suitcase full of stickers at their shows. The money in the sticker cash box was only to be used as a last resort. In an emergency, someone would dip into the cash box; in good times, there'd be over two thousand marks in there. At every show, the fans would ask us, "Y'all got stickers?" Our singer at the time was able to drive to the West, where he had ten thousand stickers made for us. We still haven't used them all up. I kept putting them on all the furniture and other surfaces in my apartment, but there are still plenty left over. Meanwhile, the band hasn't been together for more than twenty years.

The Ramones aren't together anymore either, but every day I see people wearing their T-shirts. If you're wearing a Ramones shirt, that means you're cool. And so all the real estate brokers, web designers, lawyers, and bankers who want to look young and easygoing have started wearing them. Even Brad Pitt had one on once. Meanwhile, the bassist from the Ramones once wore a Rammstein shirt. That made us really proud, of course. He was also proud, because at the time he seemed like pretty much the only person who knew our music, thus he could be considered ahead of the curve. Kind of a win-win situation. The fact that I would use that expression frightens me.

In any case, it was pretty early on that we started getting T-shirts with our name printed on them, plus individual words or lines from our songs. That worked out well, since some lines could speak for themselves, like for example "*Du riechst so gut,*" which means *you smell so good.* Somebody who had never heard of the band could wear that. Apparently the most popular T-shirt was the one with "*Ich will ficken*" on it. That's a line from one of our songs too, but it means *I want to fuck,* so of course it's universally applicable. At least if you have the necessary courage—I myself have never been brave enough to wear this shirt in public. At first we took the T-shirts to the concerts ourselves, but at some point another person started coming along to be in charge of it. And so, little by little, there got to be more of us.

This cigarette really doesn't taste good. I'm probably getting sick. They say the cigarette is the smoker's thermometer. So long as the cigarette tastes good, there's not too much to worry about. It is not a good time for me to get sick. We're in the middle of a tour, after all. I toss the cigarette away. It's lying there, still burning. Now I feel bad for just throwing it on the ground, and I pick it back up. I'm in a foreign country, you know, so I have to be on my best behavior, otherwise it will reflect badly on other Germans. And now throwing the cigarette away seems wasteful, so I take another puff. The taste doesn't get any better. I put it out on a pallet. Should I put the butt in my pocket? Then all my clothes will smell. Finally I stick it in a fencepost where there's an opening. Hopefully no bugs live there.

I walk, very slowly, toward our trucks. The slower I move, the faster the time will pass. That's the theory. To test it out, I stop altogether and just let the time go by. That's not especially exciting, so I slowly start walking again. The truckers have set up their folding chairs in front of their cabs and are sitting there drinking Red Bull. It looks nice and pleasant. They talk about tight driveways, wait times at the border, bribing the border guards, icy roads, and incompetent production managers. They don't mean ours—they're talking about past tours. I hope, at least. I always want to know what other bands are like, so I stand off to the side and listen. The guys in the Wu-Tang Clan take their pistols with them on tour. And the roadies for American bands don't stack boxes on top of each other because it's too much work—they just take twice the number of trucks. The bands are the ones paying for it. Interesting.

Personally, I still find it hard to believe that we take so many trucks on tour with us. I mean, it's not all that long ago that we were driving to shows in my station wagon. It was an AMC Matador station wagon with eight seats. The last row of seats faced backward, so you could look out the back window. Usually Till sat back there because he was the only one who didn't get sick having to face the other way. He slept most of the time. On the seat next to him was the flamethrower.

We didn't have our own sound guy yet and just relied on the guy at whichever venue we were playing to make sure we had a good mix. With a bit of flattery before the set and of course a promise of extra pay, you could up your chances of sounding halfway decent. There was no guarantee, though. At most we tried to explain to the technician that a bad mix would reflect more on him than on us, which of course wasn't true. If a band sounds bad, it sounds bad, and then people don't want to see them again.

Most of the places where we played were a lot alike; we felt like we knew them all already. Some of these places, we'd crawl out of the car and go inside, and the whole place would reek of beer, ashes, and despair. In the winter sometimes there'd be a grandma shoveling coal into a big tiled stove. By the time the show started, it was so hot in there that we were sweating like pigs. It might have been the humidity. Sometimes the condensation dripped from the ceiling and ran down the walls. We had to blow dry my sampler before it would even turn on. In order to get a blow dryer, the owner had to walk across the street to his apartment. These small-town auditoriums were mostly run as family businesses. The owner's daughter stood behind the bar smiling shyly at Till. The son was unfortunately a skinhead and would beg us to come back soon and often. What are you supposed to say to that? I mean, the shows were a lot of fun. One time, in Schinne, the fans poured a large glass of beer down our sound guy's neck in the middle of a song, whether out of excitement or by accident. He couldn't believe it. He got right up and went to go change in the dressing room. To get there, though, he had to walk straight across the stage; that was the only way to the back. We were a bit surprised to see him walking past us; I mean, we were in the middle of a song. Backstage he apparently slipped on one of the inedible sandwiches that was supposed to be our meal and fell on his back. Instead of our loud music, we heard the loud sound of glass shattering.

After the concert, we explained to the owner that there must have been a skinhead attack in our dressing room, but that smartass showed us that the broken glass was outside and not inside, and so we had to pay for the window. Such was our life. Or to take a line from the Rolling Stones: we'd piss anywhere, man.

Now it's getting to be time for dinner, and the truckers slowly get up to go get something to eat. Hidden among them, I manage to get back inside. I feel like Terence Hill slipping past the bad guys by hiding in a herd of sheep. For me, everything is an adventure. I simply imagine myself in the midst of an exciting world. Nothing dangerous can happen, and yet it's all stimulating.

Outside the dressing room area is a laminated photo with a list of the passes you need to get in. It also shows the faces of all six band members, like on a wanted poster. I show the security guard my face on the photo and try to look similar to the picture. Of course the pictures were taken right at the start of the tour, when we were all fresh and well-rested. Plus at this point I have a mustache, which nobody but me finds funny. The man recognizes me anyway, though, and I'm back in the hallway. I head for the dressing room I share with Till. He's still not there. A sly fox, that guy. He's probably still asleep at the hotel, lying in bed all nice and cozy. Though he also goes to bed later than I do. Maybe he stayed up all night writing poems again. Not even I believe that, but it could be true. I mean, he drank enough Red Bulls that he definitely couldn't have slept. Although I guess there was vodka in them. These energy drinks are supposed to be five times as strong as coffee. I should pour Red Bull on my zipper.

I root around in the ice bucket. I have to drink more; I'm totally parched and I've only got an hour left. If I drink anything right before the concert, I have to pee really badly during the set. The most unpleasant things have happened to me on that front.

I can't get away mid-concert, of course, and between songs the pauses are really short. The one time I was away for half a song the band got so worked up about it that the next time I just peed in my pants. I take no pleasure in relating this now. But it wasn't as bad as all that. A lot of times you're afraid of something you've never experienced only because you don't know what it's going to be like. It's like with sickness: the uncertainty is the worst. Well, sure, a diagnosis isn't much better. I just shouldn't think about it at all. Anyhow, I'm not wild about the idea of pissing myself every night and prefer to drink my water at such a time as will allow for a reasonable interval between the drinking and the start of the concert. And that time is now.

The water I've set out hasn't really warmed up yet, but I quickly drink the first bottle. Half a liter, that's a start. Immediately I unscrew the second one. I only manage half of it, so I sit down on the couch and stare at the bottle. This gets boring, and again there's no one here to talk to. My gaze wanders over to the wall. The wall is made of gray cement blocks. There's really nothing to indicate that musicians inhabit this room. That's the price of success.

Not too long ago, we all sat packed inside a single smoke-filled room merrily shouting at each other. Our feet stood in beer puddles. On the walls there was barely room for the tiniest bit of graffiti. If a band didn't have any stickers with them, they'd at least write or draw something funny on the wall. On the subject of sex in particular, an enormous amount of creativity was on display. The club owners are seldom so heartless as to erase these things. In a club in Oklahoma City, someone who worked there showed us a spot where Sid Vicious had signed his name. There on the wall it said "Sid," and objectively speaking anybody could have written it. But it's nice to believe it's real. Were the Sex Pistols ever in Oklahoma? If so, that would mean that Sid Vicious sat here just like us, and out of boredom he wrote his name on the wall. Musicians, not unlike retirees, have rather a lot of time on their hands. They wait till they can go to the club, they wait for sound check, for food, for doors, for their set, and then for when they can pack everything up. Finally they wait for the bus to leave. In between, they wait for beer. There really aren't that many jokes to fill up the time. So it's no wonder, then, that some bands take a tattoo artist with them to write all over their body during the tour. You can tell just looking at them how long the bands have been on the road. After that, the musicians needn't bother applying for a straight job, looking like they do. Some of them even know it, yet they still keep it up. They want to show that they're betting it all on the music, that there's no turning back.

I myself have gotten a tattoo backstage. My bandmates just shook their heads when they saw the result. I wanted it to look like I'd been tattooed in a GDR prison, but the tattoo artist didn't understand me. He didn't speak any German and didn't know what a GDR was supposed to be. The only people who got tattoos in East Germany were the ones who were in jail, so it made them seem dangerous, and justifiably so. I didn't look dangerous. When I saw the image on my arm, I had to laugh. I still do, even today, every time I pass by a mirror.

Now the door bangs against the wall and Till is standing in the room. He throws his bag onto the couch and screams: "TOM!!" Commotion in the hallway. "TOOOOM!"

Tom comes running in and greets Till ebulliently. Then he hastily begins writing down the names of the guests that Till is reading off various pieces of paper. There's no end to it.

Tom is really bubbling over. "No problem," he says, "we'll get 'em all in here." Some of the names are kind of indecipherable, but it'll be fine.

Till looks at the clock. "Shit, that late already." He starts undressing in a flash. Then he pulls on his workout shirt, which has the name of a band on it that sent him the shirt in the hopes that he would wear it in public. Pretty much the only one who sees him wear it is me. Till has already vanished into the bathroom to work out. In there is a kind of torso with a head on top that you can pound on. Every day its feet are filled with water so it won't fall over. Till has already wailed on the thing so much that its neck is broken. Does a real neck break that easily?

In our time with Feeling B, I witnessed fights that I never thought the people involved would survive. But they just got back up and went to get another beer. Sometimes, though, all it takes is for one of them to fall funny and then he's dead. The other guy goes to jail, even though he had no intention of killing him. I know this from watching *Tatort*, which is like the German *Law & Order*. It's probably best to just steer clear of fights altogether. Unfortunately it's not always that easy, especially because I can't run very fast.

I hear pounding and heavy breathing. Every now and again, Till runs out, grabs his phone, and runs outside to take a call. Soon he's back and pounding on the dummy again.

I decide not to bother him and head next door to see what the others are doing. Olli keeps kicking a soccer ball against the wall. I had been hearing the noise for a long time but I thought the sound check was still going on. Hip-hop groups get the deep sound of a bass drum by kicking a ball against the studio window. That's what I've heard, anyway.

Paul is lying on a kind of bench and lifting weights. The pleasant music is still playing. On the table are postcards from Budapest for their families. Man, do they have their act together. They even have stamps. I relax a little bit, if that's the right word for my dull non-activity, and then go back to our room.

—

WHEN I PASS BY THE sheet with our photos on it, I remember when we took our first band photo.

We had a few shows under our belt, but not yet a real concert planned in advance. We'd just been playing as a surprise opener for our friends' bands. We now meant to change that. An old acquaintance who, like so many of us after the wall fell, had set out to build a secure life for himself and direct his efforts toward something new had decided to try his hand as a concert promoter and begun organizing rock concerts in and around Berlin.

This time he wanted to establish a legit small-scale rock festival that was to take place in a field outside of Potsdam, just south of Berlin. Since we were still unknown as a band, he booked the Inchtabokatables as the big draw. Medieval music, especially the kind the Inchtis played, was very popular at the time.

But to make sure a few more people came, he wanted to get a write-up in *Tip*. That was a magazine for events around Berlin. There also used to be a lot of sex ads in there, with things we couldn't even begin to comprehend. Was there really somebody out there who wanted to be peed on? Was somebody really seeking a person with stinky feet? Were people actually looking for someone to watch them having sex? And what was a hard wave supposed to be? I only knew about German New Wave. And unlike all the punks who hated German New Wave, and especially Frl. Menke, and accused artists like her of ruining that whole style of music, I thought it was all really good. Even Markus.

I don't know what got me talking about all that. Oh, right, the hard wave in *Tip*. They were supposed to run a photo of us. Though not with the sex ads. We had no idea what the photo should look like and who should take it. All we knew was that all the bands whose photos we saw in an old issue of the magazine looked almost identical. We wanted to set ourselves apart from them somehow.

Then it occurred to me: at the junk shop in between the tram tracks, I'd seen a small studio where you could get your picture taken in historical costumes. The point was to have it look like an old photo. Everybody thought it was a good idea, so we all went to the shop after practice. The woman who worked there was a little surprised there were so many of us. Normally it was just single people or couples who came to get their photo taken. We also had to talk her into giving us the negative instead of just a print. Or was it a Polaroid she was using?

When we went to try on the costumes, we realized that we couldn't really put them on—they just consisted of the front part; in the back they were held together with rubber bands. That way they fit everybody, which was more practical.

We all went and stood exactly where the woman told us to, and she took the photo. It was never that easy again. Later on we all started coming up with our own ideas, and sometimes we were of the opinion that we knew better than the photographer. In any case, we proudly brought the photo to our manager. He gave it to the paper. The only problem was that when people saw the photo, no one could tell what kind of music we played. It looked a bit like we were going to play old favorites from the thirties. A cappella style, like the Comedian Harmonists. The article that ran with the photo promised unreservedly that we were an excellent band. Of course, you rarely see articles that say a really bad and boring band is playing, even if that might be the case.

But neither the photo nor the write-up drew any notice from anybody. Interest in bands from the East generally wasn't high at that time, so soon after reunification. This became clear to us as we were driving into Potsdam.

Normally, at a festival, the promoter knows the route that the band has to take to get there and puts up a few signs so the band will get excited and see what a good job the promoter is doing. But we were coming from another show in Dresden, where we had jumped on a bill opening for our friends in DEKAdance.

We'd had an incredibly fun night in Dresden, so we were a bit tired and hungover and took a different exit off the highway than the one the organizers had expected us to take. As a result, we didn't see a single sign, just a giant billboard that said "Say Opel—think *Piegorsch*!" What happens when I think Piegorsch, though? I think I came to the conclusion that Piegorsch was probably the name of a person who sold Opel-brand cars. Did any customer ever think of Piegorsch and go see him on account of this billboard?

I'm inclined to think not. After all, even with a write-up and our picture in the paper, nobody came to see us. It really was almost no one—in front of the stage there was just a thin row of people made up exclusively of our friends and relatives. And of course, with them in attendance, we were even more embarrassed that nobody had come.

One of the guys' parents even came. There they stood, their faces filled with eager expectation. They finally wanted to see their son play in this cool new band that they'd heard so much about. Their son nearly froze when he saw them. To make matters even worse, we had a friend with us from another band who, in an attempt to escape the depressing atmosphere, or maybe just out of habit, took a whole lot of drugs. Maybe there were other reasons for it, but in any case the effect was the same. In the middle of the concert, he came out from behind the stage and started turning all the knobs on all the amplifiers, trying to find a sound he liked. The security guards didn't want to go after him since we were in the middle of a song and he didn't seem to be bothering us. We all probably looked like we were on drugs. I doubt anyone could tell for certain who was part of the band and who wasn't. It wasn't entirely clear to our friend either. He grabbed a microphone and started singing. He didn't know any of our songs, so he sang the lyrics from his band's songs, and then he just started cursing at us at the top of his lungs. We stood there on stage like idiots and tried, unsuccessfully, to calm him down. We weren't prepared for something like this. Finally we stopped playing, grabbed him, and locked him in our bus—this way, if nothing else, he wouldn't get beat up by the security guys.

We couldn't really get back in the groove after that. We just hoped the show would be over soon. I didn't dare look at our friends in the audience and instead looked over at our bus, which was rocking dangerously the whole time. Our buddy had figured out he was locked in. When it was finally over, we drove back to Berlin as fast as we could. We parked in front of the squat where the Inchtis lived. On the ground floor, under their apartment, was a bar that was run by some people who lived in the building and their friends. You could drink there for as long as you wanted, provided you could convince them not to close. This was exactly the kind of bar we needed right then.

We were devastated after this concert. After we'd all gotten back on the bus, our friend had cheerfully informed us that he'd be up for doing something else—we left him in the bus so he wouldn't cause any more trouble. Now we all tried to get so stinking drunk that we could forget about the concert. It probably wasn't our photo's fault that the evening took such a sad turn.

Nevertheless, we quickly got another photo taken. In taking the first photo, we had learned how hard it is to get six people in the frame. Each person's face ends up being very small, and everything below is just a single black mass. After all, everybody wanted to wear black. And so we decided that only Till should be in the next photo, and he should be wearing a long trench coat and holding fireworks in his hands. Unfortunately, fire doesn't photograph well.

We put Till in a courtyard at night, and at a signal from the photographer, he had to light the silver or gold flares that he had left over from New Year's. He had his bug glasses on, so nobody could recognize him. Luckily that didn't matter—no one knew what he looked like anyway. We did still need photos of the whole band, though, and since we actually did like our first photo—it had such a serious air to it, and we really didn't look like a normal rock band—we decided to stage the photo again and get a friend of ours to take it. This time we brought our own clothes. The new photos were of far better quality than the photos from the shop. That one was basically unusable. And the edges were cropped. So now you can always tell which one's the original.

—

IN THE HALLWAY, I HEAR Schneider's clacking. He warms up on an electric drum kit. Of course it's actually called an electronic drum kit, but I think electric sounds better, like *Metropolis* or *The Electric Rider*. The instrument only sounds like a drum kit in his headphones; to me it just sounds like he's slapping some paper plates.

I open the door to his dressing room and quietly step in. He neither sees nor hears me. He also doesn't say anything, and I think of the three monkeys that my grandma had at her house. Unfortunately I couldn't play with them, since they were welded together and had no practical use. I watch Schneider a little without him noticing me, then I quietly move on.

As I go, I think about how Schneider really has his act together, way more than the rest of us. It's not only that he conscientiously warms up before every concert; he's just generally a clear-headed and upstanding guy. It's his nature. He sets himself a goal and then does what he needs to do to accomplish it. Yet another quality that I completely lack. If I accomplish anything, it's usually something I didn't even know existed when I first set out. For example, most of the music prizes we've won—I'd never heard of them until we were nominated. Schneider, on the other hand, at least from my perspective, has very clear ideas about what he wants to do and be.

When I get back to our dressing room, there's also music playing. Much louder than the music in the room next door, naturally.

Uh-oh, that's the get-dressed music. An hour before the show, Till always puts on the same playlist of songs he can sing along to. This way he can get warmed up while he gets dressed, and with every song he knows how much time he has left. A kind of sonic clock. Is it that late already? Yes, it is. I must have gotten the hours mixed up somehow. On our clock there are only lines and no numbers. So it's easy to slip up and be an hour off. Especially if the clock is crooked. But now it's time to get going. I drink another bottle of water. That's the last one before the concert. Then I go piss.

When I get back, Till is already pulling his boots on. I run over to our dresser and pull out my clothes. My God, do they stink. This is bad. This is inhuman. And they're all a little damp still too. And I'm supposed to put them on? Good thing I haven't eaten anything—I can barely fight back the urge to vomit. I put off actually getting dressed a little longer by draping them over a chair and going back to the dresser to pick out some clean civilian clothes. I'll put them on after the concert.

We inherited the dresser from the Kelly Family. As the name suggests, they were a band made up entirely of members of the same family. They sold millions of records in the nineties and put on giant concerts all over the world. Whenever we're proud of having sold out a stadium in some city or other, the organizers will take us out to dinner the day before the concert and tell us that the Kelly Family once played there for a week doing two shows a day. When Father Kelly died, the band split up and stopped touring, so they didn't need their dressers anymore. That's how we ended up with them.

I pull open the drawer where I keep my clean clothes and books. There are a few gifts in there too. I always try to bring something back for the kids that's specific to each of the countries we visit, but I often find out that the things I buy in far-off lands are available for much cheaper in Berlin. In New York I once bought an Indian doll for my daughter. It turned out to be a Barbie doll and didn't get past her mother's prescreening. How am I supposed to know what a Barbie looks like? But that wasn't all: the authentic Indian miracle stones that I bought in the desert from some self-styled medicine men can be had at every other flea market in Berlin for half the price.

It gets harder for me every time I go to Paris or London. The whole apartment is full of Eiffel towers and red buses. After the first tour in Australia, I got boomerangs and kangaroos for everybody I knew. For my daughter, I even got kangaroo in a can. It was a stuffed animal, not meat. I was surprised myself. A stuffed animal in a tin can.

It's getting harder and harder to find things. A lot of times the only solution is the flea market. But since I have such a hard time with languages, I always pay way too much. Or I completely miscalculate the exchange rate. Now what I do is I just take the pen and notepad from the hotel. They usually have the name of the city printed on them. So later I have a nice reminder of my time with the band.

All right, I've found a clean T-shirt and a dress shirt. I call a shirt a dress shirt if it's got long sleeves and you have to button it down the middle. No idea what the actual word for it is. I set the clothes on the couch's armrest so I can find them easily after the concert. Now I get undressed. If only it weren't so cold—immediately I've got goose bumps. Maybe I really am sick. No time to worry about that now, though; I have to concentrate on following the right sequence. First the so-called fuck shorts. These are leather shorts with Velcro straps in the back. The straps are there so Till can rip the shorts off, leaving my ass exposed and free for the taking, as it were. The trick here is to use the utmost caution with the zipper in front, because I'm not wearing any underwear. Today would have been a good day for the hair-removal cream, but once again I forgot. I can get to the venue a bit earlier before the concert tomorrow.

Now the knee guards. You can buy them at any workwear store. They're the kind of thing the people who lay the cobblestones for the sidewalk use. I like watching them putting those little cobblestones in place—it fills me with admiration. Recently they tore up our whole street because they wanted to put in some new cable. Then they repaved the sidewalk. Shortly after that, they installed these pointless parking areas on the street corners and closed everything off again.

We aren't laying down cobblestones, but the stage we play on has a grated surface, which allows the light to shine through from below, and if I fall, or Till drags me around, I could rip up the skin on my knees—they make the grating extra rough so we don't slip. I kneel down to test them out. Great, doesn't hurt a bit. Then again, I'm kneeling on the soft carpet. It just cuts off the circulation in my legs a bit.

I reach for my sparkle pants. The legs have a cut up the length of them so I can pull the pants off in a flash during the concert. I pull them on over the fuck shorts and press the magnet strips together to close the slit over my legs. The magnet strips didn't hold up under the strain of the concert, so we had to sew on snaps as well. The magnet strips are thus completely useless. But theoretically good.

Now for the shoes. These are my wedding shoes. I figured it would be a waste if I just wore them exclusively for the wedding, so I started wearing them during the tour shortly after I got married and have been wearing them on stage ever since. We've played so many shows in that period that the shoes are really worn out.

Around the same time I got married, Dieter Bohlen from Modern Talking also took a liking to silver shoes and could be seen wearing them on a giant billboard. I thought it was really funny that we had the same taste; I didn't think the fact that Dieter Bohlen was now wearing these shoes was any reason for me not to wear them. Plus I had no interest in buying new shoes just for Dieter Bohlen's sake.

I tie the laces as tight as I can—under no circumstances can they come undone on stage. I can't make a double knot, though, because I want to be able to take them off quickly during the concert. Double knots can be so tight that you can't ever undo them.

Then the jacket. Wait, makeup first. I hurry into the bathroom, step up to the mirror and look for a hairbrush. The rest of the band is in the bathroom too at this point, and the hairbrush is in use.

"Late to it today, huh?" Schneider asks me while he puts eye makeup on. Doing makeup is fun for all of us because we get to try out something different every day. Or at least a small variation on our general masquerade. While I'm waiting for the brush I first give myself a thorough spray-down with deodorant. It doesn't help much with the bestial smell coming off my clothes, though, and the strong deodorant doesn't make it any easier to breathe. The whole band lets out a groan. They all start waving their towels, and some of them demonstratively leave the bathroom. I probably overdid it a bit, but I find it soothing to smell my favorite deodorant every night. Then I grab the hairbrush, which is finally available, and start brushing my hair. Most of my hair gets caught in the brush. That's not normal. I've got a real hair loss problem. Do I have cancer, or what? No, with cancer you only lose your hair through chemotherapy. I look in the mirror. My widow's peak is getting steeper and steeper. It's like a small Alp at this point. The skin on my head is peeking through everywhere. Shit, I'm getting old. That's lousy in and of itself, but the fact that the aging process moves so quickly and is plain for all to see comes as a total shock to me. I should smear black shoe polish on my head, then at least from a distance I wouldn't look so bad. Instead I put a great deal of hair gel on my hand and spread it over my head. Now we get it all nice and smooth. If there were more hair there, it would look good. At most I'd just have to get it dyed. Gel doesn't mask the gray hairs. Luckily I stand near the back of the stage, so I'm not so easy to see.

Now for the makeup. I use a sponge to dab my face with powdered milk. Tom mixes it with latex so it'll stay on better. But I've spread the hair gel around too much and the white doesn't cover those spots. This results in weird blotches and makes me look like I have eczema. Next time I'll start doing my makeup earlier.

Still, painting my face white works better than when I used to paint my face with coffee. I can't remember which of us came up with the coffee idea. If I were to ask the band, they'd probably all raise their hands. In any case, it wasn't me. But at some point we started smearing really sludgy coffee on ourselves. We used instant coffee mixed with just a little bit of water. It looked absolutely intense. A little like dried blood and a little like dirt, grime, or rust.

And you can get a really subtle mix of different shades, depending on how you mix the coffee and how you put it on.

I always used a more solid mix on my face and arms, then I poured somewhat more liquid coffee over my head and let it drip down my body. After putting it on, I couldn't sit down or touch anything. The coffee felt like glue. Then during the set I was always going apeshit, as the saying goes, meaning I was all amped up and fidgety. My heart was racing too. I couldn't really play and couldn't sleep at night. I was nauseated and abnormally nervous. The band told me to drink less alcohol, which in and of itself is good advice, but wasn't much help to me at the time. I thought I was going crazy. Finally I realized that I had a godless amount of coffee on my skin, and of course it was getting absorbed by my body. I must have had a dose of twenty cups in my body every night, and that for weeks at a time.

And so I got some decaf coffee. But for some inexplicable reason, it didn't stick to the skin as well. And so I made myself a mix of both varieties. They had that in the GDR. I still remember the rhyme. *Have a girl who won't put out? Try Kaffee-Mix, it'll knock her out.* The joke, I think, was that there was so little caffeine in the mixture that you could go to sleep after drinking it. That's just the thing for me, actually. But anyway, my coffee mixture adhered well enough. When I started sweating, though, I'd get these sticky streams of sweat running down my body that would expand and crack as they dried. As soon as I touched something, it too became sticky. I couldn't really play keyboard anymore since the keys were covered in coffee gunk. First my fingers kept slipping off, and later on they would literally get stuck. Still, it smelled good—like coffee. I find that whenever someone makes coffee, it ends up smelling better than it tastes.

On that tour, we all smelled quite deliciously of coffee the whole time, since once it mixes with your sweat you can't get it out of your clothes. When we sat in the plane or on the bus, it smelled like coffee everywhere. Whenever I smell coffee in my day-to-day life, the Pavlovian response kicks in right away and I get really excited and start sweating. I think the show's about to start. And of course the rest of the band still uses coffee. In the bathroom, I always hear somebody calling out, "Has anybody made coffee yet?" And then they all go on and on about the quality of that day's coffee mixture. I can't join in because now I'm white as a clown. I think clowns are horrible, but I still do my makeup this way. At least I get to use powdered milk and not coffee.

Yet again I've forgotten to shave. My stubble is peeking through the makeup. That doesn't look good, but the people in the crowd will be standing at least thirty feet away from me, so they won't be able to see it.

Now I grab a kohl pencil from the makeup case. The point has broken off again. The sharpener's there, which looks more or less like the pencil sharpeners I had in school. So I sharpen the kohl pencil and use it to paint my lips black. I press my lips together so the coloring is nice and even, and I look in the mirror. Not bad, not bad at all. Then I carefully do the edges of my lips. If I were a woman, I'd know what you actually call that. Nice! If I'd used black lipstick, I wouldn't have been able to do it as well.

Now come the show glasses. I started wearing sunglasses very early on—I realized that with my normal glasses on, I looked as normal as an insurance agent or an apprentice electrician. Before I was in Rammstein, I didn't dress up at all for concerts. I just went up on stage in the clothes I'd been wearing—and probably slept in—for the past few days. Whenever I see a photo of a concert from that time, it's hard to tell what I'm even doing up there on stage. I don't look like I have anything to do with the band or with music in general. I discovered, however, that if I put a pair of sunglasses on, I looked a little bit better, even though, not having corrective lenses, I couldn't see clearly anymore. I'd run into posts and stumble down the stairs. So then, at a gas station, Till stole me a pair of clip-on sunglasses that I could attach to my normal glasses. But since it was really dark on stage, I still could barely see anything. What I did see, though, was nice and focused.

One day, I happened to learn from a friend who also wears glasses that you can order sunglasses with prescription lenses. And so I had an optician make my first pair of show sunglasses, which I now wear during our concerts. Otherwise I never wear them, though, because I can't stand sunglasses. As before, I still couldn't see very well in dark rooms. And the concert halls and dressing rooms are usually enclosed spaces where it's not that bright. Today's being a case in point.

I feel my way into the shower to do my East German army exercises. Somebody once saw me doing them and that's how they described them; I myself was never in the East German army, and definitely not in the West German army. I was much too old by that point, plus it essentially would have meant being forced to fight myself, since for years the West German army was our biggest enemy. An aggressive mercenary force whose purpose was to serve the interests of the imperialist world powers through violent means—that was the story they fed us, anyway.

I start by waving my arms in circles. I have to warm up, see. I throw them right up in the air. And immediately bash my left hand against the shower head. It's too cramped in here. Man, does my hand hurt! I broke a bone for sure; I can't even move the fingers anymore. Luckily I don't play that much with my left hand. I carefully shake my hand out and take a step back. Onward, back to the exercises. Twenty circles moving forward, then backward, then counter-rotate: left arm forward and right arm backward, then right arm forward and left arm backward. I start to sweat. The makeup on my face is already softening. Am I really that out of shape? It's probably the smoking. I think I'd better just move my head in a circle. Sometimes on stage I'll start unconsciously bobbing my head in rhythm, and if I haven't loosened up beforehand, I cramp up. In the band we call it the bang ache, because you get it from headbanging. Really you're supposed to have long hair to headbang, but when I saw a concert video and realized what I looked like with long hair, I went and got my hair cut very short. I looked like Gerhard Gundermann, if anybody still knows who that is. The singing backhoe driver.

After the tenth head rotation, I start to get dizzy, and I start rotating in the other direction. My vision starts to go dark, and I have to hold onto something so I don't collapse onto the tile. Since I can't really see anything, I grab the hot water pipe and burn the fingers of my other hand. I try to run some cold water over the burn so I don't get blisters, but only hot water comes out of the faucet. It hurts like hell, but I figure it's not so bad; after all, when you get frostbite you're supposed to pour cold water on it first. It's kind of like fighting fire with fire. Nevertheless, blisters pop up on two of my fingers.

I think I've had enough exercise for now and stumble back to the dressing room. I'd love to sit down on the couch and rest for a second, but suddenly there are people everywhere. No idea where they all came from. Till has somehow managed to get fully dressed. Right now he's pouring champagne and vodka for everybody. Some women are sitting on the couch, shouting excitedly. They pull out their cigarettes and blithely start smoking.

"Hello, let's fuck!" I cry out by way of greeting—I figure I'll loosen up the mood a bit, though it's already pretty loose. I said it in English, but no one takes any notice of me. They probably take me for a mentally challenged assistant who can't speak the local language. They're right, of course, at least on the latter point. The visitors have nothing against me, they're just focused on Till. I look for my sparkle jacket. It was hanging on my chair, but someone is sitting there now and he's tossed it behind the dresser. I go to pick it up. I try to weave my way through the people but have a hard time making myself heard because Till has turned the music up really loud. Now he starts dancing. Every now and then, the door opens—the guys in the crew want to see what kind of women we've got in here.

I've almost reached my jacket when a giant man who looks like—and may well be—a bouncer accidentally bumps me out of the way. He's telling Till what is apparently a very funny story in broken English. There are a lot of hand gestures involved. Till laughs loudly and keeps pouring vodka. I manage to grab my jacket and decide to go see Tom in his office. I want to see if I can use some oil to get the zipper going. I'm running out of time.

Luckily Tom is there. I show him the zipper. He takes the jacket from me and unzips it. Like I'd been trying to do for hours. I don't seem to have any strength left. We drip a little baby oil on the jacket and I put it on.

"Remember," Tom says. "At eight forty, we've got the Meet and Greet." Oh, right, that was on our day sheet, which is taped up next to the door in our dressing room. It has the schedule for that day's concert. Which band plays when and all that. Apparently the first band to play every night is the Doors. Or at least I used to think that until somebody explained to me that "Doors" means when they start letting people in. So "Curfew" isn't the last band either. It's just when people have to leave the venue. Now that I know all this, I'd name my band Curfew, that way there'd be an ad for us almost every night. At least on the day sheets. Of course, by that same token, we could also name ourselves the Evening News. That comes on television every night. We'd even be in the *TV Guide,* if it even exists anymore. The evening news will be over by now, though—it's already 8:30.

I hurry back to our dressing room. By now everybody has really started to let loose. The women are laughing and squealing for no apparent reason, at least not one I can see. They're all trying—and I believe succeeding—to drink as much champagne and liquor as they can in the short time that remains between now and when the concert starts. Till tells them they should fill some water bottles up with vodka, that way they can take them inside to drink during the concert. And so the water bottles that I had so lovingly set out to warm up are unceremoniously emptied into the ice bucket. It doesn't matter since I'm not going to drink anything else before the concert. I am thirsty, though. I'd better go pee again, make sure to get all the water out. The bathroom is occupied, however, and a few beauty queens are waiting outside—they want to fix their makeup or something, what do I know. At any rate, the doors are locked, and all I hear is giggling and snorting.

Back in the dressing room. Now they're all taking photos with Till, or at least a lot of them are. And now I'm supposed to take the photos to make sure everyone's in the frame. What they really need is a selfie stick. Stupidly enough, I can't figure out how to use these modern cell phones and I can't even manage to take a normal photo. All right, another try. And another. What happens to all the photos? Who wants to look at them all? Or maybe I should ask who has to look at them all? Are they just going to sit in the cloud for centuries? On a server somewhere in the American desert? Won't they go bad? And don't you lose your soul if you're photographed too much? Thankfully, I'm not in the photo. Now here comes Tom and our security guy to take the people to their seats. A horrible scramble ensues. The visitors leave their jackets and bags with us—the place looks like a dressing room. Well, okay, I guess it is one. Then they're all gone. Till dreamily sips his champagne, and a peaceful silence sets in.

—

SO WE WERE PLAYING a small-town auditorium every now and then, and we were slowly winning over our first fans, who sometimes asked us when our next show would be. These were all things to be happy about, but if we wanted to get any real attention, we'd actually have to put out a record.

The only record company we knew about was Amiga, the state-owned record label in East Germany. Feeling B's record had come out on the label in 1989. Now, five years after reunification, this company, like almost every other East German company, was gone. Two musicians from the moderately successful GDR group City had started their own record label. We knew them from playing a few shows together and seeing them at parties, so we approached them with our cassette or our CD—the switch from the former to the latter medium was taking place around this time—in their small office in the Treptow neighborhood of Berlin. We all sat down, or some of us anyway, and the two of them took a quick listen to each of our songs. This wasn't the kind of music they wanted identified with their label, they said. Maybe we should practice for another year or two before we thought about bothering them again. They were probably more interested in trying to keep the old GDR bands relevant or promoting the Ostrock style of music in general, which of course was an honest motivation, but wasn't much use to us.

Another company showed more interest in us, but all they were offering for an advance was 15,000 Deutschmarks, which wasn't enough for us to be able to really take our time recording an album. And so we went to the employment office and registered as self-employed artists. We got a little startup capital, but we also lost our claim to unemployment benefits. Permanently. That meant from now on we had no other choice but to make our living playing music.

Soon after that, we were supposed to play a show at another small-town auditorium. When we got there, the place was still locked. After waiting outside for half an hour, the guy who owned the place finally finished his bath and came down, barefoot, to let us in. There on the edge of the stage were a couple of tiny speakers that they'd set up for us, the kind you'd find in a home stereo system and that maybe would have been loud enough for a singer-songwriter. This was really infuriating—we'd come all the way here and wanted to play a good show, and they were so ill-prepared that there was no way it could sound good. The guy probably figured people would show up anyway, so he might as well save himself the cost of sensible speakers. A band that's driven all this way isn't going to cancel a concert on account of a couple of speakers.

But that's exactly what we did. We decided to just head back home. It's such a shitty feeling to have to cancel a show, though, so we asked our sound guy, who also managed a club, if we could play for free that night in the opening slot at the Knaack-Klub. He put it together no problem. This show was incredibly fun and also made a very good impression on the manager of a singer friend of ours. He had his office above the club and just happened to come down and see us play. It was also around then that we started wanting to leave these seemingly pointless, small-time shows in the villages of East Germany behind us and become a serious band.

In Feeling B, our way of thinking was that the manager was only there to book as many concerts as possible. We really didn't care where or when or whom we played for. We weren't even interested in how much money we would get—we assumed the fee was non-negotiable anyway, and thus kind of God-given. It was at most a hundred marks, and since everything was so cheap in the East, we could live comfortably for a whole month on that. Everything other than booking concerts we dealt with ourselves. Our singer picked out the studio, and we all worked together on the album cover. As a band in the GDR, there was nothing more we could do.

And so we didn't know, or at least I didn't, what a manager was actually there for if not to book as many concerts for the band as possible. And now here we stood, all excited, talking to a guy who was a real band manager. He radiated authority; it was palpable, even though he wasn't any older than we were. But it was probably just what we needed. We didn't doubt for a second that he knew exactly what needed to happen with us. It's impossible to say whether we took the right step or the wrong one, since no one knows how things would have turned out otherwise, but there's no denying that we've become a relatively successful band. Who deserves credit for what depends solely on your point of view. That I wasn't always happy with the progression of things says more about me than anything else. But every band probably knows this ambivalence. Either you, the musician, concern yourself with the boring business side of things, spend all your time sitting in endless, mind-numbing meetings, and then read every bit of fine print until you've understood it all, or you just make music and accept that you'll just have to live with it if sometimes things on the business end don't always go how you imagined they would. You can't do both. Maybe you do try to have a say on the business side, and it still doesn't work. Then it's even more frustrating. Better not to set foot in the office in the first place. As a musician, you've got no business there anyway. At least that's what our manager told us. Later on, we split with him too. Maybe none of it has anything to do with success, commercial or otherwise.

When I reflect on why it is that we've been so lucky, I sometimes think it's simply because we're still around and still together. Most of the bands that have been around as long as we have are successful. I've known most of the bands that play the big festivals since I was a kid. In some cases, they don't even stop when a band member dies. Some bands even tour the world with just one or even none of their founding members—ghosts of their former selves. At that point you might as well just do karaoke. When I'm trying to be clever, I whisper to people: You'd better not start anything with me, I know karaoke. Or I say I'm trained in No Can Do. That's when you let them beat you up without fighting back and you say "No can do." Of course, that's not what the bands say when one of their members has died. They say "We've got to keep going somehow." But a band's career doesn't always end with death; sometimes they break up when the disagreements between members get to be too big. Unlike your relatives, you get to choose who you're in a band with. But only once. It's like with marriage. You can work on the relationship, and you can try to change, but you're always meant to stay with the same woman.

When I joined the band, I wasn't worrying about whether I would get along well with everybody. I just assumed that when people played music together, they got along well automatically. To be honest, I would have stayed even if the other guys had been smelly, violent sociopaths. Only much later did I notice how well-matched we all were. From the start we were serious about trying to clear the air of anything that caused discord in the band. It started with food. In the beginning, everybody would lunge at whatever dish had just been put on the table. We didn't care who ordered it or who actually wanted to eat it. If that person happened not to be paying attention or was gone for a moment, there might not be anything left for him. And so we came to an agreement: whoever ordered something got the first bite before the dish was passed around. That way the person whose food it was still had a small chance to ask the others to spare some for him. By now this rule has become moot since we're all trying to lose weight and can barely manage to finish what's on our own plate, much less someone else's.

Women aren't much of a problem either. Especially not with us, since our individual tastes, where women are concerned, are pretty divergent. And the more options there are, the less risk there is of overlap. And even then, a musician will tend to act with restraint in consideration of his bandmate's feelings, since the band is much more important than a hookup or a fleeting moment of horniness, for the simple reason that musicians are with their band much longer than they are with a given woman. Actually longer than with any woman. Musicians don't even see their own mother as often as they do the guys in their band. You spend more time with your bandmates than anyone else in your life, simple as that. Aside from that, musicians also make their living from being in the band they're in, and that's not entirely unimportant. You don't put that at risk just because you have a thing for your bandmate's girlfriend.

Money is definitely the biggest source of potential conflict. I think conflict over how to divide up the money is what has led to the most band breakups. Normally it's the case that the composer of a song gets a percentage of the song's sales. Knowing that some songs sell millions of copies and can set you up for life—I'm thinking, for example, of "Last Christmas" by George Michael—every musician tries to get a composer credit. But when you write the songs together as a band, there's no sure way of determining after the fact just who it was who contributed the crucial, essential element that makes the song what it is. And if only the self-styled composer is paid for it, simply because it's easier for a guitarist to string a few chords together than it is for a drummer, the others find it unjust. The drummer is just as important to the song. For me, then, what matters is if they're part of the band.

From the beginning, we decided we would all be listed as composers and have an equal share in the songs, and accordingly we're all paid the same thing. Otherwise there might not be any more new songs, since who would want to spend forever working on a new idea only to not be paid for it? At that point, it's better to go off and look for a new band. I find it more respectful to just give everybody the same amount. And with six people, there's no risk of anyone putting too little energy into the band; really the opposite is the case. What was it they used to say in East Germany? From each according to his ability, to each according to his needs. We just went ahead and assumed that we all had the same needs. Maybe within our band we still practice a form of socialism. The dictatorship of the musicians. It used to be that when I was drunk and excited and wanted to tell a story or yell about something, my voice would crack and I would sound like Erich Honecker, the East German head of state. *Cut it out, Honecker*, the band would say. But it was all meant in fun, and there was never a serious quarrel between us. In the early days something like that would never have occurred to us. We were all just excited that things were finally starting to take off.

Once we had all more or less agreed to give it a try with this new manager, he immediately launched his efforts to get us signed with the record label where our friend the singer, whom he also managed, was under contract. The company was called Motor. We sent them a cassette with our songs. The rejection came back quickly. There was no interest in this kind of music in Germany at this time, they said. This record company supported more innovative and progressive music, they said. The person who wrote this letter would be asked about his rejection a lot in the years to come.

But our manager wouldn't let this discourage him, and he managed to arrange things such that he was riding in a car with the head of the record label. As if by chance, our cassette was playing on the car stereo. After the head of Motor had heard two songs, he asked who the band was. Our manager acted all nonchalant, and the record company boss took the bait.

Back then the record companies were almost drowning in their own riches. Suddenly there were a lot of successful artists from Germany—for example Dune, Snap!, Loona, Marusha, plus figures like DJ Ötzi and Captain Jack. This in turn lured lots of young and adventurous people to come work for the record companies, people who often didn't have the relevant experience but on the other hand had unorthodox ideas and a lot of enthusiasm. Now we found ourselves doing business with such exotic personages as Andreas Dorau or Benjamin von Stuckrad-Barre—man, oh, man, did that guy have a long name. Since these weren't exactly the standard, all-powerful, infallible, stuffy record company people, our introduction to the music business wasn't difficult. The husband-and-wife duo who ran the label was actually even crazier than us musicians. Plus, for a new band, we were already pretty old. Really we got our first record contract at an age when most bands have either broken up already or even died. And we got a whole lot of money. We must have gotten a hundred times what the first company had offered us. And so we signed the contract without even glancing at it. We just flipped through the many pages of clauses and conditions, found our names, and scrawled our signatures on the line next to them. There could have been anything in there. In the end, we couldn't have cared less what exactly was in the record contract; the important thing was that we had one. And now that we did, a lot of things were going to change for us.

We just assumed that we would never have to work another job. It was of course clear to us that we were going to record one or several albums, but what we hadn't thought about was that the label would also want to sell those albums and to call people's attention to them. To that end, we were supposed to make videos and go on a promotional tour during which the album—or rather the product, as it was now referred to—would be presented to the right journalists. Then we would be asked questions by the journalists, questions which we couldn't answer because we had never thought about such things, and also had never practiced really articulating them. We had assumed that we could express our feelings and opinions in the music and not have to formulate them in words, but apparently people heard the music differently than we did. Or they didn't even listen to the music in the first place.

But we hadn't gotten to that point yet when we signed the contract without reading it. And I don't know what would have had to be in there to keep us from signing it. Supposedly there are record contracts where it says the employees of the record label always have to put on clown noses whenever they meet with the band. Or the other way around. But the way things looked then, there was nothing fishy in our contract.

At first, nothing at all happened. Then suddenly we were asked what producer we wanted. We were totally unprepared for this question. I didn't even know what a producer actually did. In Feeling B, the so-called producer was working for the Stasi. His job was to keep an eye on who visited us in the studio and what kind of lyrics we sang. But Richard did know what a producer was, and he knew a few names, the mention of which met with nothing but laughter from the label. These famous people—nay, legends—would never work for an unknown band like us. Actually, no producer in the world has much interest in devoting his energy to a band's debut album. But our record company was putting up the money for it. And producers need money too.

It was then explained to us that on every CD, the producer is listed by name. And so we were sent off to the record store to write down a few names. As far as the writing goes, we were very successful, though we were probably a bit too excited to determine which was the actual producer of a given album among the many names listed on the CD case. Anyway, we picked out a certain Greg Hunter. We found his name on a Killing Joke CD. This was one of the bands, like Ministry, the Prodigy, Pantera, the Cult, and the Cure, who we used to sit up all night listening to. The people at the record company were happy we weren't prattling on about Rick Rubin or Bob Rock anymore and set about getting in touch with the producer. The idea was that he would come visit us in our practice space to get to know us and our music.

The person we got seemed more like a homeless person. He listened politely, but somewhat indifferently, to our efforts in the practice space and probably made some comments that weren't particularly helpful. That night we all went out, and we tried to show him the most interesting side of Berlin. We went to more places over the course of this one night than we usually would have in a whole month. We even went to watch a Turkish rap battle. Alcohol must be harder to come by in England than in Berlin, because Greg took full advantage. That night he threw up on Till's rug, and he spent the next day asleep on the couch in the practice space. By the afternoon, he had recovered just enough that he was able to eat a banana. We took him back to the airport, and to this day we don't know who he was or what he might have thought of us because we never heard from him again.

At that time, there was a really popular band from Sweden called Clawfinger, and the person listed as the producer on their CD seemed to actually be a producer. And so we invited Jacob Hellner to our concert in Hamburg—but in doing so failed to consider that we were completely unknown in Hamburg, and that Hamburg was in the West, where a club isn't automatically full just because there's a concert going on. What impression must it have made on Jacob to see us in a club that was not only tiny but empty on top of that? For our part, we liked him a lot. He didn't look at all like someone who produced rock music; he looked more like a friendly trade school instructor. My whole worldview was shaken. I thought everybody who was successful at making music had a scarred face and chain smoked. And here was our new producer, polite as can be, looking at us like a doctor looks at a patient. Like Greg Hunter before him, he came to see us in our practice space and sat on the same couch, but unlike his predecessor, he brought a colleague named Carl with him, listened to a few songs, recorded them on his Walkman right there, and suggested a few things we'd never thought of before. He dove right into the music, brought out the best—and probably also the beast—in us, and helped us to put our ideas and our feelings into the songs. Now we realized for the first time what a good producer was able to do.

He also decided we would make the record in Sweden, which of course we thought was very exciting and momentous. He probably just had no desire to leave home on account of some small-time band. I mean, Stockholm was where he lived. I was afraid of flying back then, so I drove to Sweden and claimed it was because I wanted to bring our instruments to Stockholm myself. The ferry passage alone was totally exciting. When we reached shore, a wonderful landscape opened up before me. I also really liked Stockholm itself. Here I had a chance to see what a city looked like that hadn't been bombed to bits during World War II.

Jacob took us to Polar Studios, which apparently had been built by ABBA. Everything there looked wonderful—a real seventies vibe. What impressed us most was that there was a refrigerator and you were allowed to take as many Cokes or bottles of mineral water as you wanted. The very next day, I went back to the studio eager to finally start making the record. When I arrived, there was all sorts of activity. People were plugging in cables, setting up microphones, and bringing in amplifiers. There was no place for me to comfortably sit down. All of a sudden everybody was only speaking English.

Enough time passed that I couldn't take it anymore and I finally asked Jacob what I should do. He said in his friendly way, "Flake, please don't do anything!" And so I sat on a couch in the break room and drank Coke and mineral water. If I'd known we would end up having to pay for everything ourselves, I'd have shown a little more restraint, but for a long time we thought the record company was paying for everything we did. Which of course they do at first, but then they get it back from you later on. Then, to my disappointment, I learned that to start with they would only be recording drums, so there was nothing for me to do.

So I went out walking. I was fascinated by all the water in the city. Real ocean liners—the term is completely outdated now, but I don't know what else to call them—sailed through the middle of the city, which in part was built on different islands. And the water was very clean and inviting. It was insane. I couldn't stop staring at the boats on the shore. Every day I discovered new, even more memorable streets and landscapes. I also got used to taking the long way, on foot, from where we were staying on the edge of town to the studio.

It was weeks later before I finally recorded my organ parts and samples in a tiny basement studio. You don't need an expensive ABBA studio to record keyboards; a cheap basement is enough. That's because the room sound doesn't matter, the notes are recorded directly to tape—in my case an ADAT cassette, an invention nobody knows about anymore. All my homemade samples were retuned so that they actually fit the songs. While recording, I also noticed how sloppily I'd been playing my parts up to that point. I put a lot of effort into it, which meant it took over a week just to record my parts. Most of the time I was alone in the studio with Jacob or his co-producer Carl. When we went out to lunch together, they tried to take me to good restaurants, and we went to all kinds of places.

Once Jacob even took me to eat sushi. There's a first time for everything, I guess. I sipped a brown tea that tasted like smoked meat, chewed the algae and the rubbery fish in disbelief, and waited for the real food. For a long time we sat in silence. I had no idea what to talk to him about; I didn't know anything about music or new instruments. I didn't know a single one of the bands he tried to tell me about. I also couldn't judge whether our record was coming together or not. I thought everything sounded cool, but the band was always unsatisfied in some way. It turned out to be a problem that the producer didn't speak any German. As a result, he only judged the singing by how it sounded and not by the lyrical content. I actually thought that was a good thing—after all, I loved all the English bands I listened to, and I didn't have a clue what the lyrics were about.

At night, when we were back at the place where we were staying, we'd end up fighting over Till's singing and the guitar sound. To me our guitars always sounded the same; I had no idea what the guitarists were talking about, so I usually just went for a walk. There weren't many other options available to us in terms of how to spend our free time. It's true we did manage to rent a couple of bad English-language movies from a video store in the neighborhood, but we couldn't get into the clubs in town. There were long lines out front, like there used to be back in the East. All kinds of people would be let in ahead of us, and we would slip ever farther back in line. Either we weren't dressed the right way or we had unknowingly violated some code of behavior that applied there.

The only time we did get into a club was for the record release party for Clawfinger's second album. After all, we now had the same producer. In Sweden, it seemed commonplace to celebrate such occasions in a very unglamorous manner. Actually, you couldn't even call it a celebration. It was really just a concert in a small club. And it was really hot in there. For us, the beer was prohibitively expensive and we had to stand in line forever to get it. I was dying from thirst. Then a girl offered me her beer bottle. Greedily I took a large swig—and only one swig, since it turned out to be homemade liquor. I actually had the air knocked out of me. At that point, I walked out the door and went back home.

We slept on bare mattresses—when we weren't crouched in front of an old television watching Paul play Meteorite 3. The way buying alcohol worked was also new to us. What I did most of the time was to buy a couple cans of beer at the supermarket on the way back from the studio and sit and drink them on the couch that night. Once, out of boredom, I started to read everything on the can. The alcohol content was listed. Really, just two percent? There was almost no alcohol in the beer. I hadn't noticed beforehand, but now that I knew, I didn't care for the beer one bit. I didn't even want to finish the can. And so I tried to find real beer.

To do so, I had to go to a special shop called a Systembolaget and take a number like at the employment office. From the layout of the place, you wouldn't have thought they were selling liquor—it looked more like a law firm or a doctor's office, which then again was actually kind of fitting. There were bars on the windows. After about forty-five minutes, my number was called, and upon producing my ID I was able to buy beer. I had to pick the kind I wanted out of a catalog—there were no bottles visible anywhere in the store. It was such a hassle that, whenever we went, we always bought a bunch of liquor, too, although it was really very expensive.

The Swedes probably did the same thing we did, because on the weekends an ungodly number of drunks filled the streets. I'd never seen people so drunk. They moved primarily in groups of three, with the person in the middle being propped up by the other two. They vomited all over the place and with great frequency. I saw some of them trying to board a stone wall, thinking it was a subway train. Heaters were built into the outside walls of the buildings to keep them from freezing to death while waiting in line for hours outside the clubs.

In my free time, I walked back and forth across the city, and in doing so realized how quickly I could get to the edge and out into relatively unspoiled nature. Whenever I went back to the studio and told everybody about my walks, all the pent-up anger was unloaded on me.

The mood was tense. We decided not to mix the record in Sweden as planned, but to go to Hamburg instead.

There the mood was completely different. Summer had truly arrived by then. In Stockholm, anything above forty degrees was considered warm. Girls were already running around barelegged. By contrast, the weather in Hamburg seemed like a heat wave. Plus some of our old friends from Schwerin had since moved to Hamburg and were able to show us around. For us East Germans, the city was incredibly exciting. I'd never experienced anything as wild as the Hamburger Club. Berlin seemed like a small town by comparison.

We went all out every night. It didn't matter where we went—the Purgatory, the Hans-Albers-Eck, the Mojo Club, Tiefenrausch, the Grünspan, the Prinzenbar, or even a concert at the Docks or the Star Club, where supposedly the Beatles used to play for weeks at a time. I'd never been out that much in my life.

As a result, I wasn't much use to anyone during the day. When I woke up, I'd drag myself down to the store to buy some yogurt and berries. Then I'd walk the whole way to the studio, slowly regaining consciousness as I went. In the studio, I ate my yogurt. Sometimes the berries had gotten moldy— not because I had been walking so long, but because I hadn't paid enough attention when I bought them. I had my hands full just dealing with myself. Then we all went out to lunch together. There I could drink a few beers on the sly and be gladdened by my gradual recovery. Even though no one knew about our band, since obviously we hadn't put anything out yet, our self-confidence was very high. At night we sat cocky as can be on the steps outside the Golden Pudel Club and waited for a nice woman to come talk to us. Preferably she would be so drunk that she wouldn't be bothered by our outward appearance. Or by the fact that we were completely wasted. Apparently there just weren't that many drunk women in the world, not even in Hamburg, since most of the time we remained alone. We could have sat around like that for years; no one would ever have come to talk to us.

The people whose apartment we were staying in were on vacation at the time. I wanted to wash my smelly clothes, so I put them in the washing machine with some detergent and went to the studio. I didn't know that when you flipped the light switch to turn off the light, it turned the washing machine off too—I guess it was meant to save power—and so that night I just put my wet and still smelly clothes back on. I assumed they'd been washed. At the time, I didn't have much experience with doing laundry. I did wonder why everything stank so bad, but it never occurred to me that it might have something to do with me. After we had gotten good and drunk at all the clubs, come daylight we went to the Erika—that was a breakfast pub where construction workers, punks, and pimps all ate their hamburgers together in harmony. Although one of us kept burping the whole time, the service was very friendly. The following night, the Pudel Club was closed. I say night, but it was probably closer to morning. We had kind of lost our sense of time, but not our improbably great thirst.

Since the owners of the club were supposed to be punks, we figured they wouldn't mind if we took a bottle of egg liqueur and a few beers. One of the shutters was pretty easy to slide up, and soon we were sitting happily on the bank of the Elbe, watching the first tugboats and barges of the new day. We threw the empty beer bottles at chunks of Styrofoam floating past us. We played catch with the bottle of egg liqueur—if you caught the bottle, you got to take a slug from it. We were still playing as we slowly made our way home through the Hamburg morning. Such wonderful nights—I won't soon forget them.

At the studio, we could just close the curtains and watch movies on VHS. That's when I saw *The Gods Must Be Crazy*, which made that another wonderful day. Of course I also went into the mixing room, but I couldn't be of any use in there. Criticizing the sound would have been just as pointless as praising it. In the latter case, if the band was yet again unsatisfied with something, I'd only have been undermining them.

After we'd finally finished the album in Hamburg, the record company explained to us that first we had to put out a single to drum up excitement for the upcoming album, and this meant putting out a video as well. We were actually going to make a music video!

The record company was beginning to regret the courage they'd shown in the beginning, and so they picked "*Seemann*" because it was our quietest song. The initial idea for the song came from Oliver, who thought up this great riff on the bass. Whenever we played this song at a show, he always had to really concentrate so he wouldn't mess up—as a result, he wasn't so crazy about the song anymore. But of course now he wasn't supposed to play the song, he was just supposed to act along to the music, as they called it.

László Kadar was chosen as the director. He's the one who did that weird Jever beer commercial where the guy falls down in the sand dunes. And then the lighthouse fills up with beer. We thought we had made a brilliant move in hiring a guy who made commercials to direct our music video, since at the end of the day the video was supposed to be a commercial for us, right? In our excitement, we forgot to read the script. All we knew was that it would have something to do with boats, and we figured that was good.

And so we drove to a film studio near Hamburg. Right around where Dieter Bohlen lives. I walked around a little bit just to see what ol' Dieter's neighborhood was like. If the house I saw was really his, it was pleasantly modest. But all the time I spent walking around, I really should have been worrying about the video.

Inside a sound stage, piles of sand had been dumped out onto the floor, and in the middle of it was a cardboard boat that had been slapped together as haphazardly as possible. First, we were sent off to makeup. There waiting for us were two characters who only spoke English. Their pants were sagging so low we could see their underwear. Later this would actually be in style, but we couldn't have known that then, and we considered letting the two of them know that their pants were falling off. Without hesitation they proceeded to cut all our hair off without asking. For me they left a small strip that they put gel on and made stick straight up so that it looked like I had a lump of coal on my head. Given how much my ears stick out, it didn't look good, and I wondered a bit at their decision. But Richard was truly devastated. And there was absolutely nothing he could do about it. Next they started filming us pulling the boat or whatever it was through the desert. The background would be filmed separately, something they called blue screen compositing. They'd taken footage of the harbor in Hamburg for the purpose. To increase the erotic factor, they hired a woman who was supposed to look striking and walk through a subway tunnel. MTV turned the video down, and I don't think Viva was around yet. Maybe they also turned it down. Almost no one in the world has seen this video, and that's not at all a bad thing.

—

Till starts frantically lifting weights again. It's definitely not healthy. Though it probably doesn't make any difference, since playing in a rock band is kind of the unhealthiest thing I can think of. All that noise, not enough sleep, lots of bus rides and long flights, smoke-filled clubs, smoke-filled practice spaces, smoke-filled cars, smoky dressing rooms, really just a general lack of oxygen, plus stage fright—which isn't just a mental state, it affects your whole body—also all the bad, hastily scarfed-down food, and of course the ungodly quantities of alcohol. So exercise in and of itself is a fine thing.

I myself have never exercised. In school it was so bound up with torment that it never would have occurred to me that exercise could also be something good. In my experience, exercise was simply something that hurt and should be avoided as much as possible. But when you're in as sporty and exercise-focused a band as ours, this stance can attract unwanted attention, so Till and I came up with a trick. About twenty-five years ago, I got in the habit of holding off on drinking until exactly an hour before the show started. If I drank anything before then, I ran the risk of being unconscious before the concert began, or at least getting horribly sick. I can remember early concerts we played where the whole time I had to concentrate on not falling over. But if I didn't start drinking until an hour before, the effects were manageable. The only snag was if the concert got delayed, which can definitely happen at some of the smaller festivals. Plus there were also times when we were on such a roll on tour that we'd drink from one concert clear through to the next without sobering up in between—see, they give you a big wheat beer to drink at breakfast, and I mean it's very nutritious—but by and large, I've managed to stick to the one-hour rule.

I just had to figure out what I wanted to drink during this one-hour window to get myself into shape. Beer wasn't ideal, one because there was too little alcohol in it, and two because then I would have to pee really badly during the concert. I didn't like drinking liquor before the concert either—it made me dehydrated, and I'd get drunk too quickly. I really like the taste of coffee liqueur and stuff like that, but it's too sweet and cloying, and anyone who's ever had to vomit after drinking it will understand all too well that you can't ever drink it in large quantities again. Champagne was okay, but, again, I didn't really like the taste that much. Plus the bubbles annoyed me. And I wasn't sure if the alcohol content was high enough for me. And so I decided on red wine. I was amazed at the huge differences between the different kinds—I used to think wine was wine, but now I know better. Some red wines taste really bad.

Then, at a concert in Portugal, the organizers wanted to give us a gift of something uniquely Portuguese, and so they gave us a bottle of port. I was totally surprised at how good it tasted, all soft and a little sweet, but not too sweet. I drank a big glass and I was in good shape. No one told us that you're actually supposed to enjoy port wine in smaller doses. Port glasses are about as big as a thimble. But Till and I thought we'd found our ideal drink, and since then we've always asked for a bottle of port wine before the concert.

On that first occasion, in my state of bliss and contentment, I asked Till for another drop of port wine, but since my speech was already a bit slurred, he heard *sport wine*, which he thought was incredibly funny. At which point

I did too. After all, certain witty hash smokers like to say that they're going to roll themselves a nice "sport cigarette." Or at least the German ones do. From then on we'd always take a magic marker, write an S in front of the "port" on the bottle, and tell everybody it was sport time. And then we'd start drinking.

It wasn't long before one of us would ask, without even thinking about it, "Well, is it sport time yet?" Or we'd just say "Sport time," plain and simple. If I was in one of the other guys' dressing rooms, I'd mention in a really offhand kind of way that I had to go back over to my dressing room to do some sport stuff and the others would accept it as a matter of course. Then I would sit down on our couch, drink my big glass of port wine in just a few sips, and not move for a while. And then to actually get ready for the concert, I'd jump up at some point and start flailing around like I sometimes do during the show. In an instant I'd be completely out of breath. Plus I would also have pulled a muscle before the concert had even begun. But that was before; now I do my exercises.

Tom comes back in. "Meet and greet!" he shouts, and we jump up and walk down the hallway. Here's Heike, the liaison between the band and the outside world. She hands each of us a magic marker. We're sent into a large room where the fans are already waiting for us.

There are about thirty people, all eagerly awaiting our entrance. Radio contest winners and other lucky ducks specially chosen for the privilege. I don't know what they've been promised, but in any case they're very happy to see us. We split up, and I turn to the first couple I see, smiling politely. The woman throws her arms out wide to give me a hug. Then she stops mid-motion and recoils in horror. She wasn't counting on the stench radiating from my clothes. I'm like the Olchis, that family from the children's books who live in a garbage dump. I'm used to it by now, but for the uninitiated it's a real shock. Her smile seems a bit forced as she holds her arm out as far as she can to hand me a CD to sign. I ask her name and sign. And on it goes with each and every one of them. Every now and then, I do a quick check-in with my bandmates and we compare notes on the fans, what they're asking for and what they're like. Schneider tells me that over in the back is a man who had him write his autograph on his back so he could get it tattooed later.

That's not at all uncommon. I used to be completely shocked at the idea that anyone would get a tattoo of our band name. The first Rammstein tattoo I saw was in Vienna. If someone wants a tattoo of our signature on their back or on their arm, then it's smart to have us write our name right there on their body. We're happy to do it. By now we've signed all kinds of things. Cell phones, shirts, hats, handkerchiefs, bags, sneakers, strollers, wheelchairs, newspapers, paper money, IDs and passports, pants, pretty girls' bare skin—this we're especially happy to do—sunglasses, guitars, guitar picks—on which it's very hard to fit six signatures—tickets, photos of us and of others, posters that cover an entire table, flags that are even bigger, and God knows what else. Compared to all that, a bare back is really easy. Of course I could mess with him and write something different; after all, he can't see it. Maybe I'll write "Falke." Sometimes I do that by accident when I have to give out a lot of autographs. But that's not particularly funny. I could also write "Helene Fischer" on his back. She's kind of like the German Taylor Swift.

Instead I tell Schneider that there's a girl up front who claims to know him from Stuttgart. I tell him he should look over there first and try to remember her name so it's not so embarrassing. I'm just making it up, it's not at all true, but now I get to watch his brain working as he tries to remember a name he never knew in the first place. Then a fan hands me his phone. I say thank you and start to put it in my pocket, but my suit doesn't have any pockets. The fan laughs because he thinks I'm making a joke. Like I'm only acting like I didn't know that I'm supposed to talk into the phone. And so I put the phone to my ear and say, "Hello." It's breaking up a bit. The reception in here isn't the best. Now I hear something: "Wolfgang, what's going on? Wolfgang, Wolfgang! Hello!" I give Wolfgang his phone back. "D'you hear that!" he screams into the phone. "Classic Rammstein!"

The others prefer to use their phones to take photos. Since we're walking around separately, we all have to be photographed separately. Sometimes people stop us so they can get two or three band members in the frame together with themselves or their boyfriend or girlfriend.

Tom puts an end to the confusion by putting us all together for a group photo. Meanwhile Heike collects all the phones and takes a photo of us and the whole group. Then we go back to our dressing rooms. It's five minutes till show time.

I want to go to the bathroom one last time before the concert, but Tom stops me in the hallway and asks why I haven't signed the autograph cards and the posters hanging up in the hallway yet. I grab the pen that's stuck to the wall with adhesive tape and sign the posters. There are rather a lot of them. They'll be given out as a kind of thank you to the organizers and the local crew. When I'm finished, I stick the pen back on the wall, and Tom hands me a thinner silver pen for the autograph cards. I'd estimate there are about a hundred of them. Luckily the other guys signed their names in the same place every time, so I don't have to keep looking for a new spot. Still two minutes. High time to put in my In-Ear System.

This bears explaining. Rock bands as we know them have been around since the fifties. Back then, when they went to play at a dance, they would just set up on stage and start playing. A drum kit is loud enough to be heard in a dance hall. The guitars and bass, however, weren't so loud, and so guitarists invented the electric guitar. Now they'd each have their own amplifier on stage with them. A piano couldn't really be heard over all that, and so the first electric pianos were invented by placing pickups over all the strings and plugging into an amp. All that was left was the singer. He got a microphone and a so-called PA. The microphone was plugged into an amplifier, and from there the signal went to two speakers that were placed on the left and right sides of the stage. When bands started playing in larger venues, it became necessary to further amplify the guitars and the drums, so the people standing in the back could also hear. A two-speaker PA wasn't enough anymore; you needed special bass speakers—or subwoofers—since the normal speakers weren't capable of reproducing a wide spectrum of frequencies. Without subwoofers the music would sound distorted. Now of course it was no longer sufficient for the PA to have just a simple amplifier. You wanted to be able to control the volume levels of each individual instrument, thus everything—the voice, the drums, and the guitar amps—was miked and it was all run through a mixing console. From there the signal went to the main amp, which is the blanket term for the big power amplifier or power amplifiers for the front of house, then passed through a crossover unit that divided the frequencies, and out of the speakers came the band's whole sound. The more speakers you attach and the bigger the main amp gets, meaning the more amplifier power is added on, the louder the music can get without sounding distorted. The guitarists can hear themselves perfectly well on stage because they all have their own amplifiers. But the singer can't, since he's standing behind the speakers that his voice is coming out of. Sometimes he hears his voice echoing off the far wall of the venue, but since the sound takes so much time to travel there and back, the singer hears himself on a delay and can't sing in rhythm. For that reason, the monitor was invented. From the mixing console, a second output was now fed into an extra amplifier. This powered two speakers that were placed on the left and right-hand sides of the stage and pointed back at the musicians. This comes with its own English term: side field monitoring.

Then, however, rock bands, and the guitarists especially, started turning the volume on their amps up to earsplitting levels—ostensibly this was because only at that volume could they get the full tone they wanted, but in reality I think it was probably just because they liked being that loud. Whatever the case, once again the singer couldn't really hear himself. If he turned up his channel in the monitors, the mic would feed back. And so the singer got his own monitor, which was set up right in front of him. To ensure the sound reached him, the speaker was tilted in such a way that he was basically screaming into his own face. We started calling this monitor the "cheese wedge." The bigger the band was, the more speakers and amplifiers they had, and eventually the stage at a rock concert started to look like the storage room at a furniture store. There was barely any room left to walk around.

Then someone invented the In-Ear System. Now a signal travels from the monitor amp to a transmitter. Each band member wears a small receiver on his belt that's about as big as a cigarette pack. From there, a cable leads to a pair of headphones. Now you don't need monitors on stage anymore, and it's easier to control the overall sound. At first, though, I had problems with my receiver, since I sometimes have to change clothes at the drop of a hat or jump around on stage, and the thing kept falling off or getting lost. And so I took a belt and made myself a really tight neckband. I stuck the receiver to the back of it with gaffer tape. Then I only needed really short earphone cables and had total freedom of movement without having to worry about the earphones falling out. The other guys in the band wear the receiver on their belt and have Tom tape the cable to their backs.

They're all ready to go already, of course. The monitor engineer has already turned on my receiver. I check to see if the volume is set to three. Then I carefully put the neckband on. The leather has gotten rock hard from the heat and my constant sweating, and the buckle pinches my larynx—it feels a little bit like somebody's trying to strangle me. But other than that, it fits perfectly. It doesn't move around, at least. Through the headphones, I can also hear that the band in the dressing room has started playing the first song of the set, that way right from the start things will be really grooving on stage.

That's a word that I'm not wild about using, but I don't know how else to express the feeling you get when a band is so locked in and you're completely carried away by what they're playing.

But since the concert is actually supposed to start now, they all put down their instruments and gather in the hallway. The band calls for me.

"I have to go *in die Tannen* real quick!" I shout and hurry to the bathroom. Why am I the only one who finds that so funny? I like using lines from our lyrics in everyday contexts; I get a kick out of it. Whenever I want something I ask "*Ob jemand mir etwas steigen kann*," like the line from "Rosenrot," and I also like to yell out "*Ich habe keine Lust!*"

That's another one of our lines, and really you can use it on any occasion. It means, basically, "I don't feel like it!" Now, though, I do feel like it. I just have to hurry; I myself know that I'm late. All the same, I still have to be careful with the zippers.

When I get back to the hallway, Tom is already holding the tray of shot glasses. We toast with gold tequila before every concert. My glass is lighter, because it's only got lemonade in it today, but of course I still want to participate. Looks like there's a second glass of lemonade. Someone else must have gone a bit overboard last night and can't stand the sight of liquor at the moment. Let's see who takes it.

Now Nicolai is standing with us, the tour manager—actually he's everybody's boss. He has big headphones on; he's in touch via radio with the stage crew. He says, "The stage is ready."

Then he takes a look at us, gives a quick grin, and says into his radio, "The band's ready, house lights off."

I hear it only faintly, because I've already put my earphones in and am hearing my stage mix. It's true there's no music in the hall—we're not playing yet—but there are microphones on stage that pick up the sound of the audience. I can hear them getting excited now that the house lights have been turned off. That's a sure sign that the show is finally about to start. The people have been looking forward to this moment for hours. But their joy is still a little premature since we're just now toasting with the shots. Knock it back—now here we go.

Or at least now we're walking in the direction of the stage. This is like the scenes you see in movies about rock concerts that show the band walking down long, dark corridors. God knows how many times we've gotten lost and ended up in some kitchen or storage room. Or in the middle of the crowd. The people were a little confused; after all, they were expecting us up on stage. This kind of thing happens more often than you might think, since we usually just follow the crewmember ahead of us without thinking. It can also happen that we first have to take an elevator to the right floor. Then we have a few seconds of down time to look at each other and be amazed at what we all look like and what's become of us. Sometimes we just have to laugh, realizing the kind of ridiculousness we're involved in at an age when other people are starting to think about retirement. We definitely don't look serious in these moments.

Then a door opens, and we realize from the atmosphere that we're now inside the arena. We can't see it, since everything is dark backstage. The technicians are shining their flashlights this way and that. It's a bit like camp. We climb over all different kinds of cables, duck out of the way of the spotlights, and step on stage.

In a movie, the applause would well up at this point, and we would start playing, but this isn't a movie. The curtain is still down.

This way we can take our time and get to our places. I check my keyboard, but of course I can't tell whether everything is in order. I mean, I can't see inside of it. Even if I could, I wouldn't see anything, so I can spare myself the whole procedure. Maybe I'm slowly starting to get excited now. Stage fright is a real condition, like an illness—there's no downplaying it. When you don't feel good, it doesn't matter what causes the symptoms. But aside from the stage fright, I don't feel so bad at all. The lemonade burns pleasantly in my throat.

I look to the front and see Till standing on a lamp that is being lifted up to the ceiling. Once he got on stage he was quick to put on his little pink fur jacket. I turn to Nicolai, who is standing backstage. He signals with his flashlight to say that everybody's ready, and I start the intro to the first song. It's nine o'clock on the dot. Not that I can see that. I won't notice the clock hanging across from the stage for another half hour. I just know it because we always start on time. Why wouldn't we? I'm feeling good.

II

Just once I'd like to see one of our concerts from the crowd's perspective, but of course that's not going to happen, at least not as long as I'm in the band. I saw a recording once, and I was completely baffled at how it all looked. And the whole act that all the guys in the band put on—from where I stand on stage, I can't ever see it. It cracked me up, but it was just a video, and that's no substitute for what it feels like to really be there at the concert.

And so I can only describe what I see from the stage. After a few notes of my intro, rockets are fired from the scaffolding in time with the rhythmic accents that the guitar and drums are adding. On these beats, we're illuminated for a moment, so you can see our outlines through the half-transparent screen. This way the people know we're on stage and playing, but it's only after a long break that the curtain finally falls. After that they can see the stage, the light, and of course the band.

The first song we play is "*Ich tu dir weh*"—"I hurt you"—and not counting the intro, we play it without any theatrics. This way we can concentrate better on playing, which makes it really fun. Plus I'm getting a really good mix in my ears. From a grammar standpoint, this song should actually be called "Ich *tue* dir weh," but in love and war, or I mean of course in poems and songs, the rules of grammar are suspended. The song is about—no surprise here—pain and submission. I'm not entirely sure about that, however. It could all just be a metaphor for something. Though I don't know what pain is supposed to be a metaphor for.

One of our first songs dealt with a similar subject. It was called *"Feuer-räder"*—"Fire Wheels," though in English you might also call them Catherine wheels—and is relatively unknown since it wasn't on any of our studio albums. It was, however, really fun to play this song live. We bought a dog collar and leash at a sex shop, and I rode around the stage on Till's back. If I was drunk enough and really in a good mood, then I would ride Till through the crowd too. Once, in a club, we even rode down the bar. We knocked off all the glasses as we went, but nobody complained. I also had a riding crop in my hand that I kept whipping Till with. That wasn't from the sex shop, but rather from an equestrian store. I tried it out once by hitting myself softly on the leg—it hurt like hell. I couldn't understand why I thought it was a good idea to hit Till's bare back with it as hard as I could. Both of us always felt great after this song. We realized that for it and songs like it, we could think up a few good routines for the live show.

For a while I would even break a bottle over Till's head. I can't remember anymore if in the beginning I actually managed to shatter a real bottle over his head. When you need glass to shatter for a scene in a movie, you use so-called sugar glass. I think it's actually made of sugar, but I never tasted it. In the old days, the boys in the cafés would eat their glasses to impress the girls. If they didn't regret it immediately, they'd regret it the next morning. My courage didn't extend that far; in fact, I don't think there was any courage to speak of. So I don't know how real glass tastes, either.

At any rate, on one tour we brought along a few crates of empty sugar glass bottles. Half the bottles broke in transit. Sometimes we were able to repair them with tape, but we could never be careful enough. To really sell the effect, we put a little fake blood in the bottles in the dressing room. Stupidly enough there were a couple of times during a concert when the bottleneck would break off as I was lifting it and the blood would spray all over the stage without touching Till. No one ever noticed, of course. But sometimes the thin bottles of sugar glass would break in the dressing room when we were filling them, and then all my clothes would be stained with blood. If the person doing the filling got angry, the whole room would start to look like a slaughterhouse in no time. On those tours, I wouldn't bring many spare clothes with me, and so it sometimes happened that I'd be walking around a museum the next day—or trying to buy condoms at the drugstore at night—with blood all over me. Even I would have had me arrested. Meanwhile, all I wanted to do was mess with Till on stage.

During "*Ich tu dir weh*," though—that is, the song we're playing right now—it was usually Till who was supposed to torment me. Doing it the other way around would have been too hard to believe, since Till could brush me aside with his pinky finger. In order to make our mutual dislike believable, I would keep needling Till throughout the set. I'd play shrill, wrong notes on purpose, make fun of him behind his back, and sometimes come forward to shove him or kick him in the butt. Then, during the bridge, Till would grab me, drag me across the stage, and throw me in a bathtub. Then he rode a special platform up to the ceiling, so that everyone could see him, and poured a bucket full of fire over me. All the while he'd keep double-checking that I was really dead. And the old Flake was dead, because I would climb out of the bathtub in my sparkle costume, which I hadn't had on before, and so in a way I'd come skipping back out on stage, reborn.

We did the whole bit on the last tour, when we played the song in the middle of the set, and it was kind of the climax of the show. Now we play it right at the beginning, so we don't waste our energy on such foolishness. But it would be too much of a shame to leave the song out on that account. Just playing the song straight is already so much fun—it's a real shame that it's already over. The first song is always like that. There are so many new things to take in. Until the curtain rises, I don't know what the venue looks like, how big it is; sometimes I've even been surprised to see that the concert was taking place outside and the sun was shining. Or that a giant Ferris wheel was spinning in front of the stage and the fans were waving from the seats.

—

I NEVER USED TO think about how a concert should start. In Feeling B, we would just stumble out on stage and make sure all the instruments worked before we started playing the first song. Sometimes one of us had wandered off and we had to wait. We would keep screaming his name into the microphone in the hopes that he would hear us.

Later, we started with an improvised intro which, depending on what kind of shape we were in that day, would get a good or bad response from the crowd. Most of the time, people just wanted us to start playing our songs.

I saw my first concert film when the band went to Poland. One morning, at a club, they were showing *Stop Making Sense*. In the movie, David Byrne walks out on stage with his guitar. There's nothing on stage but a boom box. Byrne presses the play button, and a beat starts up. He plays the guitar along with it and sings the first song. With every song that follows, another instrument comes out on stage. I thought that was great and would have liked to do it myself, but I mean, the idea was already taken. Plus that wouldn't have worked for us; we were more of a punk band.

Then I saw some videos of Prince's concerts. His shows were major spectacles and were exciting from start to finish. Prince came out on stage in a futuristic-looking car. The sound of the car door slamming marks the first beat of the first song. Brilliant. I'd have liked to do that too, but for one thing this idea had already been done, and for another I had no idea how you got a car up on stage, especially since we mostly played in small clubs. Not to mention how you got the car back off the stage in the middle of the show—we barely had enough space as it was.

In the beginning with Rammstein, we always used to open with the song "Rammstein"—our way of introducing ourselves, so to speak. On the first note that Till sang, i.e., *Ramm*, he would either light a Roman candle, which would ignite the gasoline we'd poured on stage beforehand, or he'd have one of us come up and light the sleeves of his coat. The instrumentation on "Rammstein" is so sparse that the sound guy could use it to make sure the mix was right. During soundcheck, the room often sounds a bit different, since there aren't any people there yet to dampen the reverb. Over time we came up with more and more songs, so naturally we wanted to change up the setlist—I mean, we couldn't keep opening with "Rammstein" for years. But it was only after we'd put out our second record that we came up with a new setlist and tried out new ways of beginning the concert. We would pay attention to the crowd's reaction but could never be sure what effect the opening had, since of course the crowd was different everywhere we went and would always respond differently.

For a while we would send Olli out on stage alone with an acoustic guitar. He'd start playing something singer-songwriter-ish, and the crowd would be surprised, since they'd expected something very different from us. At least, that was the effect we were going for. Then a line rocket would come whizzing at Olli from the mixing console and hit his guitar. We'd yank a rope that was attached to Olli's chair, so right when the rocket hit he'd fly off the stage. At that same moment, the guitars and the drums would start playing the real song at full volume, and the proper order of things would be restored, so to speak.

Later we'd open the show by seeming to magically appear on stage. First flames would shoot up the speaker stacks and then meet in the center of the stage. Then the curtain rose, and you'd see the empty stage. With the first note, a firecracker would go off. When the smoke had cleared, I'd suddenly be standing there. I had of course been hiding there the whole time. I started playing. At the start of the next measure, there was another flash, and the next band member appeared. It went on like that until only Till was missing. When the verse started, you could hear Till singing, but you couldn't see him. But Schneider's bass drum would keep moving forward and then would suddenly be lifted up. Till had the drum on his shoulders as if it were his head. He stood there singing, looking like a cartoon character. When the first chorus came, he threw the drum on the floor.

We thought up ever more complicated ways of opening the concert. On the tour for the *Mutter* album, the whole stage set looked a bit like a clinic. Surgical lamps hung from the ceiling. We'd had an old dentist's chair repurposed for me to use as a keyboard stand, and I wore a white doctor's coat. Tom came up with the idea of pinning a blood bag to it. Lord knows where he got hold of that. In any case, I walked out on stage like a kind of Frankenstein—it was the doctor whose name was Frankenstein, not the monster—and went to work at my dentist's chair, turning the lamp on and pressing a few keys. Then I started playing the intro. Slowly a giant pregnant mother started to descend from the ceiling, inside of which the band was waiting. When the uterus made it all the way down, one band member after another fell out naked through the birth canal onto the stage. They only had little loincloths on, and they acted like they'd actually just been born. One by one they crawled over to a kind of shower, where they were rinsed off with carbon dioxide. This was supposed to fill them with energy, and they went to pick up their instruments and started playing. Then, when the first verse started, Till was lowered down from the ceiling on top of a surgical lamp.

On the Reise, Reise tour, we dressed up the crew so that they looked like we did on the tour posters. When the concert was supposed to begin, six members of the crew who were supposed to be us stepped on stage in front of the curtain and finished the last preparations. The crowd wondered why we didn't start playing. No one knew what this weirdness was all about. Then the curtain fell, and at the same moment we, the real musicians, started playing the first song, the crew members went off carrying the curtain. The song we were playing was "*Reise, Reise*," which we thought was very appropriate, since *Reise, Reise* was or maybe still is the wake-up call for sailors when they're about to go on watch.

For the *LIFAD* tour, which is the abbreviation for *Liebe ist für alle da*—"Love Is There for Everyone"—we kind of wrote a song especially to serve as the opener. Even as we were recording it, we had it in our heads that we could use it to start off the set. It was called the "*Rammlied*"—the "Ramm-song." We started playing the intro behind a transparent curtain. Till had had a dentist install a lamp in his mouth. For the power cable, they had to punch a hole in his cheek and put a pipe in for the cable to fit through. He had a little plug that he always had to keep in the hole when we weren't playing, otherwise whenever he drank anything it would leak out of his cheek.

I admire Till a lot for doing this, because first of all it's incredibly hard to sing with all that stuff in your mouth, and second the lamp gets pretty hot. The first time he said "Ramm," the curtain fell, and things really got going.

—

THE FIRST SONG IS over way too quickly. I start the next one right away so there's no break in between. What I'm playing is the intro to "*Wollt ihr das Bett in Flammen sehen.*" I think it was our producer who suggested the title of this song—"Do you want to see the bed in flames?" Before then, the song was called something completely different, since nobody wanted to say, *Hey, let's play "Wollt ihr das Bett in Flammen sehen."* That would sound pretty goofy. When we first wrote the song, we called it "*Der Bringer.*" Basically the same in English: "The Bringer." We liked the main riff a whole lot. *That riff just brings it,* is what we thought. The lyrics came much later. But since the record has the other title, the official one—I'm not going to write it again—a lot of times the crew didn't know which song we were going to play when we said "*Der Bringer.*" And so now we always write the official title on the setlist.

I really love playing it. In one spot, I suddenly start jumping around like crazy, then go back to standing stiff as a board in front of my keyboard for the next verse, as if nothing happened. I once did this without thinking when I was really drunk, and since then I keep having to repeat it, or else it might look like I didn't feel like it or my heart wasn't completely in it that night. Of course it's completely pointless to repeat such a spontaneous thing, but otherwise I'd spend the whole concert just standing there, and that would be disappointing too. Unfortunately, after the little bit of jumping around I'm completely out of breath and have already broken a sweat. And it's only the second song.

At the end of the song, Till stands in what we call the ring of fire. Everybody in the band likes Johnny Cash. I don't know a single person who doesn't like Johnny Cash. His song is about love. Our ring of fire is made of actual fire and doesn't have that much to do with love. Although I'm standing a few meters away, it's already too hot for me, and I have to hold my breath. The most dangerous thing about fire isn't the heat itself, but rather the chance that you might get it in your lungs. The heat on your body just hurts. Especially if you already burned yourself the day before. It's a little like when you get a bad sunburn.

Before we thought up the ring of fire, this was the flamethrower part. Here Till got to really let loose with the flamethrower—basically he emptied it, because this song usually came last. Now it's the second song and it's already over.

I leave my finger on the key to let the last note ring out until the bass starts the intro to "*Keine Lust.*" This song has a particular charm. It's in 6/8 rhythm, a fast blues. It was one of the first things we came up with when, after a long break, we started collecting ideas for what would eventually be the *Reise, Reise* album, though we didn't know it at the time of course. If we hadn't already had a song that we called the bringer, "*Keine Lust*" would have been it.

On stage, I stand between two keyboards, a sampler made by a company called Ensoniq that went out of business a long time ago, and a Roland organ, which sadly isn't made anymore either. I guess that's just how life works: most of the really good things in this world are quickly replaced by things that are supposedly better but in reality much worse. At most they just leave out all the old ports and plugs so they aren't compatible with anything. Just so long as there's always something new. For example, when my glasses broke and I went to the optician to buy a new pair, the optician looked at me like I was from outer space and told me that he'd never seen this model before, it must be from an ancient collection. The fact was, though, I'd bought those glasses just two years earlier at the same store. Or, well, at least it only felt like two years.

I bought the sampler that I use on stage, along with a backup, on Ebay, and luckily I know someone who can repair this kind of gear. If he ever moves away, I'm screwed. I had the same kind of sampler when I first joined Rammstein, and I don't know where I would get all the sounds if the two I have now stopped working. Because these samplers are so old, they have a very limited amount of storage space, so limited that young people can't even imagine it. Early on I used to have to insert a floppy disk into the drive before every song to load the sounds I needed. The whole band would have to wait on me. For that reason, I had a hard drive built into one of the samplers. But I didn't know how finicky these machines were, and during one concert I got all excited and hit it with a microphone stand. It must have broken the hard drive, because I couldn't play for the rest of the show. The sampler didn't want to read my floppy disks anymore either. I stood there on stage like an idiot, gesturing apologetically. The band was pissed, of course, since we were also missing the sequences that they all used as cues.

Even then our music was built on us, as human beings, playing along to a groove made on a computer. In order to produce this, I would tap out a rhythm or a melodic line with my fingers and then quantize it. That meant the notes were arranged into a rhythm so perfect that I could never actually have played it. Sometimes I also dropped in a break beat, which is a drum part that I sampled, i.e., recorded, and then altered in such a way that it fit our song. Schneider then just played along by ear. When each particular part came along, I would press start on the sampler, and when there was a pause I pressed stop. If another loop was needed in the chorus, I had to switch. On beat, of course, so that the sampler—which is to say the sequencer built into the sampler—would play the right thing on the first beat. And so I had my hands completely full on stage and had to really concentrate because the band was following me. To make sure something like what happened to the hard drive couldn't happen again, we took the sequences off my sampler and recorded them onto a MIDI player. But since it was still me who had to work the thing, there was just as much room for error. Now the backliners take care of it. I'm up to my ears in it as it is, as the people say—assuming they still actually say that.

In making the album *Reise, Reise*, and on tour afterward, I also used an Apple laptop. I bought a program called Logic and downloaded a massive number of instrument plug-ins. But I kept having to update the operating system so I could download all the latest innovations, and then the old instruments wouldn't work anymore. And when I tried to download the updates for the old instruments, then either they didn't exist anymore or precisely the sounds that I used for my songs were missing. And at crucial moments, to my horror, the whole computer would freeze. Plus there were thousands of different sounds available for every single instrument. If I were thinking of a particular sound, I would spend hours searching through some databank only to end up forgetting what I'd actually been looking for. I probably had a million options, but actually they all sounded like shit— pardon the language. And if I ever did happen to find an interesting sound, it would turn out that it only sounded good on its own and wasn't even audible when combined with other instruments. I just about went insane, and finally just went back to my old sampler. For sounds that I use again and again, like the choir and the strings, I've got the other organ, so now I just jump goofily back and forth between the two instruments.

Man, "*Sehnsucht*" has already started! I was completely lost in thought, I didn't even notice. That's been happening to me more and more often recently. We've been playing these two songs back to back for such a long time now that I start playing "*Sehnsucht*" automatically. By the way, "*Sehnsucht*," which means *longing*, is a word that Americans really have an awful time trying to pronounce. When they say it, it sounds like *chainsaw*. That's *Kettensäge* in German and actually fits the song pretty well. In fact, it fits better than *Sehnsucht*, but of course we don't want to sing our songs in English.

Right at the outset, a few explosions go off over our heads in sync with the drum hits. When we started, we had to work on this song forever before the explosions fit the drumming exactly. That's really important, since they're so loud that we would get completely off beat if they exploded at the wrong time. It's incredibly hard to synchronize the pyrotechnics with the music, because the fireworks have to be ignited first, and you never know how long it's going to take.

During the bridge a green wall of fire climbs up the side of the stage, and I'm happy to see it burn evenly, since it looks really good. A bit later a foul-smelling cloud of smoke blows my way. It really burns your nose; it doesn't just smell poisonous, it probably is poisonous.

On "*Sehnsucht*," Till also does his famous hammer. Every singer has his own idiosyncrasies, and Till once had the impulse at a show to incessantly pound his fist into his knee. Now he does it whenever it's musically appropriate. At certain intense moments he even does it with both fists. That's the double hammer. When Till first started, his thighs were always black and blue afterward.

In the final chorus, he bashes the microphone into his forehead as hard as he can. He hits it so hard the microphone breaks. Or maybe that's his skull. You can hear the crack over the speakers. Who says that only guitarists get to break their instruments? Then he throws the microphone into the crowd. The guy who catches it gets really excited and takes it home. He won't be able to use it, but that doesn't matter. It won't occur to him that tomorrow night Till is going to repeat the same procedure with a new microphone, and because Till bangs it against his forehead every time, the skin there gets rubbed raw. When we play several days back to back, his forehead is like a disaster area. The wound doesn't have time to heal.

One time they wouldn't let Till in the swimming pool—as the lifeguard on duty saw it, he just had too many open wounds. And the thing is, we love swimming pools. There's nothing better than going to the pool the day after a concert and swimming till all the alcohol has left your body.

Though actually it's even better to stay at a hotel where you can go swimming right after the concert. Hotels would rather close their pools at night, but a lot of times Tom manages to convince them to leave the pool open for us. He tells them we urgently have to relax our muscles. Naturally Tom doesn't mention that we also really want to party. We used to take as many women to the hotel with us as we could, and we'd immediately throw them in the pool. Then most of the women would take their clothes off. As a precaution, we'd then throw their clothes into the pool, so they couldn't run away so quickly. And right afterward a few liquor bottles would go flying into the water, and whenever we swam by one, we'd take a big swig. After that we couldn't really navigate the hallways and went wandering naked around the elevators. The next morning, the hotel staff acted really sullen around us. Floating sadly in the pool were the empty bottles, those ugly plastic pool chairs, and a few articles of clothing. At the bottom of the pool were two leafy plants, along with their pots. Now they finally had enough water. No one knew how it had all gotten in there, since actually we hadn't had anything to drink and had all gone to bed early.

Now comes "*Asche zu Asche*"—"Ashes to Ashes." My God, the time is flying by. I feel like the concert just started. Sometimes I'm afraid my life is slipping by me just as quickly as a concert. I've only just gotten into the swing of things and already it's a third over. At this rate it won't be until the encore that I can really start having fun. But we're not there yet. As for my life, I'm hoping I'm just at the halfway mark.

Paul steps forward and stands at center stage. He's the only one playing. He's just shredding on this distinct guitar riff. Then Richard walks up alongside him and joins in. They stand there like a wall, and since both are playing the same riff, the effect is even more powerful. They each voice the chords somewhat differently, and a friction emerges between the guitars. When two instruments play the exact same thing, sometimes what happens is that instead of getting louder the notes cancel each other out. I love it when the guitarists stand next to each other and play in harmony like this. They really look like a force. Like in chess when two rooks are stacked on top of each other. Nobody's getting past them.

You might think that with two guitarists in a band there might be a bit of a rivalry, and maybe that was the case with us at one time, but by this point we're all old enough to know that, fundamentally, we're stronger when we work together rather than against one another.

Now the drums come in. Small explosions go off above our heads to match the individual drum beats. Even though I should really know it's coming—I mean, it happens on almost every song—it startles me again and again.

—

IN THE EARLY DAYS of Rammstein, we would never have imagined that there were real pyrotechnic effects they would let you use on stage. Never mind that you might need some kind of certification for them. Once we realized how fun it was to shoot off rockets during a show, we simply bought as many fireworks as we could in the days leading up to New Year's Eve. Unfortunately, with us, they didn't last long, and it was hard to use some of the rockets indoors.

Luckily a few friends of ours were able to find stuff for us from stores of old army supplies. There was this great fog that parachutists used. Basically they were grenades that, once they were lit, would put out really thick orange-colored smoke for five minutes. We tested one out at a show once and soon we couldn't see a thing. We also couldn't breathe and sank to the floor gasping.

Naturally we couldn't keep playing in that state. We crawled over the stage, blind, till we'd all found each other. Then we discussed what to do next.

For the next few days, we still had the smell of smoke in our noses, and I felt like all our stuff was covered in a layer of orange grime. My suspicions weren't far off. Shortly before that, while driving to a show, we saw an abandoned LPG—the initials stand for *Landwirtschaftliche Produktionsgenossenschaft*, basically a collective farm from the GDR days—and on the property were two big fans built into one of the barn walls for ventilation. They were still turning sadly in the wind. We wasted no time in de-installing them, and after that we'd put them up on stage. We taped the smoke grenades to the fans, and once we'd lit them, we plugged the fans in. That way the fog was blown away from us and into the crowd. We could meet up behind the wall of smoke and have ourselves a shot of tequila—no one could see us through the thick smoke, plus now the people had enough to worry about. If the club was too small or too humid, you couldn't even begin to see the stage after this song. We always felt ill after these concerts, and when we blew our noses it was all black and orange. But we quickly got used to it. When we played at festivals, the smoke dispersed more quickly, but the problem was that you couldn't stop these grenades once they'd been lit. If the wind wasn't right, the smoke would get blown off toward another stage and ruin another band's set.

Sadly we don't use these smoke grenades anymore, since they're strictly prohibited, but if we did have them, we'd light them in the second chorus of "*Asche zu Asche.*"

On our first real tour, which we did as the opener for Project Pitchfork, we got to know someone who had been in the Foreign Legion. He showed us how easy it is to build bombs. Soon after that, we would go to toy stores before concerts and buy all kinds of animal balloons, which we'd fill with small amounts of explosive. Thus primed, we'd hang the animals in a prominent place on stage. During a certain song, one of us would touch a battery to the fuse, and then there'd be a loud explosion. Since most of the band had already forgotten when the explosion was supposed to happen, we were so startled sometimes that we dropped our instruments and had to stop playing. At first we couldn't control the timing of the explosion that well and so it almost always blew unexpectedly. On top of the fright it gave us, thanks to the explosion everything we heard for the next few minutes sounded like it was coming through gauze. My hearing has never really recovered. The animal balloons simply weren't there anymore. It was like they'd been atomized. There weren't even any scraps left over. But since no one had really noticed the animals in the first place, no one noticed they were gone either, and we really could have spared ourselves all the effort. But we had so much fun blowing things up that we didn't think about such trivial details.

To accompany the song "*Laichzeit*," which means *spawning time*, we bought a big dead fish that we then blew up, but even a big fish is hard to see on stage. And afterward our instruments and amplifiers stank horrendously of dead fish. The explosion got the dead fish in every nook and cranny, and it sat there rotting. So after that we stopped blowing specific things up and just had explosions for explosions' sake.

On that note, it occurs to me how we once planned a whole concert to be one big firework spectacular. Unfortunately I myself wasn't there. I don't know if this was something that was unconsciously instilled in us in the East, but any rate I always try to get out of things when it's not absolutely mandatory for me to appear. Never look too eager, that was our motto. A painter from Dresden whom we're friends with sometimes puts on events. Each one is planned around a specific theme and they're always really fun. This particular event was supposed to be a Venetian night, and he absolutely wanted us to play. The only thing we could think of that was Italy-related was the song "*Azzurro*." I knew the version by Adriano Celentano and the one by Die Toten Hosen, but not the original. We decided to play our own version.

Richard went home and came back with an interesting take on it, but the central riff didn't have much left in common with the original. The rest of us transferred the Adriano Celentano version from a cassette tape onto my sampler. In mono, of course, so it wouldn't take up as much memory. Despite all our technical wizardry, my memory bank was full after the second chorus. We then played the sample back and pitched it down a few steps, which sounded nice and sick. Plus, by pitching it down, we made the song a little longer. Music is math. But we couldn't really play along to it, because the rhythm of the original song was too uneven. And so we used the sampled recording as an intro, and then Richard's riff started up. It became a kind of remix, and the whole thing was about twelve minutes long. We packed up every kind of pyrotechnic we could find, and then off the band went. Olli and I stayed home, since at the show they were only going to play the sample off a cassette, so our musicianship wasn't urgently needed.

The party took place just outside of Dresden at Nickern Castle. It had just been lovingly renovated and smoking was absolutely prohibited everywhere on the grounds, so Till made sure no one saw him as he built the bombs, and they put up a wall of chairs covered in paper in front of the stage. They'd bought gasoline at the gas station. Next the instruments were prepared. Two band members were playing acoustic guitars, and Till sang along. The first explosions were relatively controlled; the acoustic guitars blew up once the hard riff set in. But to trigger the explosions, Till had to leave the stage. The explosions were too loud for Schneider, and he left the stage. Richard took cover behind a column. After that Till threw his microphone into the air, where—it goes without saying—it also exploded. Schneider's bass drum blew up after that. It was filled with gasoline-soaked sawdust and strips of paper so the flames would spread better. Same as the floor tom, which blew sky high only after Schneider had gotten out of dodge. Now Paul was the only one left on stage, and he erected a kind of pyre with the remains of the instruments and kept it burning with some gasoline. The fire spread to the chairs set up in front of the stage. As a precautionary measure, Paul threw them on the pyre. Oh, he was also wearing a black floor-length monk's habit and a Fantômas mask, as was the rest of the band. No one in the crowd knew what was going on. The organizers were so horrified that they couldn't speak. In hindsight, I was very sad that I hadn't gone with them. And I haven't let myself miss out on any show since.

—

I TURN ON MY treadmill. I almost said my hamster wheel, since that's an appropriate metaphor, and that was originally the idea. I never have to worry about being bored on stage. More the opposite, really.

"*Asche zu Asche*" is a pretty fast song, but I'm still fresh and merrily take off running. Everything seems to be working. When we're on one tour, we sometimes start thinking about the effects for the next one. I had an idea that I could stand in a kind of ball that would hang from the ceiling like an ape at the zoo. The whole thing was supposed to spin. Then the problem arose as to what would happen with the keyboards. You could secure them in place somehow, but what about the cables? They'd be wrenched out after one turn. And so we thought we'd leave the keyboards on stage. But I don't like standing behind the keyboards. Who wants to be hidden behind two slabs of plastic? There's a reason I didn't become a drummer. They've got it even worse. Some of them build whole fortresses around themselves. I've seen drummers whose kits take up the whole stage—there's no room for anybody else. They shouldn't call it a drum kit, they should call it a drum rig. Then again, the guitarists also like to plop a bunch of speakers on stage. They say it makes the sound better. That can't be the only reason, though. I've seen a lot of bands, at least in the GDR, where the guitarists set up all these extra prop speakers. No sound came out of them. After the concert, they were able to fold them up nice and small.

But even to us it became apparent relatively early that there wasn't any space left on stage after we'd set up all our instruments and amplifiers. And so we started putting our stuff behind or under the stage. Now we could have a little more control over how the stage would look. And we could also position ourselves so that people could actually see us. What I wanted was for people to be able to see my legs. Thus the treadmill was what remained once we ditched the rotating ball idea.

First we borrowed a treadmill from a gym. I'd never been in a gym before and found it very hard just to run on the belt. I mean, there was nothing to hold onto. If I adjusted the speed, I immediately got queasy.

Unfortunately, almost everything makes me queasy. I can't go on hardly any of the rides at the Christmas fair. Basically just the bumper cars. But even there I once got a nosebleed when I bumped into somebody. The kids who go to the fair with me are always disappointed because I'm so boring. All I like to do there is eat. Definitely potato pancakes, then those Dutch mini pancakes, quark donuts, yeast dumplings, almonds, recently too there's been a kind of stuffed bread with mushrooms, and of course kale and *Knacker*, which is a kind of sausage—I refuse to order kale and *Pinkel*, even though that's what it says on the board. If you want to know why, just look up the word *pinkeln*. Back in the day no one ever called a Knacker a Pinkel either. I always tell the kids that before the wall fell I used to work at the Christmas fair selling raffle tickets. The first thing I noticed was how cold it was. Never in my life had I had to sit on a chair for seven straight hours in the freezing cold. I wanted to look cool, too, so I didn't have nearly enough clothes on. In this case, cool was fitting in a literal sense. I prefer not to mention to the kids that I took a little cash from the till every night. The first day, at quitting time, I just stuffed some money in my pants pocket, along with some West German money that some schoolkids had given me because they'd already spent all their East German money. Nobody was supervising me, so every night I pocketed a little more money. I felt guilty about it and wanted to stop, but I figured it would look suspicious if one night I didn't take anything out, since then there would suddenly be more money in the cash box than on the previous days.

I can't even give the excuse that I was drunk, since there wasn't a single drop of alcohol in the many cups of mulled wine that we ticket sellers took turns buying for each other, just rum flavoring. The people who worked at the mulled wine stand told me that after I confessed to them that we sold a massive number of fake tickets that the owner dumped from a sack into our ticket boxes.

In any case, during the first rehearsals with the treadmill, I got queasy. Nevertheless, I set a keyboard up beside it and tried to play while I ran. I fell down immediately. It didn't work at all. Then I hit upon the trick of adjusting the speed of the treadmill so that I could walk or run in rhythm to the music, so that my legs practically moved on their own. I just had to figure out the right speed for every song and then it more or less worked. For the stage, we had the treadmill rebuilt so that it could also spin around. When it was spun around 180 degrees, I had to run backward—that I had to practice a lot. I fell down a bunch of times before it started to look somewhat natural. Well, okay, it's probably never going to look completely natural. As a joke, our bassist got on the treadmill and was able to run and play normally without having practiced at all beforehand. But, I mean, he can also surf.

On the side of the stage are boxes that shoot fire out of them. They look like window boxes, just, you know, without the flowers. After the second chorus, comets start falling from above, land in the boxes, and light a wonderful red fire. All the fire in the concert follows our own unique choreography which, for the most part, was thought up by Till. The stage fire has a really biting stench to it, by the way. The best thing to do is hold your breath during the bridge. I keep trying to remember that, but of course it never works, because I'm running on the treadmill while still playing and trying to look elegant, and as a result I'm gasping for air, completely out of breath. When we used to play in places where the power grid wasn't as stable, back when we didn't have the power truck, sometimes the treadmill would cut out for a second. Depending on which direction it was facing, I either flew from the riser onto the stage or was thrown against my keyboard. Today everything's been going well up to now. If only it weren't so hot!

And now it's about to get even hotter, because the next song is *"Feuer frei"*—"Fire at Will". This song is actually about fire. Although now I'm not so sure, maybe it's also just a metaphor. At this point, I've started to get the feeling that we only play this song so we have a part for the whole flamethrower thing. Till developed mouth torches for the song—you put them on and it looks like flames are coming out of your mouth.

People liked the effect so much that we were invited to perform this song live in the movie *XXX*. We were so proud to be in this movie, even before we'd actually seen it. To film it, we drove to Prague and from there to a small village about a hundred kilometers away. As I had been in the past, I was endlessly enraptured by the Czech landscape. It was freezing cold and there was snow everywhere. Making a movie, as some of you may know, means waiting around, and so we waited. To keep themselves and us warm, the film crew had gotten hold of some homemade liquor, which tasted incredibly good. These days you'd call the stuff organic moonshine. Or you wouldn't drink it at all because you'd be afraid it was poisonous. At any rate, we were soon in the best of moods and didn't feel the cold at all anymore. We were introduced to Czech pyrotechnicians who didn't bother much with all the precautionary measures. When flames were needed, they just cranked the valves on these giant gas canisters; when they weren't, they turned the gas off. There were no check valves or anything like that. There was only the pure, unadulterated joy of lighting things on fire.

Every time we play this song, I think of that film shoot and I start to feel good. In the last chorus, everyone's firing on all cylinders, and it really starts to cook on stage. And then this song is over too. I take a deep breath. Unfortunately there's not much oxygen to breathe. Until this point in the show, each song has been faster or harder than the one before, so now we play a schmaltzy number. This term isn't exactly the most current, so I'll say ballad instead. Now the crowd can also catch their breath a bit and gather their strength. All that singing along is taxing. Not to mention the jumping around. I wouldn't be able to keep that up the whole time. When I go see a band, I tend to stand in the back and just bob my head a little bit so nobody can see. I never pogo danced once in my whole life. I just stood off to the side and imagined I was dancing. When I look back, though, I feel as though

I were one of the people dancing. And it's not just with dancing that I feel this way.

And so now here comes the ballad. The song is called "*Mutter*." The stage set has also changed by now, but I can't keep track of such things because I'm looking straight ahead. Behind me a curtain falls, and I look out at the audience. Nothing has changed there; at most, the people are sweating a little bit more. Our guitarist Richard came up with the song "*Mutter*," I think for his daughter. At that point it didn't have any lyrics and accordingly wasn't called "*Mutter*" yet. Till then wrote lyrics to it that were for a mother, maybe even his own, so it's now a multigenerational song. There are also multigenerational households. I think the idea of several generations all living under the same roof is great, but I don't know if I would really want to live in the same building as my parents. They do say you're supposed to think globally and act locally, so I guess I've already failed on that front. I think a little bit and then don't do a thing.

On "*Mutter*," I now play a part that was actually meant for strings. I didn't compose the melody; that was a friend of ours. He's standing right across from me at the mixing console doing sound for the whole band. Watching him work is pure joy, and I think about how he came to Miraval, France, where we recorded the album, especially to work on this song. Angelina Jolie and Brad Pitt later stayed in the house we were staying in. I can immediately recite the names of all of their kids, but I get my cousins all mixed up. Really makes you wonder.

And so I play this string part, and as I do I recover from the previous songs. The treadmill is off, and I can relax. A glance at the clock—a half hour has already elapsed. I can watch Till for a second. When we play the final chorus, a shower of sparks rains down from above. Till stands in the middle of it and keeps on singing, unfazed. I admire that a lot, because I know how much it hurts when the sparks hit him. They hit his skin and then burn for a good long time. If they land on his head, his hair will be coming out by the handful when he takes a shower. If the wind shifts I get hit by a couple of sparks too, but that's not so bad since I have my jacket on.

Slowly the song fades, and I keep holding the final note. This isn't really well thought out on our part since I have to change clothes before the next song starts. We can't let the crowd see, or else it would ruin the surprise. And so I take my finger off the key and tiptoe down the stairs. I'm already tearing my jacket off. But the stupid zipper won't open, and I painfully twist out of the jacket like a yogi. Or an escape artist. Like Houdini. Apparently he died from being punched in the stomach by a student of his. Of all things. Houdini had explained to the student that you can block a punch by tightening your stomach muscles, but after the lesson, when he relaxed, the student sucker-punched him. This story left a big impression on me as a child.

But now I need to get out of my clothes as fast as I can. I can't do it quite as fast as Houdini, especially because I'm sweating so much and the jacket is sticking to my body. Plus, as I mentioned already, the zipper isn't working as it should. I could pour a bit more soda on it tomorrow. Then it suddenly occurs to me that this whole thing with me undressing was something we did last tour. No, we do it on this tour too, but at a different time. Where's my head at. Now I have to put the jacket back on. Putting it on is harder than taking it off. And the intro to the next song is already playing. If only I knew what was supposed to come next. This whole time, two guys from the pyro crew have been standing next to me. What the hell do they want? Oh, right, they're tying a belt of strobe flash pots around my waist. It pinches a bit, but there's no time to change that now. Good thing I didn't eat anything. I run around the back of the stage to the other side. There the giant iron pot is waiting for me.

—

NOT LONG AFTER WE signed our record contract, our label, Motor, asked us to take part in a so-called industry tour, and since we'd never been on an actual multi-date tour and were chomping at the bit to play, we said yes, not knowing what was in store for us. The point of the events was to honor and motivate the sales and marketing people while also introducing them to the new crop of bands. Record company marketing people weren't exactly our target audience, but we were able to make the parties a memorable experience, at least for them.

We played in select venues like breweries, ships, and castles, and after every show there was an opulent buffet, which probably nobody was as excited about as we were. We literally ate all we could. We were put up in real hotels, which of course was also a first for us. We even stole the towels, proud to show off the Kempinski Hotels logo. Every room had what we learned was called a minibar, a refrigerator filled with drinks. We thought that since the rooms were so expensive these little bottles had to be complimentary, and so we tried to drink all of them—which, however, we weren't able to do, since we were coming back from a party every night where everything was already free. Every morning then, Till would make the rounds with his medicine bag and completely empty out the refrigerators so that absolutely nothing was left. Then right after leaving for the next show we could keep drinking in our little rented bus.

Of course the record company wanted us to pay back the hotel bill, which reached a total of 46,000 marks. They couldn't believe we were so dumb that we didn't know everybody has to pay for their own minibar. When they talked to us, though, they realized that we were telling the truth—we actually were that dumb. And so they forgot about the money, so far as I know.

Back to the concerts. The invited guests came in evening dress, and the mood was very stiff at first. The bill consisted of four bands who played in a different order each night to ensure fairness. The bands were announced by an emcee who only thought he was funny. We wanted to push back against this stiff office party atmosphere, and before our first performance we discreetly poured gasoline over the nice floor. We'd bought it at the gas station earlier, just for this purpose. During the first song, Till directed a shower of sparks at the floor, which immediately burst into bright flames. The people who weren't able to jump away in time were rather incensed. Afterward the label had to give one woman a paid vacation to Mallorca so she wouldn't sue them or us. Her dress got burned up, I guess.

As soon as the fire started, the people went completely nuts. They hadn't ever seen anything like it, and no one who was there ever forgot us. The head of PolyGram sat down with us backstage after the show and kept saying, "I'll make you boys big in America!"

We've been quoting this line ever since, whenever we meet with record company people. After that a lot of people wanted to party with us, and we kept it going for a pretty long time and woke up the next morning with various record company bosses lying tenderly in our arms. They were endlessly happy and could barely manage to stammer out a few words. On the drive to the next show, we were in rough shape, as you can imagine. During the concert one or two of us had to throw up, but, feeling it was his duty to keep playing, didn't leave the stage, which came as a real shock to the spruced-up crowd.

Funnily enough, it was the bosses in particular who were happy when you didn't show them any respect, and I took full advantage of the situation, shamelessly cursing at and insulting a whole group of them again and again in the nastiest way. They laughed and laughed—they were relieved at not being submissively sucked up to for once. One of them wore a sweater his aunt had knitted for him with a rhombus pattern on the front. I urged him to take that cunt sweater off, only to find out later that this actually very charming person still gets called "cunt sweater." We learned that it paid to ignore the rules and just do whatever we felt like doing. And we saw how unspeakably ugly West German cities were. When we were driving through Essen, I thought I was in a nightmare. I couldn't comprehend how people who lived in cities like this could talk bad about East German architecture.

After that it was no more industry tour for us, just individual industry retreats. For accuracy's sake I should actually say marketing retreats. All the marketing people in Germany were invited to a particular place for the weekend. Again, everything was free. Our record company always thought up something special. For example, one time everybody had to hike through the Bavarian forest equipped with nothing but a backpack, a pocket knife, and some summer sausage. Then all of a sudden you'd see Marusha, who was that singer with the green eyebrows, singing on the ski lift; sitting on a throne up on the mountainside was Phillip Boa, the somewhat sullen singer of a typical indie band; and we were in a cart that was actually meant for straw being pulled across a meadow by a tractor. As we went, "*Du riechst so gut,*" which was supposed to be our hit, was playing from hidden speakers. The song never became a hit, but at least the attendees remembered our name— these stunts left a lasting impression on people. Of course, we had to get into the cart twelve different times to surprise each new group. Before each of these brief performances, we all did a shot. The whole thing started at ten in the morning.

At night a giant amusement park was set up, with bungee jumping, a swing carousel, and hot air balloon rides. In the hotel we'd all received freshly minted money, the so-called Peine Mark. Mr. Peine was apparently the head of PolyGram. You could even use this money to pay for things in the shops in town. Later that night there were stacks of it lying around everywhere.

When the official part was over, the whole group rode the cable car to the top of a mountain. We were in the Alps, after all. I was excited. Finally, for the first time in my life, I was on a mountain that was over two thousand meters high. When I stumbled out of the cable car, I immediately started climbing to the summit. It was actually just a few meters up, but it was tough going, because I only had clogs on. Till had stolen them for me at a gas station and they were a little too big, since I wasn't able to try them on first. By mistake I had left my old shoes at the house we'd crashed at after a concert. We'd had to flee in a hurry when the men who actually lived there came home. They didn't think it was such a bad thing that we were in their house, but that we also seemed to be sleeping with their girlfriends—that they didn't like. For the record, I was lying in a bed by myself, but the men didn't care. At that moment they weren't really making distinctions.

All of which explains why I now kept slipping out of my shoes and back down the mountain. Finally I just stood there with my socks in the snow and marveled. Also, I was hopelessly drunk. Over in the mountain hut, yet another band was playing, or several. The waiters kept placing big trays loaded with shot glasses on the table. Eventually even the most serious, buttoned-up industry people let go of all their inhibitions. In some cases only as the cable car was bringing us back down to our hotel in the valley. For some reason, everyone there only ever referred to this hotel as the sperm bunker.

First thing the next morning, we all went to the sauna to get ourselves back into shape. We weren't the only ones, naturally. There was this one woman there who really flipped out at us. We were supposed to put our feet on a towel and not talk so loudly. When she left the sauna for a second between sessions, we peed on the stones and then left ourselves. Kind of an infusion, so to speak. Then we all watched through the window as the woman smugly sat back down. Pleased with ourselves, we went off to eat and forgot to warn our bassist, who smelled suspiciously of urine for the rest of the day.

That was also the last time the record company put on such a giant party. I don't want to know what these weekends must have cost. Record sales started going rapidly downhill soon after that. At the meetings we have now, only the coffee from the vending machine is free.

At Motor, though, they always came up with some new idea. For example, the marketing people would get to shoot their own versions of our videos alongside a few guys in the band, so we'd split into pairs and go to Bremen or Stuttgart, wherever the film set was built. I'd be only too happy to see one of these videos again.

One year Motor put together a giant sports festival. The guests were to compete against the musicians in ten events. Ours was tug-of-war. We pulled in rhythm, so we won every match. They gave us traditional Bavarian garb to wear—shirts, knee socks, lederhosen, the whole deal. They took photos of us wearing it. We thought it didn't look half bad. And all over the world people would be able to tell we were German. From then on, we used Bavarian garb as the basis for our stage outfits. Even though these days I wear a sparkle suit, the fuck shorts are a relic from the Bavarian era. And all because of an idea our record company had.

But the most out-there idea the record company had was to send us to Hong Kong. Another marketing retreat was taking place in the city. They were always somewhere different. A few bands were supposed to tag along to promote their company—in our case Motor—and also to kick off some kind of cultural exchange program. At the closing event, we were supposed to play three songs for all the PolyGram employees who'd been invited. The waiters were the only Chinese people who saw us. For whatever reason Hong Kong gave me the creeps, and plus I had my fear of flying to deal with on top of that. The band bought travel guides and looked at the trip as a chance to do some sightseeing. But I don't like being away from home and thought that since they were just playing three songs for German marketing people, they didn't need me. I talked to a guy I knew who also played keyboard; he was supposed to go in my stead.

Two days later I was, of course, sitting on the plane and looking down at the Great Wall of China from 30,000 feet up. Better than being six feet under. As we approached Hong Kong, we flew right into the middle of an unbelievable downpour. At this time the airport was actually in the city, and we flew in between the skyscrapers. Some of them had red and white signs on the side, probably a sign to turn away. I could look through the windows and watch a woman cooking in her kitchen. Finally we landed and were amazed at how rundown Hong Kong was. The tall buildings were completely dilapidated, and there was standing water everywhere. We were driven to our hotel. You couldn't tell that it was a hotel from the outside— the bottom floor was a subway station, then came a department store, then a shopping mall, then a few floors of offices and apartments. On the seventh floor was the hotel lobby, and the rooms were located on the fourteenth to the seventeenth floors.

What we didn't know, but soon discovered, was that our rooms had no windows, since they were in the interior of the building. Rooms with windows must have been impossibly expensive. We couldn't sleep like that. I mean, we were used to a window-filled life, so at night we rode the elevator to the very top, broke open a fire exit, and finally got out onto the roof. Unfortunately the ledge was barely six inches high, so you had to be really careful not to fall. And me with my fear of heights. But we could breathe at least, or we almost could, since the air was unspeakably humid.

During the day, you could sweat through your shirt in five minutes. The streets were teeming with people, and I longed for a bit of calm. At a seemingly endless market on Canal Street, they were selling every type of animal imaginable. And indeed, as I realized to my not inconsiderable horror, they were being sold exclusively to be eaten. Sweet little puppies and beautiful birds—they were tied up like a bunch of parsley, then had their beak and legs cut off with a rusty pair of scissors. Naturally they were still alive. Every variety of crab and lobster, turtles that were scooped alive out of their shells with a kind of shovel, and of course frogs. The stall keeper grabbed them by their hind legs and spun them around until their hind-leg-less bodies flew into the wall and dropped onto a sad heap of other frogs, all of whom were trying to crawl away on their front legs, pathetically croaking—assuming, that is, that they hadn't already been crushed by their fellow frogs falling on top of them. On this street a very nasty smell hung in the air, but it didn't come from the animals. It was the durian, better known as the stink fruit, which looked so appetizing that we excitedly bought one. This began a fun game. We all tried to deposit the fruit in someone else's room without being noticed. Finally we stuck it in the elevator and sent it up to the top floor.

We did have to eat something, though, which meant we had to get used to food being brought to us by waiters in stained undershirts with cigarettes in their mouths. It was always the same, whatever we ordered, namely a plastic bowl with rice and a kind of chicken soup, naturally with all the bones and cartilage and innards, which you just spat out on the table, where the waiter swept it up with his hands. Then they brought the next dish. We also didn't know at first how we were supposed to eat soup with chopsticks. Then the waiter came to the table and cut the noodles and the chicken into our bowls with a rusty pair of scissors. It was, however, very reasonably priced. Once, when we ate at a place with somewhat higher prices, the waiters folded up the tablecloth after the meal and carried it away with all the plates and dishes and drinks and whatever else was still left on the table. We wondered if it was all thrown away or if some pitiable creature in the kitchen had to sort through everything.

When we played our show, we experienced the opposite. A giant hall in a grand hotel was set up for the event, and they spared no expense. In the bathroom, an old man was waiting with a little washcloth to respectfully catch the last few drops, which was so unpleasant for me that I tried not to pee, or just went when there were so many people in the bathroom that the man didn't have time for me. I don't know whether our show left any impression on anyone, but I'd be surprised if it did. After our set, we watched the other performances, not really knowing what was going on. They were all by various Chinese superstars singing Top 40–type songs. We noticed that the waiters would bring you anything you asked for free of charge, so we had every one of them bring us two packs of cigarettes.

While out walking the next day, I felt sheer terror when I saw the unimaginable misery in which people there lived. Twenty-five people living in a three-hundred-square-foot, one-room apartment was considered normal. Four million people lived in a few sprawling apartment blocks, and they all had to eat. If they were looking for something, it definitely wasn't us. What business did we have there as a rock band? What business did we have there at all?

WHEN OUR FIRST RECORD came out, the response was decidedly modest. The only thing to do was to play shows. And so we played for what felt like an eternity. We played as an opening band, we played alone, we went on tour, we gave one-off concerts, we played on MTV—in short, we played anywhere they'd let us. Well, except at political rallies, but of course no one ever asked us. Though we did play at a benefit show once at a youth club in Riesa, which was for the starving people of Rwanda.

We were even invited to a fashion show. The whole thing took place in a club in Munich where the Isar River splits and flows around an island. The high point of the show was that the models acted like they were the band and mimed playing our instruments, while we put on strange clothes and did our best to walk down the runway like models. Another word for the runway is the catwalk; that's because when cats walk, they place their feet, or rather their paws, one in front of the other. That looks more elegant than when you waddle along with your legs all wide. Unfortunately this was only explained to us years later.

It was all very exciting in any case, and we'd never been surrounded by so many beautiful women. The models seemed absolutely out of our league, or at least my league, but the dressmakers and choreographers were also incredibly exotic and attractive. Lucky for us, we were all staying in the same hotel. Thanks to alcohol, I was somewhat hampered in my ability to correctly assess the situation and assumed that the women would be overjoyed to receive a nighttime visit from me. True, when I knocked on one of their doors no one answered, but I assumed it was because they didn't know that I was the one at the door. Our room was just two doors down the hall, and so I climbed out the window and inched my way along the ledge till I was outside the room. I was relying on the assumption that since the women had also been drinking, they would also have opened their windows—after all, nothing beats fresh air. And so I climbed through the window into the pitch-black room and lay down in the first bed I could find. The woman wasn't exactly thrilled at my being there, but had nothing against my staying in bed with her so long as I behaved myself. I fell asleep pretty quickly, and when I woke up I was looking directly in the face of one of my bandmates. He was in the other bed. Somebody else had had the idea to pay the women a visit before me. He told me what a fright it gave him when I fell through the window. I went back to our room and got a massive fright of my own when I looked out the window again. We were on the sixth floor, and there was absolutely nothing to hold onto outside. So much for fashion shows.

Mainly, though, we played at conventional venues all across Germany. Tom joined us as tour manager and drove the minibus. We also had a three-person crew, by this point, who drove a different bus with the instruments and amplifiers. One guy for sound, one for light and pyrotechnics, and a third who was responsible for the stage and the instruments. Naturally we had to set up everything ourselves. Every night we were excited to see how many people would show up. Sometimes, a half hour before the show was set to start, there wouldn't be a single person there. Fearfully we would ask how many tickets had been sold. Tom would try and buck us up: "Well over sixty-seven." I preferred not to imagine how many people "well over sixty-seven" could be. Maybe a thousand? Or more like sixty-eight? "But here the usual thing is for people to just show up the night of the show and buy tickets at the door." This line was repeated often and never proved to be true.

For that reason, we often played as the opening band. There was less money in it, but at least people came to see the headliner. These bands were, without exception, very fair and friendly to us. That surprised us; we hadn't expected that these big and famous bands would take such good care of us. When we played with the Ramones, we had the same rights they did. All they asked was that we not root around in the buffet before Joey had gotten his meal. We were also excited about their groupies, who in our eyes had reached an almost Biblical age. The Ramones had simply been around a bit longer than we had. And they were still really good.

We went to Frankfurt with them, where we played in front of a lot of Americans who were stationed there. We had no idea going into the show. The city of Ramstein was also nearby. So it really did exist. At our party, there were real Americans sitting around with us. We had some intense differences of opinion. I especially started ranting and badmouthing America in the most senseless way, without having any background knowledge whatsoever. When two Americans tried to throw what I was saying back at me, they discovered how much they liked each other and married a short time later. So some good came out of it at least. The concert itself didn't help us much aside from a few interesting experiences. If you were a Ramones fan, you usually stayed a Ramones fan; you didn't switch over to us just on account of one concert.

Still, these shows were useful in other ways. At the soundchecks, we practiced our new songs. We had already come up with a few ideas that we quietly slipped into the setlist. This way we were able to try out certain songs in front of an audience before we recorded them for the next album. That was really good for the songs. And we never doubted that we would make another album. For one, we had signed a contract for three records, and for another, things were only just starting to get fun.

—

I STEP ON ONE of the wheels fixed to the bottom of the pot to pull myself inside, but once again I realize that, what with all the gas canisters for the flames, there's barely any room for me in there. There are lights built into the bottom that I can't touch because they get brutally hot. Once during a rehearsal I tried to grab one to steady myself and got a horrible burn on my hand—my skin actually stuck to the thin wire cage that covers the bulb. It smelled really hideously of burnt flesh. Makes you wonder: why does it smell so good at a barbecue? Is it the salt or the beer? Or the kind of meat? With me, it just stank.

I have to twist to get past my keyboard, too—it's also in the pot. I am a musician, after all, and I'd like to be able to contribute my part to the song. Sometimes even I forget that. I grab my keyboard in my hand and wriggle into the pot. Then I roll up on the bottom. Here comes the stagehand to spray as much fog into the pot as it can hold. I hurry and take a deep breath. A little too late, unfortunately. Then the lid is put on and Till, who has also changed outfits, pulls the pot on stage. I can't see that, of course, but I deduce it from the rattling all around me. It's a mystery to me how he manages it, since the thing must weigh a ton.

The band is really playing flat out now. Or, well, the song is called "*Mein Teil*" and not "flat out"; what I mean is, they're playing with a lot of energy. Full of spit and vinegar, you could also say, or at full throttle. It just depends what your particular set of interests are. Cooking enthusiasts, for example, say that something is on the back burner when they mean they aren't actively concentrating on it. To describe someone who has a lot of different things going on, they say that person has their fingers in many pots.

Apropos pots: Till now takes an occasional peek under the lid, and this lets out some of the smoke that was just poured in. Earlier there used to be a little canister of oxygen in here for me so that I could breathe despite the smoke, but I'd keep finding it unexpectedly empty, and since I'd be counting on getting some nice fresh oxygen, I wouldn't breathe beforehand and would end up almost suffocating. Now it looks like I have actually managed to choke on my own spit. This kind of thing usually only happens to me at the movies, when something really tense or moving is happening on screen and everyone is really quiet. I start coughing and breathe in the smoke inside the pot. Now I'm starting to get dizzy, so I switch on the light. This way I can at least see up from down. That was just in time, because now Till takes the lid off the pot and throws it on the stage. It clatters loudly, and I can sense the vibrations in the pot. Now all the smoke clears, and everything is beautifully lit up by the lights beneath me.

Till starts singing the first verse, and much to everyone's surprise I jump up out of the pot and play my line; I've quickly hooked the keyboard onto the edge. Till uses a knife for a microphone and keeps coming back to the pot to poke at me and see if I'm done yet. I don't seem to be cooking fast enough for him, and so during the bridge he grabs a flamethrower to really heat things up. It must be pretty obvious by this point that everything tends to happen during the bridge, but it's really just the only part of the song where we don't all have to play or sing. At any rate, now Till is shooting the Flammi, as we lovingly call the flamethrower, right at me. I've been expecting it of course, so I manage to duck. Nevertheless, it's hot. It was hot during the last concert, but I've still forgotten how hot it is. This is just unreal. My skin has probably gotten thinner. I pop up for a second to show Till that he won't be rid of me that quickly. Then comes the next burst of flames. It's just as hot, but I'm less shocked. All the same, when I pop back up again I'm not laughing quite so loudly. To show what a tough guy I am, I try to stay up for as long as I can, till the next burst of flames is right in my face. The third burst is again really bad, and I can only bear the fourth because I know there's a short break coming. And so I pop back out of the pot again and wave mockingly at Till to show him that he can't kill me that easily.

In reality I'm just trying to breathe—breathing while the flamethrower is shooting at me would be fatal. I would pull the flames right into my lungs. But now I can't really breathe properly either because the fire has sucked up all the oxygen. It feels like trying to breathe cement. Well, I guess I'll just breathe afterward. Till looks really furious because I'm still not cooked. But he won't give up that easily. Now he pulls out a flamethrower that's three times as big and points it at me. I duck at exactly the right moment. It's not just the flamethrower that's bigger, but also the flame that comes out of it. Before I was sweating. Now I'm bone dry—all the moisture evaporates. My jacket is really hot, too, and I have to be especially careful with the zipper, because it's even hotter. You might have experienced that at the sauna, where you're not supposed to take any metal objects in because you might burn yourself.

When I pop up after this burst of flame, I have to force myself to grin. The next one is even hotter, and I consider whether maybe I shouldn't just stay in the pot until the situation has cooled off a bit. If the heat had lasted for even a tenth of a second longer, that's what I would have done, but now I pick myself up. Till seems to be enjoying himself, and he shoots for a little bit longer. I feel like all my skin has been burned off. I just come up for a second so as not to be a spoilsport, and Till shoots again. We've tried out a lot of different ideas to make things a bit more bearable for me, but the more blankets and stuff we threw into the pot, the more I had to work around and thus the greater the danger that I would seriously injure myself. I came to the conclusion that the simplest thing was just to knuckle down and deal with the pain. You can apply this lesson to a lot of different things in life. Whatever it is, just stick it out—it'll be over soon enough.

Just like now. Till is done, and I lie here at the bottom of the pot and look for my slippers. Now I'm really turned around; I'm of course looking for my gloves. Where did I get slippers from? Even at home I don't wear slippers. I've been resisting it since I was a kid, and I still don't like going to people's houses where I'm supposed to take my shoes off. Probably on account of my socks. I also don't like wearing gloves. It feels like I don't have any sensation in my fingers. Now I need them, though. I can't see anything in all this smoke.

During rehearsals for the tour, I didn't have any gloves, and when I tried to climb out of the pot after countless bursts of flame, my fingertips would get stuck to the now almost molten-hot edge. During the first shows after that, I almost went crazy with pain, since I was still trying to play with these same fingers, but at some point they healed. During that time I simply tried to play as few notes as possible. For a while I didn't have any fingerprints and could maybe have robbed a bank, but I never got around to it.

I've now found the gloves. I put them on. I have to hurry or else the song will be over before I get out of the pot. And then Till will have won the game, so to speak. And so I swing myself up out of the pot, in what I would call an agile manner. I quickly throw the gloves back into the pot—I'll need them again tomorrow. At this moment, the pyro guys trigger the effects on my waist. I run wildly around the stage and hope that Till doesn't catch me. When I finally try to catch my breath, I find I've turned the wrong way and breathe in the smoke from my strobes. That's pure poison, maybe even radioactive—it's made of strontium or something like that. Now here comes the song's finale. I run straight across the stage while comets are shot down at me from up above. They land right next to me so that to the crowd it looks like they're hitting me. Sometimes, if I don't run straight enough, they really do hit me, which hurts a lot, and for the next few days after that I have a kind of giant hickey.

But today everything is going well, and all in all this song was pretty low drama. Why did I get so worked up? While the outro plays, the pyros, as we call them, take the belt off backstage, and I carefully take a few breaths. Then I hurry back to the other side, where my keyboards are, as the rear curtain falls. Again I skillfully avoid the cables and spotlights in the dark. Till comes toward me in the best of moods and gives me a pat on the ass.

We grin at each other, and slowly I start breathing normally again. I climb back on stage from the rear. I'm only a little dizzy now, but still pretty hot. I try and remember which song could be next. But I can't think of anything. I'll just have to wait till the band starts playing, then I'll recognize the song. But I don't hear any of us playing. Or can I not hear anything at all anymore? I press a few keys on my organ. No, I do hear something. And so I wait a little bit. I don't think a short pause can do any harm in a concert like this, so I stare at my organ. It looks nice and dirty. There's an actual layer of ash on the keys. It comes from all the fire. When we play open-air concerts, there will even be masses of charred insects on the organ after the first bursts of flame. I try to wipe off the muck, but it's really sticky. I'd need a washcloth or a towel.

Suddenly my face is burning with horror. I just realized that everyone's waiting for me—I'm supposed to play the intro to "*Ohne Dich*." I hectically switch to the strings setting and start playing. It's not such a bad thing that I waited so long, since Till has to take off his chef gear. It's no different for us than it is for Madonna or somebody like that. But Till is already standing on stage in his new clothes, and now he starts to sing the first verse.

Immediately there's this feeling that even I get when I hear a typical song of ours. Sometimes somebody will try and imitate Till and make fun of our music. These people start grunting in their lowest possible tone of voice and think they're doing the same thing as Till. They think they're demonstrating how easy it is to make music like ours and how unoriginal we are. It can be funny, but it doesn't do us justice. Till sings beautiful melodies and his voice goes right to my heart. People also like to label us doom rockers or violent rockers, but of course it's never people who seriously engage with heavy music. For people who do, we're more like kiddie music. They would never categorize us as a heavy metal band. For them, our songs are more like pop songs. Or Schlager. Schlager is a special German term. What kind of music is it, really—*Schlagermusik*, I mean. Does it come from the English word "hit," which of course is "*Schlag*" in German? If so, I guess they did have to translate it rather than tack a German ending on it, like Radler or Daimler, since otherwise the songs would be called *Hitler*.

It's amazing all the thoughts that go through my head while we're playing. Maybe this song isn't challenging enough for me. Or the fumes from the last song have gone to my head. That guy who blackmailed the department stores, the one who called himself Dagobert—originally he didn't have any criminal tendencies, but then he worked at a paint shop, and all the fumes made him depressed. He told himself that his wife would leave him if he continued to be so unsuccessful, and so he thought up the blackmailing idea. Things went well the first time, but the next time there was no handoff—the police just stuffed scraps of paper in the briefcase. A sad story. And I was there. Not in person of course, not for the handoff, but I don't just know it from hearsay. Like all of Germany, I was fascinated, I read all the articles and tuned into all the radio reports and listened to the people at the bar who all apparently knew exactly what was going on. You could also call a phone number and hear his voice. I thought that was exciting and kept calling again and again. Thankfully all the fumes on stage haven't turned me into a department store blackmailer, but I do seem to have trouble concentrating.

Now here's the outro already. I don't know what else to call it when the song has basically ended but there's a part that keeps on going. Even with the outro, this song is over, and again way too quickly. I think I'm starting to hallucinate, because now I hear a gramophone. Who here is playing a gramophone? Oh, right, it's Till. That means we're starting to play *"Wiener Blut."*

This song is about those girls in Austria who were imprisoned for years before they were finally able to free themselves. I start to feel really awful when I think about how many girls are out there who are still imprisoned. A lot of times no one ever hears about them. Since the story was brought to light, I look at normal-seeming neighborhoods of single-family homes through different eyes. Often it's the well-respected, friendly neighbors who turn out to be the monsters. The weird ones, on the other hand, whom people are always talking about behind their backs, are in reality much more normal than the people who act so proper. On *Tatort*, too, it's usually the doctors and lawyers who are the criminals—they're the ones who would do everything to maintain their power and their lifestyle. Some people seem to lack all capacity for empathy. How could you ever think of locking up a child? What goes on in such a person's mind? Since the media focused so much on the scandal aspect of the story, we decided to write a song about it that would delve a little deeper. Simply saying that you think something is bad doesn't do justice to it. We thought about what must have been going on in such a person's mind—or if anything was going on at all. Some criminals of course are firmly convinced that what they're doing is right. From their perspective, their actions are completely justified, and they lack a corrective, like a spouse, who questions what they think. "We never had a clue!" all the coworkers say about their punctual and friendly colleague. Many of them don't think how little it sometimes takes to push a person completely over the edge. How quickly someone can become a criminal.

For this song, Till imagined that he himself was the criminal. He did it so well that I'm actually frightened of him when he sings this song. I'd rather not know the darkness into which he welcomes whoever this person is.

Musically the song is also really brutal and insistent, and even though the subject matter is really serious, it feels good playing it. Aggressive music has a very cathartic effect. It's the same for those who listen to it as for those who play it. Of all the people I know, it's the heavy metal fans, the ones who go completely nuts at concerts, who are the most strikingly gentle people. I myself might need heavy music to channel my negative feelings.

When I was younger, I always used to listen to the Dead Kennedys, the Sex Pistols, and the Clash really loud. Now I've got it easier because I play in such a band myself, so I don't have to go out and buy CDs by other heavy bands on top of that. Then again, we don't play live as often as I want to hear the music. So I need our CDs, too—though of course we have to make them first.

—

MAKING THE FIRST RECORD was relatively simple: we went in the studio and recorded the songs that we'd been playing at shows leading up to that point. Now we were trying to come up with new songs. We had a few already, but they weren't nearly enough for a whole record. For me, being creative on command is just one of those things that's impossible to do. The record company was waiting for our second album, and suddenly there was a huge amount of pressure on us. We didn't want to disappoint anyone, and we also knew that other bands would listen to our new record very critically. What we didn't know was what kind of music we even wanted to make in the future or what direction things would develop in. We didn't want to repeat ourselves, but did that mean throwing out all the knowledge we'd gained? And never again using all our proven formulas? Just to do something else? Wasn't our music good exactly the way we played it? What even was our music?

We once thought up the term "dance metal" as a way of describing it, but nobody knew what to make of it, and they definitely didn't want to actually use it. It was a bit like we had come up with our own nickname and were now hoping that everybody would start calling us by it. But that was beside the point. The important thing was to somehow put a record together with new, good, maybe even better songs. Earlier we'd laughed about the pretentious terms the record company used—for example, making an album was called "production"—but now we realized how out of hand things had gotten: it had ended up becoming real work. Little by little, we were starting to feel like we actually were producing something. Even if we didn't yet know what that something was

Every now and then, one of us would bring in an idea and we would plug away at it for hours. If we felt like we'd developed a halfway decent version, we'd record part of it on a DAT cassette. At first we used two East German microphones, also called *schwarze Teufel* or black devils. You can imagine how these recordings sounded. Most of the time, when we listened back to the songs the next day, no one wanted to keep working on them. That didn't necessarily change later on, when we were able to sit before a proper mixing board to put our ideas to tape.

I was in charge of the DAT. That meant I was supposed to start recording whenever I thought I heard an interesting development in a song. I thought there was a lot worth recording; the bigger problem was labeling all the fragments so that we could find them later on. The names I came up with were as imaginative as "Monday," "Monday 1," "Monday new," "Monday really new"—and then on it went to Tuesday or whenever it was we'd had whichever idea. In order to find an idea again it of course made sense to mention a band that you could attribute the idea to. Thus we had the killer Björk sequence, the Depeche Mode chorus, and the Coldplay part. Coldplay later told us that they, in turn, have a Rammstein part in one of their songs. But of course we clearly didn't come up with the idea of naming things after other bands.

Soon I'd filled a whole notebook to go along with our DAT cassettes, trying to take as many notes as possible on every recording so that we could actually find the recordings we wanted to hear again. Of course, to make things even more miserable, this was spread out among countless different cassettes. And then of course there were several different versions of each song, some fast, some slow, some punky, some more hard rock-ish. Some with this chorus, some with that chorus. On some only the bass played on the verse, on some there was a kind of techno-like sequence on the synthesizer. We bought a chalkboard and, just like in school, we wrote down the different ideas that could turn into a song. This way we could at least keep a general picture of things in our heads. Then we came up with a few categories. It was like in soccer—we had the Champions League, the Bundesliga, and the Premier League. Now we could at least see a few names that could maybe turn into something. But so long as Till hadn't come up with lyrics for them, these ideas remained adrift. If we didn't know what a song was supposed to be about, then we also couldn't change or improve it in a meaningful way. A lot of musical ideas lose their purpose or meaning once certain lyrics are attached. It can happen that the best-sounding parts then become completely superfluous. Or worse, if you can't come up with lyrics for the song, you might as well throw out the whole idea. But in order to ensure that Till really gets inspired, the musical idea that is presented to him also has to sound good enough that it speaks to him. And so we have to work painstakingly on an idea without knowing where it's going to lead. It all sounds pretty complicated, and it is.

If we were really going to concentrate, there was only one thing to do: we had to go off somewhere together. So we went looking for a house where we could live and make music. The house should of course be in a pretty area, ideally on the Baltic Sea. We thought about Rio Reiser's house, since it was already set up as a studio. Rio was the lead singer of Ton Steine Scherben. He wasn't afraid of being associated with us—other musicians always understood us better than any uptight journalists.

When we left to start rehearsing, however, we learned that Rio had just died. We didn't want to unpack our things, so we just kept driving with all our gear along the Baltic and tried to find another suitable house. Then, as if in a fairy tale, there stood this old East German *Schulungsheim*—kind of a mix between a boarding school and a summer camp. If you studied a trade, you might spend some of your summer in a *Schulungsheim*. There were countless rooms spread out over several floors. And everywhere these great East German radiators and steel railings. Right away we called our friends and started throwing crazy parties. After every weekend, it would take us several days to recover. In between we learned how to ride horses at the farm across the road. Not me, though—I don't know what I'm more afraid of: horses, pain, or making a fool of myself.

We didn't spend that much time in the practice room. It was a real classroom like we remembered from our school days. Naturally we didn't have many good memories of classrooms. Sealing the windows was fun, but then when we wanted to start playing, we still couldn't think of anything. The drums were so loud they gave me headaches. I went to my room to read or went looking for a beer in the kitchen. A poster of the Kelly Family that we had torn out of *Bravo* hung over the kitchen table to inspire us. On the kitchen table itself lay a few dead fish that we'd talked a fisherman into giving us so we could fry them up that night. And then, before we knew it, the next weekend had already arrived. Even the record company people came to visit, both for fun and to see how we were getting along. At night, over red wine, we played them our pitiful results. We called it preproduction.

Years later, when making the next record, we tried to do it all differently, with no pressure and no stress, but in the end things went the exact same way with every record. And it really wasn't all that bad, since there kept being these great moments when all of us sensed that a good idea had just been born, and we were all hyper focused and trying to preserve the exact essence that we had just discovered, more or less by accident. No one can take those moments away from us.

—

It was my thirtieth birthday. I'm actually not a fan of big birthday celebrations, but this wasn't what I'd had in mind either. I hadn't really slept for the past twenty-four hours, which I'd spent on a train. Now I was in Catania in Sicily and I'd just gotten out of a rickety cab, only to find out there was no ship waiting in the harbor to take me to Malta. I kept looking at my ticket for passage. It had been sold to me in Berlin, on Sredzkistraße to be precise, but of course here it was no good to me at all. There was no ship there, and there wouldn't be any ship either, not for the next three months. The cab driver must have been wondering this whole time what I wanted down by the harbor.

Before he could drive away, I quickly jumped back in his car. It was nice and warm in there. I would never have imagined that it could be winter in Italy. A few weeks later I would even see it snow here. The taxi driver took me to the airport. That was a port too. Or, well, port, harbor, same thing. He didn't know that I had planned to put myself through the whole long train ride and ensuing ferry passage only because my fear of flying was in its worst phase. Now I was faced with the pleasure of having to book a flight on my own in a foreign country for the first time in my life. I would have to fly to Malta by myself. And from Italy at that. If only I'd stayed with the band. Then I wouldn't even have had time to think of my fear of flying, what with all the dumb jokes the guys would make on the plane. Now I sat squished between two sweaty strangers who talked really loudly.

Two hours and one bumpy flight later, I was on the island. Naturally no one was waiting for me, since the nonexistent boat wasn't supposed to arrive till the next day. What was I even doing on Malta, anyway?

We planned to record our second album here. Phillip Boa had a studio on the island. And he was of course also signed with our record label. Sometimes it's that simple. We were nice and far from home, and for us that was really the most important thing. It used to matter what kind of technical equipment the studios had, but that got ever less important as the equipment got smaller and cheaper—you could take it with you wherever you went. We had to get away, otherwise we might never play together. In Berlin, by the time the last of us got to rehearsal, the first had already left. He'd gone off to the dentist, to see his accountant, or to dinner at his parents' house. I don't exclude myself from this—I was proud if I even made it to rehearsal at all.

But the biggest problem on Malta turned out to be the food. I don't know if it was all the years of British occupation or what, but it was as good as impossible for us to get anything halfway decent to eat. If we went out to dinner at the one restaurant in town, we stood to lose hours of our valuable time waiting for our food to arrive. And then everything would be swimming in grease. In one of the larger towns, we went and ate at an Indian restaurant. When Paul threw up that night, he left behind a vomit stain of such intense color that you could still see it six months later. At a disco in the capital, no one wanted to talk to us, let alone dance. And of course the name Rammstein didn't mean anything to anyone.

The most exciting thing that happened to us during that time was a visit to Popeye Village, which is called that because the movie *Popeye* was filmed there. The sets from the movie were all still there, clustered around a small bay. We wanted to see the place from the other side of the bay, because we didn't feel like paying for admission. Not to mention that this bay was the only pretty place for miles. We stood around a bit on the pier across the way and admired the view. Then we got cold and went back to the car. Thus we didn't notice when a wave came up and swept Olli into the sea. The undertow was so strong he couldn't get back to land, so he swam across the entire bay and finally surfaced from the deep in the middle of Popeye Village, to the great excitement of the children. This way he spared himself the entrance fee.

Later, one rainy night, we managed to crash the rental car into a wall. They drove on the left side of the road there, which takes some getting used to. The car was completely totaled. Worse, though, was that at the time of the collision we were stuffing our faces with hamburgers. Shortly before then, around midnight, we'd gone to pick up some food at Burger King, and now we were wondering how our lives could have turned out this way. Where did we go wrong? We couldn't imagine. All we wanted was to record our second album, and they say that's the hardest one for every band. At least until you have to make the third one.

AND THEN WE'D DONE it. We had recorded all the songs for the album. We'd mixed and mastered them. Ideally we would have put the record out immediately—we could barely wait to get the songs out into the world—but we weren't quite there yet. We had to learn that there's much more to putting out a record than that.

Long before the album was actually finished, the promos had to be made. That meant we had to do interviews, something we really didn't care for. And above all we needed cover art—we needed a couple of photos for the album. Plus there were supposed to be new photos of us for the music magazines that would give some indication of what the new record sounded like.

We looked for suitable photographers. Or at least our manager did—we didn't know any photographers. That is, I knew a few of them by name from the books that my parents had borrowed from their friends, but I didn't know how to get in touch with them. I didn't even know if they were still alive. It was the same with Gottfried Helnwein. I had seen a few photos by him that I liked a lot. I also knew the cover of that Scorpions record, though without knowing that Helnwein had done it. I wouldn't ever have guessed that the Scorpions were a German band, since they sang in English, and so I also would never have guessed that Helnwein lived in Germany. Then we learned, through a mutual friend, that Helnwein lived near Cologne and that he was into rock music. He had even met the Rolling Stones and Michael Jackson once.

He came to the Bizarre Festival in Cologne to meet us. We were so little known that we played early in the afternoon in the sunshine. I'm sure it didn't look very impressive. Later we were backstage hanging out and we saw Gottfried Helnwein—he was the only one there who really looked like a rock star. We barely had the courage to speak to him. The next day we drove from Cologne to his castle in the Eifel Mountains. I was a bit confused—I'd thought the Eifel Mountains were in France. Probably because of the Eiffel Tower. Wrong again, I guess. We drove up a huge mountain, looked through the gate, and were speechless. In the GDR, it wasn't possible to own such giant cultural treasures privately; they weren't even available for the public's use. At most you would have been led through the rooms after they made you put felt slippers on. Here there was a group of assistants peacefully at work. Servants silently set the table and brought out lunch. Then Helnwein led us through the rooms where his paintings were on display. They were larger than I'd expected, and meticulously executed, down to the last detail. The surprising thing, though, was that it was the assistants who had painted them. I also saw a lot of paintings and posters that I remembered seeing as a kid—they were also by him. I hadn't known he was a painter, too. And that he was so famous.

His photographs were housed in another building. The first photos he showed us were all black, and I thought something had gone wrong in the darkroom, but of course it was intentional. With a lot of effort, you could make out a few dark faces against the dark background. *This must be an extraordinary artist*, I thought—*he makes portraits where you can't see anything.* And then he showed us his wall of fame—that is, the wall where he showed photos of famous people, and of course himself. There he was, arm in arm with Muhammed Ali and Mick Jagger. We'd felt shy about speaking before then, but after seeing this wall we were really intimidated.

Then off we went to the studio wing. There we had makeup put on, and Helnwein started photographing like mad. I tried to keep track of all the film he used, but I lost count. He then told us that he'd taken about 1,500 photos of us. That in itself was a bit different from our first photo session. Who was supposed to pay for all this? Then he sent an assistant into the city to have the photos developed. They were meant to be finished by that night. We couldn't believe it. Whenever we dropped off film to be developed, it was a week before we got our photos back. But this way we could just relax and wait for the photos. And so we wandered around the castle grounds and talked to pass the time. We still had makeup on and were covered in fake blood—now we could well imagine how Helnwein had gotten the reputation of being in league with the devil. What else were all the tourists who were at the castle sightseeing supposed to think when they encountered us? Even without having seen the photos, we knew they were perfect.

And so after a certain time had passed, we picked a portrait of each of us to be on the album cover. To ensure that no band member was given preference, we designed the CD insert in such a way that, depending on how you folded it, a different band member would be on the front cover each time. In most bands the singer is placed above the rest, and we wanted to avoid that. And it was exciting to see who was on the front when the record was advertised in the newspaper. It was only at record signings that there was confusion, since we would sit in a certain order and would keep having to page through the insert to find our own faces. Some of us would sign the wrong face by mistake, and when the owner of this face saw another name under his, the perpetrator's photo might end up with a pig nose, a mustache, or glasses. But in any case, we finally had a wonderful album cover for our second album.

The song "*Engel*" was chosen as the first single. And we were going to make the video with DoRo, a company which, at the time, was producing the majority of music videos in Europe. Everybody in the band was crazy about Quentin Tarantino. I'm always a bit skeptical when so many people are into the same thing, but I did like *Pulp Fiction*. I didn't like *From Dusk Till Dawn* as much, but I kept my opinion to myself when the band decided they wanted to recreate the movie for the "*Engel*" video. Or reference it. That's a nicer way of saying steal the idea.

Unfortunately there's no group of six people in the movie, so we had to split up. Three of us played in the band, and the other three were patrons at the bar where the movie and our video were set. We couldn't be the only ones in the video, so all kinds of shady characters from the Hamburg club scene were also invited. That was a good idea, since it made filming a lot more fun, and we became friends with some of the people and went on to work with them again on other occasions. They didn't have far to travel for the shoot, as it took place in the Prinzenbar behind Docks. Docks was a really good rock club on Spielbudenplatz.

In *From Dusk Till Dawn*, there's a kind of snake dancer who drips tequila down her leg into the mouth of one of the men. I guess the band hadn't watched the movie all that closely, because they all thought that I, in taking on this role, should try and fit the woman's whole foot in my mouth. I thought it was really strange, but of course I went along with it, because I didn't want to hold up the shoot. We were already way behind schedule. There were these two kids there who were supposed to sing the chorus from inside a cage. At some point they would have to go to bed, and it would disrupt things even further. The shoot lasted all night. We were still missing the part where we were supposed to turn into vampires. We just got drunk to make it easier for us to act. A method that would prove effective on many different occasions. The next day we filmed the final scene where we all leave the bar together. It's the best scene in the movie, because the camera zooms out to show all the countless trucks whose drivers have already fallen victim to the vampires. We couldn't do that, but we did walk out of an old warehouse in Hamburg that would be torn down soon afterward.

By today's standard, the video is very tame, but at the time there were strict guidelines at Viva and MTV when it came to sex and violence, and the chances that our video would get played were already very small.

—

Now it's time for "*Du riechst so gut*," and I turn the treadmill back on. "*Du riechst so gut*" was one of the first songs that all six of us came up with together. Before I joined the band, there were already five songs. These were "*Rammstein*," "*Der Seemann*," and "*Weißes Fleisch*," which back then was in English and called "White Flesh," though I heard "White Flash" and thought it was about a nuclear explosion. Then there was also "*Tiefer gelegten*," which means *deeper down*, and was called that because for this song the guitarists had to tune their low E string down to D, which let them play one step lower than is usually possible for guitars. And finally there was *"Das alte Leid,"* which used to be called "Hallo, Hallo."

When we recorded this song on our eight-track recorder for the first time, Till said "hello, hello" into the microphone beforehand to make sure he could be heard and that he could hear himself. This "hello, hello" was accidentally recorded, and from then on it was always the first thing we heard before the song started. So then we called the song "Hallo, Hallo." I even sampled the words so I could drop them in unexpectedly at shows. And of course also in the right spot, which is to say before the song started. Even when we were making the album and recorded the song properly in the studio, we added this "hello, hello" at the start.

There's something else that's special about this song, too. Before the second chorus, there's a small, tension-building pause. For this part we were missing something distinctive from Till. We were at his house, in the small town where he lived, to work on the song, and we wanted him to scream or something like that. But he didn't know what he should scream. We asked him what he wanted to scream—just generally, it didn't have to have anything to do with the song. He didn't have to think long before he shouted out, *"Ich will ficken!"* Which, again, means "I want to fuck!" We wanted to record it immediately. It was important to us though that Till really belt it out. But because he sang so loudly if singing is the word for it—his voice was completely distorted, and so he had to scream it again and again before we could really capture it on tape. The whole town could hear him. The people must have thought Till was really hurting.

Later on, the people from the record company got really worked up over this line. I guess we would have been disappointed if they hadn't noticed it. They said this line would never appear on the record. Naturally we insisted on it, and astoundingly enough the record company gave in. At every concert we played, I always looked forward to this spot, and Till never disappointed me. I would look into the crowd to see if the people who didn't know the song yet were surprised.

And then I even got to play a solo with my dinosaur sound. That was the first solo I ever had in this band, and now that I think about it, it was more or less the last, too. Unfortunately we aren't playing this song today.

Right now we're on a so-called *best of* tour, and in the band's opinion this song doesn't belong. Of course it doesn't matter one bit what the tour is called, we always want to play only the best songs. Who goes on tour and just plays the bad songs? We've made six records at this point, so we don't play more than four songs from each record. Otherwise it would be unfair. What that means though is that there are a lot of songs we can't play. And this song in particular is from our first record, where we first really came together musically. A lot of the songs on this record are important for us for that reason.

Of course, we never put out any actual records, but rather CDs, and we had to call the resulting product an album, but I still always just call it a record when we put out something new. Funnily enough, right now record sales are rapidly increasing, while CD sales are on the decline. Well, nobody finds it especially funny. But it could be that in a few years I might accidentally be onto something with my habit of saying "records." My father also completely missed CDs. He just kept listening to his cassettes, and when he was finally ready to switch, there weren't any CD players anymore, they even stopped building computers with CD drives, and he found he had to listen to songs on Spotify or something like that. When I feel like listening to a particular song, I just search for it on YouTube. Then I'm really amazed to see what the musicians look like, because it's the case with a lot of bands that I've never seen live recordings before. As a child I never saw the faces of the musicians that I heard on the radio; still today I don't know what many of these bands and artists look like; sometimes I don't even know if the singer is a man or a woman. What I heard in the music was just the song itself. I didn't associate it with the people who played the music or sang the words; I considered the individual notes of the song to be a kind of living being that spoke to me. For me the voice was floating in a river of melodies. The choruses were the islands in the stream. No, I don't take any drugs, I just love music—and above all, music that I don't understand. Music where I can't explain where the melodies and rhythms come from.

As it happens, there was a music magazine in the GDR that was called *Melodie und Rhythmus*—I guess the combination of words made a deep impression on me. In any case, I don't have to see the musicians for a song to capture my attention. Later on, there was a TV show that showed music videos. *Formel Eins* with Kai Böcking. Naturally I wanted to watch it. Unfortunately, in order to do so, I had to skip school and work my bad influence on a friend who had a television. When they played the songs currently in the top ten,

I was baffled. For all of these songs there was a video. How could the bands have known that their song would reach the top ten? If they hadn't, they wouldn't have had to make a video. Or did every band make a video for all of their songs? I couldn't understand it, but suddenly I knew what Prince looked like, and that was exciting. I kept having to skip school, because now I wanted to see Michael Jackson too. Or Die Toten Hosen. They were dancing around a soup pot and singing something about chilled schnapps, I couldn't really figure out what was going on. The other bands had names like Ultravox or the Thompson Twins. And I saw Modern Talking play "You're My Heart, You're My Soul" for the first time. Everything I missed on *Formel Eins*, I now watch on YouTube. I dig around for hours trying to find really old recordings.

Now, on the treadmill, I'm trying to approximate dancing. The hard thing about it is that it's supposed to look really natural. Like I said before, the things that look natural are often the hardest. Meanwhile the things that look hard aren't necessarily easy; in fact, they're hard too.

In the chorus, the song quiets down a bit. At this point there's no more driving riff; the guitars are playing open chords. Every now and then, at this point in the concert, one of us will hold a finger under his nose like a mustache. When we were kids, men with mustaches were the enemy. We thought they were respectable types with clean middle-class cars and bad taste in music. Some Ostrock musicians were also very proud to wear a *snotblocker*, which was our name for that particular type of facial hair. We saw a connection between mustaches and the mentality of a somewhat phony, somewhat sleazy pop singer or businessman. Or, well, what counted for a businessman in the East. A lot of times mean waiters also had mustaches, for example.

After the chorus comes the bridge. I could also say the in-between part or the break, but they don't sound any better. Astoundingly enough, most rock songs have a similar structure. At the beginning the riff is introduced, and then comes the first verse. Then there's a short chorus, and after that the second verse. The second chorus is built up a little bit, and then, so things don't get boring, there's usually a bridge.

In the bridge we usually depart from the harmonic structure in order to give the song a new flavor. From a lyrical standpoint as well, the message of the verse is presented from a different perspective. For that reason we also call the bridge the "but sometimes" part. And in this particular song we usually save the pyrotechnics for this part. This time the guitars are lit on fire. That is, one of each guitarist's arms—the arm closest to the side of the stage—bursts into flame. This has a nice effect—two people collectively forming a single image. Ah, now they start spinning, and it reminds me of figures in a music box. I turn off my treadmill because the crowd's attention should be directed solely toward the guitarists. I'm standing in the dark anyway and don't need to exert myself, since nobody can see me. I use the time to catch my breath. I try and fan a little air under my jacket. Then I wave at Schneider, who also has a little time, since he's only keeping the rhythm with one foot. Olli doesn't have anything to do right now either. He might be drinking a beer for all I know—he's in the dark too so I can't see him. Now he sees Schneider and me and waves to both of us. We wave back. And shortly after that, we jump back in with renewed strength for the last chorus. The people want to dance and sing along too; after all, just staring straight ahead the whole time gets boring after a while.

Last tour the guitarists threw their instruments into the crowd at this point, but we don't do that anymore because it was such a hassle getting the guitars back. Naturally the people in the crowd had no interest in parting with them once they'd caught them. Or was it last tour that we actually lit the guitars on fire, not just the guitarists? I can't even begin to keep track of it all.

So, now comes "*Benzin*." *Benzin* means *gasoline*, but we're not about to pour any gasoline on stage, since of course we play on a grated stage. It's like the subway grates on Schönhauser Allee in Berlin, the ones with warm air blowing out of them in the winter. After the wall fell, I used to park my cars there in winter so they would start in the morning. It was great for my old diesel Mercedes, and at that time not a single policeman came by to tow me away. Cars that run on regular gasoline start much easier in cold weather. Of course that wasn't the reason we wrote a song about gasoline. Nevertheless, the song "*Benzin*" was a commissioned work. Till asked the rest of us to start thinking up lyrics so the whole burden didn't fall on him. Paul came up with a couple of subjects and wrote them down on a few slips of paper that he pinned up in the practice space. This piece of paper with the word *Benzin* written on it has been staring us in the face since 1999.

Still, the song wasn't finished until we started working on the Rosenrot album. Musically speaking, the song is a bit atypical for Rammstein. This is because of the way the guitars are played—more like a punk band. The song is also faster than "*Du riechst so gut*," the one we just played. We do that intentionally, to build up the intensity level of the set. The next song after this will be even faster. I can't even imagine that right now—I can barely manage to keep up as it is. Now is when it comes in handy that the treadmill can rotate. See, I have to play both keyboards on either side of it. So I have to rotate at the right time, otherwise I won't be at the right instrument for the chorus and thus won't be able to play along. I also can't stop running if I don't want to fly off the belt and onto the stage. Where of course there are now these giant flames. I mean, what's the point of playing a song called "*Benzin*" if the stage isn't on fire for practically the whole time? Right at the start, during the intro, Till drags an old but very beautiful gas pump out onto the stage. A friend of his welded some wheels to the bottom so you can move it this way and that. During the chorus, the flames pass pretty close to me, so it's important that I'm really mindful of standing in the right place. When we play outdoors and the wind is blowing, sometimes the flames don't go exactly where we planned, but because of this we tape little strips of fabric to the trusses so that we can see at a glance which way the wind is blowing. It feels like you're at the airport, where they've got those windsocks. I think that's actually what they're called.

Now here comes the bridge again, and surprise surprise, Till takes the nozzle from the pump and shoots massive flames across the stage. At every concert, Paul tries to get a little closer to the flames without burning himself. I mean, he really lets Till shoot at him. I get him—it's a good feeling to get shot at every now and then and feel things get really hot for a second. Sadly I can't sit back and watch, because I have to concentrate on the treadmill.

For the last chorus, I have to be pointed back toward the organ, which means I have another 180-degree spin ahead of me. I start to get a little bit dizzy. I could leave the treadmill in its current position and start running backward, but that's impossible for me at this pace. I did so for "*Mein Herz brennt*" and was stupidly proud of my agility, but no one in the audience noticed—on that song, I'm standing, or rather running, in the dark. I only noticed it when I saw a video of one of our concerts. I was a bit surprised to see that I was completely invisible. Or almost completely. I'm sure the others in the band have also had the same thought about themselves. I mean, we do it on purpose. It's a way of making the stage look immense and atmospheric— we play with the lighting in such a way that it's only adding certain accents and the total effect is really mysterious and dark. I mean, we don't want the stage to look like a Deutsche Bank branch.

That's the impression I had when I saw the Rolling Stones at Olympic Stadium in Berlin. Even though it did mean that all the band members were clearly visible the whole time. Even if it's absurd, I myself would rather keep playing in the dark than to stand on such a sterile stage. I could of course make things easier on myself and only run on the treadmill when people can see me, but it wouldn't be the same. The crowd would probably sense it. Paul once said that even when getting your portrait taken it's important what shoes you wear, because even if you can't see the shoes in the photo, your face reflects how you feel, whether you're wearing nice shoes or just going barefoot.

Now, after the last bursts of flame from the gas pump, comes the song "*Links zwo drei vier*"—or "*Mein Herz schlägt links,*" I don't know what the name is exactly. I set the treadmill another notch faster, the fastest speed for tonight. I used to have it turned so that it was facing the audience, that way I could be marching toward the crowd without having to leave my spot. Man, is it fast today. Sweat is dripping into my eyes, and I'm so hot that I've started shivering. For the concert, we've lengthened the intro so the crowd will pick up on which song we're playing. This way they can all start clapping along. Now the rest of the band comes marching onto the stage. And with a massive bang, the song starts in earnest.

—

NOW THAT WE WERE a little more well-known in Germany, the desire grew in us to go and play in the US. Only then would we be a real band, we thought. At the end of the day it was no great feat to become famous in Germany with German lyrics, but if Americans, who didn't understand the lyrics, thought we were good, that would mean that we actually made good music. Plus we felt like the European music market was dominated by America anyway. When it came to music, America set the tone for the entire world.

Naturally no one was there to roll out the red carpet for us. Strictly speaking, no one was there to welcome us at all when we flew to New York for the first time for a test run. Nevertheless, we were totally excited. We checked right into the Chelsea Hotel and immediately felt like we were part of the international art scene. Although the hotel was anything but luxurious. I had never seen such filthy rooms in a hotel. Not only could we not lock the door to our room, we couldn't even close it—it had been kicked open too many times. Apparently our room on the tenth floor was the same room in which Sid Vicious had killed either his girlfriend or himself. Thankfully a painter who had lived on the top floor for years let us up on the roof, and we sat up there every night, drinking beer, eating untold amounts of food from plastic containers that we filled up at the steam tables at the deli, and staring up at the skyscrapers. We couldn't believe it. How did this happen? When I was a kid, I never would have thought it possible.

Back then, in my childhood, there was a long time when I considered the radio the highest authority. Actually higher than God. Everything that came out of the radio was good and true. And every now and then, or even most of the time, what was on the radio was really good music. If I was lucky, the radio was on and I was there when a good song was playing. I was as happy as a child, and no wonder, because I was one. I had no notion that there was such a thing as a radio station where a disc jockey sat playing records; I thought someone was singing a song and I just happened to be able to hear it through the radio. What I imagined wasn't a radio station, but rather a kind of intelligent cloud that was always just there, and music came out of it. I listened very carefully, because it could well be that the good song that was playing would never be played again. Sometimes they also said what the musicians' names were, but I didn't really know what to do with that information. Then I learned that in the West there were supposedly records by a few of these bands. I felt that records were made for people like me—that is, for people who couldn't go to concerts. I didn't know anything about concerts, I didn't even know if the singers or bands I heard on the radio were still alive. Because it was a West German station I was listening to, I assumed that music only existed outside of East Germany.

And so I was completely surprised when I saw my first band at the Free German Youth's Tenth Youth Festival. But they too came from abroad. It was a long time before I finally went to see an East German band play a concert, in Plänterwald in Berlin. I think the band was Reform, either that or Magdeburg. I was impressed by the volume—it hit me so hard it was almost painful—but the music wasn't close to the kind of music I liked. Still, though, the band was living proof that you could be a musician in the GDR.

Without a trace of doubt, I decided I also wanted to be a musician. This wasn't a career choice—the idea that making music could be a career would never have occurred to me. I mean, you might like collecting stamps or eating cabbage, but you wouldn't call either a career. Nor is it a career to love a woman and raise children. Or to grow up. None of these things are particularly easy, they're just inevitable. Since I couldn't sing—I would have liked to try, of course; even as a kid, it was clear to me that singers were special—that meant I had to learn to play an instrument. Most of the instruments I knew about sounded really pitiful on their own, and I couldn't count on being able to find friends who would play with me. And so the only options I was left with were guitar and piano. By simple arithmetic, it was clear to me that I could make considerably more music with eighty-eight keys and ten fingers than with six strings and one hand. Piano was also harder to learn, though, and what good were two hands when they always seemed to want to play the same damn thing? And if the only notes I could come up with were so strange. But even with my first attempts to think up a song on my own, I noticed how little it mattered whether I could play well or not. So long as someone sang along, one or two notes were enough accompaniment.

Sometimes my brother brought a few classmates over after school, and they thought it was fun to mess around a little with me on piano. We just acted like we were a band. My brother's friends sang lyrics from songs they knew from the radio. I had never heard these songs before and thought our versions were simply brilliant. You couldn't say what we were doing was in any particular musical style, but when German New Wave groups like Trio started to appear, we felt completely understood, like we also were a part of it.

Meanwhile, my piano lessons were the complete opposite of this. There I pounded out sonata after sonata without any emotion and was just happy not to make too many mistakes. Unfortunately I had to play these pieces at recitals every now and then. I would get so nervous beforehand that I felt physically sick. I just wanted to go to bed and let the music be music. I was amazed to discover how sweaty my hands could get. From then on, I considered it a good idea to pour cologne over my hands before a recital. This made them feel really strange, and you could now smell me before you heard me. The cologne didn't help with the trembling, but I somehow managed to play my pieces and continued to suffer through my lessons.

But later on, when I met real musicians, I realized that bands usually didn't need a piano. Maybe for a few little twinkling notes in a love song, but otherwise they would all get along perfectly fine without me. And piano sounded so boring—it always just sounded like a piano. If only I'd learned guitar! With guitar at least you could put that awesome distortion on it. But there were more than enough guitarists. Then I heard about keyboard players. That seemed to be a better kind of piano player. These people could also play organ or synthesizer. I didn't know what a synthesizer was supposed to be. Actually I still don't know. Something with oscillators and a mod wheel that squeals like something on a Pink Floyd song. But I was assuming there weren't bands like Pink Floyd in the GDR, so I didn't need that part. And then Trio came along with their Casio. And I went out and got myself a keyboard like theirs. And now here I sat with my band in New York City.

I used the early morning hours when I couldn't sleep to explore the neighborhood around the hotel. Like a little insect, every day I dared to venture a little farther away from the hive. I often went past Madison Square Garden, though without noticing it. First, I had no idea that the place even still existed, since all the live albums I knew that were recorded there were over twenty years old. And second, I wasn't looking for a music venue at all—I was convinced that it really was a garden, or at least a park where bands recorded their live albums. The actual venue looked almost dainty among all the gigantic skyscrapers. Also, I couldn't see how the trucks were supposed to drive up to it. Really it didn't look like a venue at all.

My impression wasn't all that far off, as our technicians would later confirm. They had all kinds of trouble getting our gear into the venue whenever we played there.

But back then we were playing in tiny clubs. It was because of these concerts that we were here in the first place: we wanted to spark Americans' interest. But the shows weren't very glamorous. We tried to take a taxi to the club, but the taxi driver had never heard of it and of course couldn't find it. We wandered around on foot, and when we did arrive it was only to discover that a musician isn't afforded the same respect in New York as he is in East Berlin. No dressing room, no drinks, not even a firm set time, and of course barely any people in the crowd. We'd end up playing at around four o'clock in the morning, which on account of the time difference felt to us like ten o'clock in the morning after a night of heavy drinking. Well, we contributed the heavy drinking part. When it was finally time for us to play, we were almost sober again. On top of everything else, it was strictly forbidden to light even a match inside the club, which we cleverly circumvented by having Till enter the room through the emergency exit to the side of the stage with his coat on fire. So we didn't light anything inside the club.

Even without jet lag, the crowd was pretty tired and seemed not to get too much out of our show. At our second concert we had to change in our rental van, which made us curse our stage costumes. Around four o'clock we got to go on stage. This time, however, fire was strictly prohibited. And so we fell back on our old show gimmick, which we used to do during the song "*Feuerräder*": I ride on Till's back S&M style and use a fluorescent tube as a riding crop.

The idea came to me in a town auditorium in Thuringia, where there was a whole box of fluorescent tubes sitting in the hallway. We were able to do it again and again, as we could find a fluorescent tube at every venue—we just had to unscrew it from the ceiling. At the end of the song, I always broke it across Till's back. Normally it worked great. And so off he went, crawling on all fours through the moderately excited crowd in the direction of the bar, where several glasses were broken. Back on stage, Till planted himself in front of me and waited for the blow. I whacked him in the chest as hard as I could, but nothing happened. I kept trying. In America, the tubes are simply much harder. Till screamed at me—the song was almost over. And so I summoned all my strength and whacked him again. Finally the tube broke, in two, and the other end flew over Till's shoulder and stuck into Schneider's arm, where it remained. What was more, the jagged edge cut Till's chest open down to the ribs. The bottom half shattered in my hands, and the shards cut deep into my palms. Luckily that was the last song in the set. I went with Till into the little bathroom. Not only was he bleeding like a stuck pig, I actually saw the fatty tissue under his skin poking out. A woman who said she was a doctor came hurrying over to provide first aid, but when she asked what she could do for him, Till's friendly answer was to suggest oral sex—she clocked him and then went off. I doubt anyone in the audience registered any of it, and as we stood bleeding and half-naked on the street, none of the passersby took even the slightest notice of us. A great city. New York was just as crazy as I'd imagined.

—

Now for "*Du hast*," I can slow the treadmill down a notch. "*Du hast*" is kind of like our "Satisfaction." We never had a real hit in the traditional sense, which is to say a song that you can hear on the radio every day and see the video on television.

When the song "*Du hast*" came out, only a small group of initiates knew who we were. And most of them really liked the song. We hadn't necessarily counted on that. When Richard came up with the idea, I didn't have a clue how the song was supposed to go. In my head I heard a different count. I thought the riff was starting on the downbeat; what was actually the second beat I heard as the first. As a result, to my ears, the chorus came out of nowhere and started way too early. I tried to explain the rhythm I was hearing to the band and to play the song as I heard it. Naturally that didn't work.

It happens all the time—I'll start listening to a song and come in on the wrong beat. Either the station isn't coming through all the way or the radio is playing in another room. Only when I recognize the song do I maybe slip back into the right rhythm. But nowadays I'll even try to intentionally listen to a song as though the beat count were different. It's like exercise for me. I end up hearing a completely different song than the one the band thought up.

Anyway, after a while I understood how "*Du hast*" was supposed to go, and I was really excited by the sequence that runs the whole time. I would never have come up with such an idea. That's Richard's biggest strength; he comes up with ideas that are completely atypical for a rock band like us. He studies music more than probably any of us. Even in his free time. In his room, there's a giant bookcase full of CDs. Earlier, when we would sign autographs in record stores, we sometimes got to take a few CDs with us as a thank you. Richard always knew exactly what he wanted, and he put together a top-notch record collection, though I guess it's more of a CD collection.

After the second verse in "*Du hast*" comes my favorite part. There's a beat-long pause for catching your breath. I always draw myself up to my full height, only to collapse into myself on the next beat. I learned that in gym class. That's how the gymnasts on the horizontal bar build up speed. In the bridge we get really quiet and encourage the crowd to sing along. The lyrics are relatively simple: "*Du, du hast, du hast mich, du hast mich,*" etc. Though I guess I don't know how to write it exactly, since the spelling determines whether it's "*hassen*" like *to hate* or "*haben*" like *to have*. I don't think it matters to the people in the audience. I'm sure most of them don't have a clue what the song is about. I myself have trouble on that front.

Then Till shoots off the line rockets. We came up with the line rockets idea because you can send them flying out over the crowd without any danger, since they can't leave the wires they're attached to. Most pyrotechnic effects require there to be a massive amount of space between the effect and the public, and you lose the sense of really being there. At the start, we just shot rockets off in every direction, but later the organizers started insisting that we only use tricks that are permitted. We have to present a list of them before every concert. Actually, though, there haven't ever been any complaints about the line rockets. I love them so much because they also give off this nice whistle when they zip over our heads. Thunder claps go off to mark their hitting their targets. The rockets mostly hit the mixing board, so I'm not standing right next to them, but it's still extremely loud. After that the flames shoot up from every direction. It's a joy. We're basically luxuriating in flames. You almost forget the pain. I look at the other guys to see if they're feeling the same way I am. On every one of them, I see the same sick grin. I'm sure I don't look any different.

I don't need to pay attention to what I'm playing; my hands do it all by themselves. We only had to rehearse this song once before the tour, and the notes all came right back to me. You could pull me out of a deep sleep in the middle of the night, and I could immediately play this song without making any mistakes. Unfortunately I quickly forget most of the other songs after a tour's over. I don't even remember what key they're in.

When I find out that we have to practice a few old songs to get ready for the next tour, I try to find live versions on YouPorn. I mean YouTube. Unfortunately, the fans' recordings don't really help much since the microphones on their phones are so small, so the sound is completely distorted. And it seems to me that we don't always play our songs that well live. Speaking for myself at least, I feel like I should clean up my act a little bit and play tighter. Seriously, nobody can hear whatever it is I'm trying to do.

Amazingly enough, the best recordings I find are of Rammstein cover bands like Feuerengel, Völkerball, Weißglut, Stahlzeit, or others. I play along to the live recordings at home with a toy keyboard until I can actually play the songs again. I guess I could also go find our CDs, but I can never manage to put the disc back in the case, and then they get all scratched up or I lose them. But like I said, "*Du hast*" basically plays itself. And now it's particularly easy for me, because after the chorus I turned off my treadmill. It wouldn't have fit the quiet mood if I'd kept on running like that. I realize how nice it is when I just stand at the keyboard and play. And it doesn't even bother me that Till keeps pelting me with water bottles the whole time. I don't know what I've done now to have incurred his displeasure, but I assume he finds my behavior on stage unacceptable, just in general. I can well understand that, but I've also tried to stand still on stage and put on a grim face, and that hasn't worked any better. Of course, it wasn't as strenuous. But after the concert, I didn't feel like I'd given all I had for the crowd.

I have to get out of the habit of trying to think for the audience, since for the most part people's taste is completely different from mine. And besides, they can think for themselves and are perfectly capable of deciding what they think is good or not. I'm sure they just want to see a good rock concert and can do without my opinion. And if our band didn't exist at all, they would simply be fans of a different band and would be just as happy. They wouldn't be missing anything. Nobody cries for all the bands that haven't even been started yet, even though, if they existed, they'd definitely be able to play much better music than us. It's like with children that were never born. Barack Obama and Angela Merkel could, theoretically speaking, have a child together. Since that probably won't happen, though, the world is now, in a certain respect, missing out on this child. I wonder if this child is already present with all the others waiting in vain to be born. That is to say, I wonder if the potentiality of each individual being is already predetermined.

Once again it becomes clear to me what a stroke of luck it is that I even exist in the first place. Amidst the great mass of humanity, my parents had to meet each other. That wasn't at all easy, since my mother fled Poland, while my father lived in Thuringia. They must have met in Berlin. It must have been real fun there in the sixties. When my parents tell stories about the parties they had and all their crazy friends, it doesn't sound like the gray East. It sounds more like I missed out on a whole lot. At any rate, my parents got together, which was very good for me. Then a child was born, but it wasn't me yet; it was my brother. I've often asked myself why I wasn't born first instead of three years later. And why am I not my brother, and he not me? I would really like to know why my brother and I are so different, even though our DNA must be almost identical. And what would have happened if my parents had had another kid—would it have been me or just my little brother?

Actually, I feel really sorry for all the kids who weren't ever born. But of course I know that the ones who really deserve my sympathy are the ones who were born and who have really tough lives. I try of course, with the band and with music, to make some of them feel good and give them some courage to go on living. Or I just tell myself that, because I don't want to admit that I'm too comfortable to actively help the children who aren't well off. I still think about it, at least. That, as anyone will tell you, is the first step toward action. And whenever I meet someone who actively volunteers, I can see that this person is very happy. These people seem happier than all these really important artists who want to tell you about their projects and deadlines.

Now "*Du hast*" is over, and here's another spot where I have to change. But like I've said, it's dark between songs, so I have to feel my way down the stairs. As I go, I pull off my jacket. Paulo is standing by ready to help me, but getting undressed goes quickest if I do it alone. First the jacket, then I sit down and pull off my shoes. Next to the stairs, the waders from the bait and tackle shop are waiting. They might actually be called waiters. Fishermen use them because they allow them to stand waist-deep in water for hours without getting wet. They're only available in green, but we spray-painted them black. But they got so saggy from the paint that we had to shorten them at the top bit by bit. As I thread my feet into the boots, a really evil smell comes out of them, which helps me get in the mood for the next song. Then I put on the S&M gear. I hope Tom or Paulo actually did disinfect the ball that I put in my mouth. Rarely, but still every now and then, it can happen that in the rough and tumble of a concert we start yelling at each other, and to get me to put a dirty ball in my mouth would be a good way of getting revenge, since I wouldn't have any time to do anything about it.

Today the ball tastes normal, i.e., like rubber that I've had in my mouth hundreds of times before. I clip the dog leash to my collar and stagger out on stage. Till grabs the leash right before the first verse to tug me over the stage. It's not just women who can multitask—Till can also sing and push me around at the same time. Shortly before the first chorus he gives me a firm kick and sends me off to my instrument, so I can play along. For the second verse, he pulls me out front. This time he doesn't let me go, rather as he sings he pulls out his giant dick. It's not his real dick, of course, but you can only see that if, like me, you're standing right in front of it. Strictly speaking, I don't see his dick now either, since I'm trying to crawl away from the two of them, i.e., Till and his dick. Naturally I don't get far because Till is holding me by the collar and the belt. But it occurs to me that I've seen the dick a bunch of times, since I'm there when Till puts it on in the dressing room. There's also a hose that runs down his pant leg, so he has to pay close attention to the order in which he puts it all on. I suppose I'm revealing a secret here, but who out there seriously thinks that Till is ejaculating for two minutes straight? The whole time Tom is standing under the stage and pumping liquid from a kind of pressure tank.

It took a lot of experimenting before we found a liquid that would look like ejaculate. For our first mixture we used milk. The problem was that the milk would spoil very quickly. We didn't play every day, of course, and when we had an off day the gear sat in the truck, which in the summer meant significant heat. You can't imagine how bad spoiled milk can smell. That's where the famous butyric acid comes from, which is used to make butter, but also for fish bait. You can level a whole neighborhood with it. With us it was never that bad, but it did get us into trouble a few times.

We were supposed to perform in a real Hollywood movie. In one scene, there was supposed to be a decadent party at which we would be playing the song "*Bück dich*." *Bück dich* means *bend over*. We had been in the US for about ten days by that point, appearing at a few festivals. Then we spent a few days in Los Angeles and started to look forward to being in the movie. Or, well, to being at the film shoot, since the finished film never found a distributor and was never released. It's hard to believe, but sometimes movies get made and it all ends up being for nothing. But we didn't know that at the time.

When we got on set on the day of the shoot, Tom immediately started assembling the apparatus for the spurting dong, if I may describe it as such. The whole time lots of extraordinarily beautiful people kept walking past us, and they were all very busy and important. Elsewhere, an appropriate distance removed from us, the stars were waiting. I can still remember Michael Caine. That was the only name I recognized. Then we rehearsed the scene a few times with the actors. There were a lot of them, since it was supposed to be a big party. It all went really well. But only when we actually started filming was Till supposed to start spraying everybody with his dong. It was impressed upon the actors several times that they were meant to really enjoy this sperm shower and should feel free to swallow some.

Then we started playing, and in the second chorus the dong let loose as planned. As soon as Till started spraying me from behind, I noticed that something had gone horribly wrong. It started to stink so much that I immediately started gagging. Without showing any signs of noticing, Till turned and directed his spray at the actors. I could see the surprise on their faces, but because they were pros, they stayed in character, as if it were completely normal to have spoiled milk sprayed all over you. They all got to the end of the scene, and then the screaming started. The worst thing was that all the clothes had taken on the smell and the actors had to keep wearing them for the rest of the day. At least. In that respect, I had a key advantage over them in that I had learned to deal with the stench. All the same, my clothes stank for weeks afterward. The whole film crew shouted and swore and said horrible things about us Germans. Tom, unfazed, kept repeating that the milk was perfectly fresh.

Since then we always quote his words—"The milk wasn't spoiled!"—whenever someone makes a claim that stands in clear contradiction to reality. Now, more than fifteen years later, we still sometimes ask Tom if the milk really was fresh, and he still hasn't changed his story. But even he has to laugh.

In any event, after this incident we thought about alternatives to milk and came up with Pernod, since it also gets milky and cloudy when you mix it with water. We knew this because, after the wall fell, we went to drink in the newly opened cafés like all the other idiots. I mean, we just had to try out all the drinks that we only knew from movies or books. We didn't really like any of these new drinks—tequila in particular was thoroughly gross. I thought it tasted like ladybug piss. But it did at least seem cosmopolitan to order Pernod and water. So we also knew that this mixture smelled much more pleasant than milk. After this decision the fans started pushing up to the front just to get a taste. It burns the ass a bit, but alcohol is supposed to be a disinfectant, so it's a good tradeoff. Besides, Till is only pantomiming sexual intercourse, or at least that's the agreement anyway.

For the police in Worcester, Massachusetts, however, even the suggestion of sexual intercourse—or rather the exposure of sexual organs, no matter if they were real or not—was sufficient grounds to arrest us. When I went to go take a shower after the show, the police were waiting in our dressing room. I thought they were fans, and I took their yelling to be a funny way of saying hello. They tried to stop us from taking a shower—they wanted to take Till and me with them right away—but I just pointed at my smudged makeup and went to shower anyway. The policemen started to get fussy, and one of them posted himself right outside the shower so I wouldn't run away. That was completely unnecessary—where was I supposed to run to in Worcester, Massachusetts? Besides that, I thought it was all incredibly exciting. I was even happy when they led us to a paddy wagon and handcuffed us to a pole— it was all like a movie. Of course it was also very touching that Till had been arrested with me, but I would have been even happier if our tour manager or some other responsible party had come along to bail us out right away, since we actually still wanted to go to the afterparty.

Instead we waited forever in a holding cell until our names were called. The policemen took their time. And more people kept being put into the cell with us the whole time. Everyone who got arrested that Friday night was in there with us. One of them had been shot by a policeman and was bleeding heavily. Another kept trying to get in touch with the outside world—he needed to find someone to milk his cows so they wouldn't have to suffer. Things got nice and cramped in there after a while. The officer called the prisoners up one by one—he was in no hurry. While being questioned, they were handcuffed to the desk. We were no exception. The desk was all worn down in the spot where the prisoners had to rest their arms. The policeman was very friendly to us and he brought out all the German words that he knew: *Leberwurst, Sauerkraut, Volkswagen*, and maybe also *Autobahn* and *Beckenbauer*. He wrote down our names and rattled on a bit. I understood very little of it. Then he wrote my name on an old chalkboard in the column that said No. 10. At first I thought it was the cops' shift schedule. But when I had to hand over my shoes and my glasses and was told to follow a giant policeman, it was clear to me that I was now going to cell number ten.

The cells were divided by metal bars and Plexiglas. The air conditioning was running at full blast, and I was mad at myself for only having a T-shirt on. I really could have thought of that. Whenever we went to eat somewhere or tried to go see a movie, I always took a thick sweater with me. Otherwise I would freeze. It's a mystery to me how the Americans can put up with it without constantly getting sick all the time. I once made the mistake of going out to dinner in only a T-shirt, and I was so cold during the meal that I kept having to step outside to warm up.

Here in the jail, there was no use asking if I could just pop outside for a second. Nor did I have to ask anybody if I had to go to the bathroom, since I had my own toilet right there in the cell with me. Albeit one without a toilet seat. The sink was built into the tank in the back. Very practical. I immediately positioned myself in such a way that I was a little shielded by the bars and peed. I hadn't been able to the whole time. When I flushed, a chorus of shouting broke out. I myself hadn't expected the flush to be that loud, and I was really startled. Now I had woken up all the people who were asleep already. So right at the outset I hadn't made any friends. In my head, I went over everything I knew or thought I knew about jails. That I was in a cell by myself I considered a good sign, since it promised a degree of security from the other inmates, but things weren't necessarily going to stay that way. To warm up, I did a couple of push-ups. After the fourth, I was out of gas and I stopped. The inmates who could see me stared with incomprehension. I was able to return this with a blank stare of my own because I didn't have my glasses on. Till was unfortunately far away from me.

Then another massive commotion broke out. A four-hundred-pound man was being driven through the cell block and past my cell by six policemen beating him with billy clubs. It was really hard physical labor for the policemen, since the man was fighting back with both hands and feet. He was put in the cell next to mine, and I was happy for the thick bars. The man screamed so loudly it was like his mouth was right next to my ear. And it basically was; I mean, there was only the Plexiglas between us.

Over the next few hours I began to think. Since they had put me in a real cell, that meant I was probably going to be here a while. Though actually after twenty-four hours a judge had to decide whether they could keep me locked up. At least that's how it worked on *Tatort*. Did the judge even work on weekends, or did he not come back from a nice relaxing stay at his *dacha* till Monday morning? The people here wouldn't call it a *dacha*, of course, that's a Russian word, but there had to be weekend houses in America too, right? I was worried. A little bad luck and I would have to stay here in jail. When it comes to certain things, Americans don't have much of a sense of humor. There are movies where things start off nice and harmless, then suddenly you're caught up in a prison gang war. At night you get your teeth knocked out and have various things stuck up your butt. Well, that I know from our concerts. But it was more likely that nothing would happen and I would just have to wait.

I got bored in the cell, and so I tried to at least sleep a little. It was a very discomfiting feeling to know that I couldn't just leave if I got sick or something. Plus I'm a big fan of fresh air. I made a promise to myself then and there that I would never again put myself in a situation in which I was at the mercy of circumstances or prison guards. All these thoughts, plus a wicked buzzing sound, kept me from falling asleep for a long time.

When I woke up, a man was standing in my cell. He led me to the booking counter, where I was handed back my glasses and my shoes without much commentary. I went through two doors, and there in a hallway Till and our tour manager Nicolai were waiting for me. Till was also looking very relieved, while Nicolai, walking quickly, led us to the bus, which was waiting outside the building with the motor running. We had to hurry to make it on time to the concert in Montreal. During the ride, Nicolai told us about having to fight for our release. Really we were supposed to keep waiting in jail, but since the concerts would have to be canceled otherwise, an exception was made and we were allowed to go play them. But on our off days we were supposed to check in with the court. And so we kept having to fly back to Worcester. We missed a couple more parties, but at least we were sitting on a plane and not in a paddy wagon, which was certainly an improvement.

In court we met with our lawyers, who of course had to be licensed to practice in Worcester. My lawyer cheerily explained to me that I shouldn't say anything in the courtroom. That was just fine with me. It was less than ideal, however, that the trial would be taking place a few weeks after the tour was over and we two weren't allowed to leave the country before then. At that point, the rest of the band was already relaxing back home.

Still, all that time I never had any misgivings about our performance; if anything, my misgivings concerned the limits of American tolerance. In Salt Lake City, out of respect for the Mormon religion, we agreed not to expose any sexual organs, real or fake. But why were we arrested in Worcester, which to our eyes didn't seem much different from Mecklenburg? We really didn't expect to encounter any difficulties there. Later on I heard that the daughter of the mayor or the police chief was in the crowd, and that's why the police had to step in.

Meanwhile, "*Bück dich*" doesn't seem like it's ever going to end. I'm still kneeling on stage and can feel the brew running down my whole body. The dong keeps on pumping, the pressure's good and constant. Now Till stops pumping me and directs the spray at the crowd. The people open their mouths and press forward to get some. There are even older people and really pretty women among them. None of it has anything to do with the lyrics. The show is based more on our love of mischief. As the song ends, I keep senselessly bending a note up and down with my pitch wheel while Till keeps spraying the people in the face, happy as a clam. Then he points the spray at his own mouth and looks utterly pleased.

—

OUR FIRST REAL TOUR of the US was as the opener for KMFDM. They were a German band who had moved to America and built up a considerable fan base there. But we didn't know if their fans liked our music or whether they would come see us again. The only way to find out is to headline your own shows. But we didn't dare do that yet.

Instead, we went on a tour across the US with four other bands. It's not uncommon there for several bands to go on tour together. The tour we took part in was called the Family Values tour. We were a bit surprised at first when we saw that there was a concert scheduled for almost every single day. But as the tour progressed, we got less worked up about it since every evening unfolded about the same way. Most of the concerts took place in sports arenas located outside of town, which meant things looked almost identical every night, and our dressing rooms were always in the same spot. There was really no need for us to think about anything. Not even about food, since we had our own cook with us. From our previous visits to the US, we had learned that it wasn't so easy to eat well or healthily there. Now, every morning, the local runner was sent off to buy groceries for us, plus underwear, stamps, batteries, and aspirin. But mainly ingredients for the cook. In our bus, we had a gas stove, and the cook would start preparing our meals on it with the groceries the runner had bought. The aroma traveled throughout the backstage area, and the other bands would come by to see what sort of delicious things the *fucking Germans* were cooking up now.

The bands played in the same order every night. First up was Orgy, a fun young band that had an incredible amount of confidence, especially given that this was the first tour they'd ever been on. After that came Limp Bizkit, whom I'd never heard of, even though they were world famous by that point.

Their show was indescribably good. At the beginning, the spaceship from *Mars Attacks!* was up on stage, and the band climbed out of it. The guitarist wore a skeleton suit. The music was so infectious that everybody in the venue had to dance, whether they wanted to or not. They wanted to, of course. These bands were a hundred times better than us, really they never should have had to play before us. Then Ice Cube was up. He was a rapper whose crew consisted primarily of bodyguards. Ice Cube had himself driven the five hundred feet from the hotel to the concert venue in a giant limousine. He had a singer with him who called himself WC. I once asked him if he knew what his name meant where we were from. West Coast, was his answer, and whenever he saw me his face lit up and he formed the two letters with his fingers. After Ice Cube, known to friends as simply Cube, we got to take the stage.

We weren't in top form on this tour—most of the time we were hopelessly drunk. We figured the other bands would be drinking just as much, I mean after all we were in America, but all the others were much more reasonable. They of course knew how strenuous these long tours across the US are. This wasn't like a few concerts in Saalfeld and Lobenstein—there was no comparison. And we had already made the mistake of drinking too much on tour once before, when we were touring with Clawfinger.

Clawfinger went completely by the book and only drank on the off days. We drank every day and only took a break on the off days to give our ruined bodies the chance to recover a bit. But as a result, we never got to party with the people from Clawfinger. You might have noticed by now that "party" is a synonym for alcohol and drug abuse, but that's the kind of thing that establishes and deepens friendships. And so we decided to also drink on the off days, with Clawfinger. You can imagine what we looked like after this tour.

And this time it was even worse, since in America we were so far away from home and felt like no one was watching us. Nevertheless, the other bands never said anything about us playing badly. Or at least we never heard them. It was hard, see, for them to communicate with us, and we didn't make it any easier for them with our stiff German manners. Whenever somebody came around with a camera and a microphone, we ran away. That was just about the opposite of what the Americans did. Naturally, because of this, we don't appear in any footage of the tour or anything else written about it. Looking back, it seems like we weren't there at all.

One day I sent my mother a postcard with an image of one of the stadiums we had played in. I wrote to her that we had played to a sold-out crowd, not mentioning the fact that it would have been sold out even if we hadn't been playing. The people were there because of Korn, who played after us. They were pretty much the most popular band around at this time. The place really went nuts when they came out, and we felt even more pathetic. We hoped we'd at least be able to go to their afterparty. That's where the prettiest women were—during the concert, they would be handpicked from the crowd by staff brought along specifically for the purpose.

Mostly, though, we partied with Orgy on our bus. There might have been a few girls there who couldn't get into the actual party. We only ever played two songs on the bus: "Blue Monday" by Orgy and our version of "Stripped." And then "Blue Monday" again. It really was just the same two songs over and over again, and it put us in a state of near ecstasy. We danced till the bus shook. Eventually that woke the driver up, who screamed furiously at us, kicked everybody off the bus who wasn't in the band, and drove off to the next city. Drunk as we were, a lot of times we didn't even notice.

Sometimes all the bands went to a strip club together. There you could sit on a chair and have the women dance at you, a ceremony that I watched with bewilderment. Under no circumstances were you allowed to touch the women. But the women seemed really wild about meeting the musicians in the other bands, which was also typically American, I guess. The important thing was that they were musicians. It didn't always make sense to me, since some of the musicians, to put it delicately—well, character-wise, there was room for improvement.

Then we got back on the bus. We had a panties-blue tour bus. The Spice Girls had had it right before we did. They had slept in the same beds as us, so naturally we found that very exciting. At first it smelled really good in the bus. There were real leather couches in there, and in the back there was a great spot to veg out, and there were TVs and VCRs everywhere. But the best thing was that you could open and shut the door. On German buses, the doors were operated by compressed air, and you couldn't open or shut them when the bus had been standing around for a while or the engine was off. Here in America, that couldn't happen, because the engine was left running day and night on account of the air conditioning, which took some getting used to. That had no effect on the doors, though; they were just plain old regular doors, and the windows too you could just open and shut. Since for me nothing beats fresh air, the bus had won my heart.

And given the massive distances we had to cover, having a good bus was an absolute necessity. Early in the mornings we would laze around on the couches. There were slippers on our feet, and we wore our so-called bus pants—especially comfortable and worn-out sweatpants. No one was going to see us in them anyway. At most when the bus stopped at a rest stop in the middle of the night and we had to go to the bathroom. Sometimes the bus driver wouldn't notice that one of us was missing, and after filling up the tank he'd just drive off. He didn't always feel like going to check every bed to see if we were all there. If the one who got left at the gas station was lucky, he wasn't left standing there in just his underwear, but at least had on his bus pants. On our first few tours in America, we didn't have cell phones yet, so you really had to work to get back to the band. The only thing to do was hitchcock, I mean hitchhike, but you had to move quickly, since the bus drove pretty fast and the distances were long. A lot of times nobody would notice that someone was missing, since on long rides we usually just stayed in bed. Or we sat like slugs on the couches and watched one movie after another. As we watched. we would heat up these horrible prepackaged meals in the microwave—Hungry-Man, they were called. Or we would make ourselves a sandwich, to the extent that it was possible with the American ingredients on the bus. All the packaging landed in a giant built-in trash can. We just had to lift up a big lid on the kitchen counter. Someone told us that every day a giant container ship full of trash left New York for West Africa, where all the stuff was sorted out again and searched for anything that could be salvaged. After we heard that, we also tossed in a bunch of CDs and other stuff that was still in good shape. Plus whole cans of root beer. We really were drunk most of the time.

Like when we got to Las Vegas. I couldn't believe what I was seeing. There was essentially only one street, which was where all the hotels and casinos were, and just beyond that the desert began. But down this one street flowed a constant stream of excited people. Most of them wore T-shirts that said *Las Vegas—The Best Day of My Life*. I didn't want to see the bad days.

After two hours, I had seen all I needed to see and wanted out. But of course we had a show that night. Then Schneider got the idea to rent us a car and drive out to Death Valley. We went to Dream Cars and got a Corvette convertible and a badly photocopied page from a road atlas. I was supposed to navigate, and I immediately miscalculated the distances. We soon turned off onto a gravel road and struggled our way through the desert at a crawl. All of a sudden there were no more buildings, and instead we just saw a few wrecked cars with bullet holes in them. We thought it looked just like a ,movie, which is ridiculous, since movies are supposed to look like real life. The sun was so brutal that we had to put the top up. When we finally realized that we were going the wrong way, we turned around, but we took a wrong turn somewhere and got completely lost. When we started getting thirsty, we realized we really didn't know what to do. We thought about what the people in movies always did, and decided to just keep driving straight until we got to an actual road. In America, you can drive for an amazingly long time without seeing anything.

When we finally reached the paved road we'd been longing for, we had no interest in and definitely no time left for visiting Death Valley. We had our hands full just trying to find the way home. When we got back to the car rental place, they were completely horrified at how bad the car looked. It was covered in dirt, and all the little rocks from the gravel road had gotten lodged in the undercarriage. We had to pay a large fee, and I've still never been to Death Valley. And I don't need to, either—I almost died just trying.

Even if that's an exaggeration, I did have a bad cold throughout most of the time I was in America. Then I noticed that at the rest stops they sold these big bags of pills. I read the label, and it seemed to me that all of my problems would soon be a thing of the past. It seemed these pills contained every kind of vitamin and mineral that my body needed to stay healthy, and above all, to be full of power. That's actually what it said in English—*full of power*. The different pills were split up into daily doses, all individually packed. I was supposed to take ten or twelve a day. I couldn't figure out which of them I was supposed to take in the morning, which at midday and which at night, so, with some hesitation, every morning I just gobbled down the whole day's ration. It wasn't too long before I had orange diarrhea and green piss. Then my heart started racing. The worst thing, though, was that I just couldn't sleep anymore. I thought it was because of the bus, especially since I wasn't the only one who sat like a slug on the couch behind the driver every night drinking himself senseless. It took a few weeks for me to trace my symptoms back to the funny pills, and when I stopped taking them, I slowly started to feel better. But by then the tour was already over.

After or maybe before that, we went through South America with Kiss. I asked my friend Paulo if he wanted to come with us, since the tour was supposed to go through his home country of Chile, and off we went in the best of spirits. But the concert in Chile never took place—someone apparently pocketed the ticket money. Paulo assured me that in Chile that was nothing unusual.

And so we went on to Argentina. Because the cities in which we, or rather Kiss, were set to play were so far apart, we didn't get a bus; instead we took a plane to each different stop. There we stayed in hotels, which we still weren't used to, but which was very pleasant. In Buenos Aires, we wandered around town, happy to be alive. Olli even forgot his own birthday. So then of course we didn't remember it either. Something like that was possible back then, because we didn't have cell phones. An innocent time. To play in South America meant to really be far away from home. In all that time, I only once managed make a brief call home from our hotel.

We played at River Plate stadium and two days later were invited to a soccer game there. Kiss too, of course, but they didn't come; rather, they voiced their wish to go to a flamenco concert. Of course there is no flamenco in Argentina, the people there play tango. Or vice versa. I would have liked to see the guys in Kiss off stage sometime. But even without them, the soccer game was an unforgettable experience, even if I did miss the goals. I was distracted for a moment. I guess I found the sausages there more important. Unfortunately, we were led out of the stadium fifteen minutes before the game was over—they couldn't guarantee our safety otherwise.

In Brazil, we were escorted to the stadium by mounted police officers. The fans had taken over the official route and blocked it off, so they took us on a dirt road through the favelas. Whole families stood out on the street and stared at us. They were probably trying to get a look at Kiss. Who knows what they look like without the makeup on? We could have been them, for all anyone knew. And so we briefly basked in unearned fame.

In São Paolo, we played where they held Formula 1 races—i.e., right on the track. We were still on our first song when all of a sudden there was this earsplitting noise. I concentrated on my instrument and was surprised to hear the applause coming at such an unusual moment. Then I looked out at the stage and saw that Till was being pelted with bottles, beer cans full of piss, and whatever other objects came to hand. Every direct hit unleashed a torrent of applause. Apparently the point of all the noise was to get us to leave the stage immediately. We tried to keep our heads down and to stay out of the way of the flying goat heads and fire extinguishers. Everyone in the crowd who was close to us tried to spit on us. They all seemed pretty well practiced. When finally, reluctantly, we left the stage, the organizer came over to congratulate us, beaming. He predicted great success in South America. We saw things a bit differently at that moment and actually wanted to go straight home, but the organizer was all excited. He had never seen a band opening for Kiss in this stadium last as long on stage as we had. Then he explained that Kiss fans show their admiration by preventing the opening band from playing. They run them off, so to speak. No band could even come close to Kiss, and any band that dared think they could share a stage with the gods had to be punished. It wasn't personal—it had nothing to do with us. Also, the organizer explained, the people weren't spitting at us, they just wanted to kiss us and couldn't get close enough. So they just sent the kiss on a journey to us. Right. That was certainly one way of looking at it, and of course we did keep playing on that tour. We took a practical view of things: it was a long flight back, and our instruments were already there anyway.

Bafflingly enough, the organizer turned out to be right. A few years later, we were supposed to sign autographs at a record store in support of whichever album had just come out at the time. This was in the middle of Mexico City. We had barely left the hotel when we saw a whole bunch of police vans. We looked on with interest and figured there must be some kind of unrest somewhere in the city. Then we kept having to drive down these narrow side streets because all the major streets were blocked off. Only when we got to the store did we see what was going on. The whole square out front was packed with fans. The police tried to make room so we could get into the shopping center. We made it as far as the door, but a few of us lost our sunglasses in the process. The fans just grabbed at our faces. Till fell over when our security guard took a wrong step and knocked into him.

But once we were inside the department store and in the music department, no one came to get our autograph. There was no way they were going to open the doors. The people were going completely nuts. I don't even want to know how far they all must have traveled to see us. In any case, they started to just lay waste to the square. I saw little trees, benches, and trash cans flying through the air. To calm the situation down a bit, the policemen sent us up to the roof. From there we were supposed to speak to the people. When we opened up the roof hatch and crawled out, we saw people, an untold mass of people—and they were everywhere. On all the surrounding roofs, in all the stairwells; they leaned over balconies and ledges, they looked out the windows—no idea how they got into the apartments—and down in the square an endless surging crowd. I don't know how many thousands there were. And we weren't even playing a concert; it was really just about a couple of autographs. This was a clear illustration of how the word *fan* comes from *fanatic*.

On that tour with Kiss we also played our last show in Mexico City, but back then nobody in Mexico knew us. During that performance, we didn't get anything thrown at us for once, and apparently Kiss watched a feed of our set in their dressing room. I mean, it took them two hours to get dressed and put their makeup on, and since we played during that time, they were never able to see us live.

The day before, we had gone to see the pyramids. We had to drive two hours while the driver instructed us on how we should comport ourselves. Tom, who was sitting up front, kept turning back to us and translating: "If somebody at the pyramids offers you something," he shouted, "then say *nicht danke*." A valuable tip. But because Tom was speaking German it took a while for me to understand what the driver was actually saying. "No, thank you."

Why am I talking about this again? Oh, right, because of Kiss.

One time, when I found an open seat in the catering room, two old building superintendents sat down at my table. They said hello and were very friendly and then went back to their meal. Long story short, it was Gene Simmons and Ace Frehley—or maybe Paul Stanley—from Kiss. I hadn't recognized them.

—

NOW WE'RE PLAYING "*ICH will.*" Apparently we have trouble coming up with good names for our songs. "*Ich will*" is hardly a proper name for a song. It's hardly anything. All it means is *I want*. An electric company once used it as an ad slogan. They had it on all their bags. So I would go around holding one of these bags to promote our song. Free advertising, you could say. Still, I always had my issues with this song. This has less to do with the song than with me. From a purely musical standpoint, I somehow never understood it. It didn't sound bad, but every time we played it I kept waiting for the real song to start. The rest of the band was excited from the get-go, and while we were recording it they were already looking forward to the crowd's reaction when we played the song live. And as it turned out, they were absolutely right.

Before the choruses come accents on the drums that we've highlighted with bombs. Or, well, we call them bombs; the trade term is flash pot or air cannon or something like that. On stage the explosions are much louder than the music, and of course they startle me every time. Then the sound of the explosion comes back as an echo, and it can make you get off beat really quickly. The best thing to do is to pretend there are no explosions at all and to concentrate on playing.

Recently we played this song at a rehearsal without the bombs. I mean, it would have been ridiculous to set off all the bombs during rehearsal—we're not that sick. This time I was able to just sit back and listen to the song, and I thought it was really good. With bombs of course it's also good. Besides that, I know it's the last song in the main set, which means that we've just about made it. It's not that I'm always longing for the end of the concert, but I am happy of course when everything goes as planned. And so, spirits high, I dance around a bit on stage and imitate Till's way of pounding his fist against his thigh. He doesn't like that, so he tries to push me off stage.

A few bombs later, the song is over. The concert too, and so I leave the stage. For a long time I thought that a concert really was over when the musicians left the stage, and that it was only because the audience cried so enthusiastically for an encore that the musicians would change their minds and decide, just this once, to make an exception and come back out and spontaneously start playing again. In a small number of cases, the concert really was over once the musicians left the stage, but what happened in these cases was probably that the band had started fighting or the schedule was so tight that there was no time left for encores. Otherwise the band always came back on stage, and usually it was only then that they played their three biggest hits. That seemed strange to me, since without the encores they wouldn't ever have played them, and why should a band not play the very songs that get the best reaction from the audience?

In Feeling B, we didn't need encores, since most of the time we couldn't even manage to end our concerts in a halfway dignified manner. And at the first Rammstein concerts, we simply didn't have enough songs to plan for an encore. If the people still wanted more after we'd gone through all of our songs, we'd just have to pick a few of the songs we'd just played and play them again. At our best shows we would play the same song three times. But eventually the day came when we too started saving songs especially for the encore. If we did play them, it would be as a kind of surprise. I mean, we could always get together after the main set and discuss whether we wanted to keep playing or not.

For today we've planned three songs for the encore. So now we don't have to discuss, since the three songs are already written in order on the setlist. See, it can happen sometimes during a concert that you suddenly forget what song comes next, and for that reason the backline techs always tape a piece of paper with the order written on it somewhere nice and visible.

In the first song of the encore, I'm supposed to play piano, so I have at least as much time as it takes the crew to get it set up on stage. Which means I can go ahead and relax. The crowd can also see that a piano is being set up on stage, so they have a clear sign that the concert isn't over yet. And actually they don't have to keep cheering for an encore, but maybe they're not looking at the stage, or they're just cheering for fun, or so they'll feel like they've done their own small part to contribute to a nice evening.

A crewmember comes up to me with a cigarette. He lit it especially for me. I think that's very nice of him, and although I want to quit smoking, I thank him kindly and take the cigarette from him. I can't just leave him hanging; how would that look? Never mind that smoking is prohibited everywhere in the building. The cigarette tastes even worse than the one this afternoon. I'm completely out of breath and what my body really needs is something healthy. Cigarettes generally don't taste good after exercise anyway. I don't know how I know that, since I don't ever exercise, but clearly this is a really tough cigarette for me to get through. It looks cool, though. At least I tell myself it does. Meanwhile, no one can see me because I'm hiding behind the stairs. The technician triumphantly raises seven fingers in the air. That means that we have just seven concerts to go. I wave my hand in a friendly way. Again I'm happy that nothing went wrong tonight.

On the last tour, I still had to ride in the inflatable boat. I was always terrified beforehand. Now, you might be asking yourself just what I was doing in an inflatable boat, since in a concert venue there's no water anywhere. Yes, well, as perverse as it sounds, I sail the boat over people. Or rather, sailed.

It was like this. At the last concert of a tour, the technicians always have a little harmless fun with the band. It's a bit like summer camp, where on the last night you have a big pillow fight. While we were playing "*Seemann*," Tom had himself pulled across the stage in a little rubber boat that they'd put on one of the dollies they use to move the heavy amps. He was making silly little paddling motions as he went. Till, who was standing at the front of the stage, didn't notice him at first, but when he finally saw him, he grabbed the boat, shook Tom out of it, and threw the boat into the crowd. Now we could all see how the boat sailed over the outstretched arms of the people in the crowd. And so we thought it would be cool if we were to have someone man the boat. And I was the only one eligible for this task, since I didn't have to play during that part. Plus I'm nice and light. Or I was then, at least.

So from then on I sailed the boat. And the people moved me around pretty well, too, but I hadn't thought about how they would be looking toward the front to see what was going on onstage, and in so doing would keep pushing me toward the back. At some point I'd run out of people, and I'd fall. In the beginning I wasn't able to catch my fall very well and I'd land directly on my head. Then I'd have to make my way back to the stage on foot. Through the crowd, of course. As I went, I often lost my shoes and other articles of clothing. Once I got back on stage, I would try and determine where it was I'd hurt myself and how I could keep playing.

One time the crew—again on the last day of the tour—put a girl in a bikini in the boat with me as a little gag. The people weren't able to hold us both up, and I fell and landed back-first on one of the metal barriers. Then I started kind of twitching funnily. I was taken to the hospital, where a lot of fans were already waiting for treatment. They were very happy to see me and they let me go ahead of them. It was just a bad bruise, but man, it hurt. As I mentioned, though, it was the last concert of the tour, so it didn't matter.

Since we didn't play "*Seemann*" on the next tour, we just slotted the boat into another song—we didn't want to give up doing such a fun gimmick. Unfortunately, this song was much faster and more aggressive, so now I really got shaken up. Sometimes the excitement was so great that I was pushed up the rows and then flew back down again like a bobsledder. When I got to the bottom, the boat tipped over. Then I was back at the hospital while the next day the band went to the beach.

And so I'm very happy that the boat isn't part of the set today. I stand up contentedly, neatly put my cigarette out, and go around to the other side of the stage to look for the band and find out if anything's changed or if some other interesting thing might have happened. They're all standing comfortably in a corner, each one of them drinking something. I even smell ginger tea. They're in the middle of a friendly conversation. Sadly I can't understand them because I still have my earplugs in, but I don't want to take them out because they're fitting so snugly right now. And so I smile feebly and give a friendly nod to everything they say. That's what I do most of the time anyway. Even without earplugs, I hear just as little of what people are saying. It could be that I don't hear so well anymore. Now Nicolai gives me a sign with his lamp, and I go back around to the other side of the stage where the piano is. The plan is for a spotlight to follow me on my way to the piano, so that the crowd can see me and above all so that I can see where I'm going, but the spotlight operator, as the man behind the spotlight is called—probably one of the truck operators who does it to make a little extra cash on the side—hasn't noticed that I've stepped on stage, because of course it's dark. By the time I've reached the piano, though, he's found me, and I start playing.

The song is called "*Mein Herz brennt*." The song we're playing today isn't the original version, but rather a version that a friend composed for the video. He took our rock number—now that sounds really unfortunate—I mean he took the song as the band played it and made a piano version, that is, a song that only consists of the song and piano accompaniment. Since I'm the keyboard player in the band, it makes sense that I should play piano. We've removed the strings and the real keys from the piano because otherwise it would be much too heavy to take on tour with us. So the piano has a new set of keys and the sound comes from a sampler that spits out piano sounds that correspond to the ones that I play on the keyboard.

It wasn't easy for me to learn this piece. In fact, it was extremely hard. It's the first real piece of piano music that I've played on stage. And I'm almost fifty. But I've discovered a really good trick: I just have to keep on breathing calmly and not think about it, then my hands just play by themselves.

Now Till joins in. It sounds wonderful. On a song like this, you can really hear his voice. I think the crowd is also happy when the band isn't playing at full volume the whole time. You can hear them singing along, and there's a really momentous atmosphere.

It reminds me of how I used to get goose bumps when I watched *Rockpalast* at night with my friends and the whole stadium sang along to a ballad. It seemed to me like the biggest hits were always slow songs. They had strings, too, or at least a piano. The number-one spot on the Hit Parade was always a schmaltzy song. The songs I liked never got past number three. The people who were into heavy music probably didn't have as much money to buy records. Even songs like "We Are the Champions" are really slow.

And now we're playing a slow song, with a piano even, and it's still not a hit. Even though it's nice and emotional. As a kid, I couldn't stand to even hear the word "emotional." That was something for old people. What was I supposed to do with emotions? "I'm getting emotional!" the boys in the schoolyard would shout when they saw a pretty girl. What they meant was that they were sexually aroused, or rather horny, as we would later call it.

I think when I was young they played more fast music on the radio than they do today. The song we're playing now, though, would definitely never be played on the radio, no matter what era. That has less to do with the music itself than with the fact that it's a song by us. It's also generally hard for me to find a station that plays music that I like. I probably just go to bed too early at night. I can remember times when I would kneel by my tape deck at night to record music off the radio. I knew that if I missed my chance, I might never hear some of the songs again.

I'll definitely hear the song we're playing now again, and often, because it's part of our set. Unless for some reason today is our last concert. I mean, something could always happen. Now all of a sudden I'm totally sick with fear. If this really is the last time, then I wish I'd sat back and enjoyed it more. You get so mad about little things, but it can be so much fun to play in a band in front of so many people. Hopefully we can keep doing it for a while. From now on, I'll be happy at every concert. And if there aren't any more concerts—if maybe our plane crashes—then it won't matter, because in that case I won't be at all interested in whether I'm going to play more concerts or not. Amid these thoughts, this song too comes to an end.

I tinkle the keys for a little bit at the end, then I hurry behind the stage and back over to my side. In an instant the piano is cleared off and Schneider starts the next song. He plays like a machine. Only better. It's a joy hearing him. It is our great luck that we have a drummer who doesn't try to prove himself on every song. There are drummers who try to fit as many hits in a beat as possible. Or who play really complicated rhythms. But the drummer is the heart of the band. He keeps the band and the song together. And the best way to do that is with simple, clear rhythms. For this, Schneider possesses the necessary discipline. That might be due to the fact that he's the only one of us who was in the army, but that was more an oversight on his part. He didn't live in Berlin at the time, so he didn't have people around him who could have helped him avoid compulsory military service. He says that when, on his first night as a soldier, he had to pack up his civilian clothes in a cardboard box to send back home, he realized he'd made a huge mistake. But by then it was too late.

And now his self-discipline is once again serving him well. With the rest of us, you can see what becomes of people who never had to follow orders. Sometimes it's hard for us to see an activity through if at first glance it seems pointless. But that's exactly what you have to do every now and then in order to make a good song. And in order to play a song good and tight. This song is called either "*Sonne*" or "*Hier kommt die Sonne.*" It'd be nice if you didn't always have to name the songs. Sometimes you'll see paintings where it just says *Untitled* under them. It would be funny if the disc jockey on the radio said: "The next song is 'Untitled.'" Okay, maybe not that funny.

We just call the song "*Sonne,*" which means *sun*. I'm so jazzed that I turn on the treadmill, even though it's completely unnecessary. Of course it's never strictly necessary, but we spent so much money having the treadmill modified that we feel like we have to use it. To work off the debt, so to speak. I'd be very curious to know when the treadmill will have amortized.

It's moving slowly now, so it's not so demanding and fits the heavy guitar riffs well. A riff is a constantly repeating figure on guitar that forms the basic foundation of a song. Heavy metal music consists primarily of guitar riffs. Just not the ballads, and of course every kind of music has those. We've got ballads too, but even in them there's usually a guitar riff at some point, and that's another reason why even these songs aren't played on the radio. Guitar riffs are considered too hard for normal people. At least in Germany. All the same, I like to play this music, because a riff like this one is really powerful and truly grabs hold of the listener. This particular riff here I find especially well done, and I feel great as I run along. My job during the verse is really simple. I have to play a single note on piano with my finger. It's a D, in case anybody's interested. That is, it sounds like a piano, but I play it on my sampler. I guess I explained that already. I raise my hand really high and let my finger fall on the appropriate key like a hawk swooping down on its prey. On the chorus, I play the inevitable choir sound. And for the *allerletzter Braten*, which means something like *the very last sausage* and is what we call it when the riff plays out at the end, flames shoot out at us from literally all sides. It's the hottest point in the concert, and sometimes it can happen that one of us can't keep playing and drops to the ground like a roasted fly. We call this part the rotisserie. Today I myself have to duck down and blindly search for notes on the keyboard with my fingers.

It's a shame that this song is over now too. I'm not always as happy to play it as I am today, since we play it on almost every tour. Which means at almost every concert. The so-called hits are always in the setlist, so it's a bit hard for us to muster the same excitement every night, but I can understand the people in the crowd—when they come see us live, they want to hear the songs they like. I'm sure the Rolling Stones don't want to play "Satisfaction" all the time, either. But the one time I was at one of their concerts, I got totally excited when they played that song. I was only going to see them once and probably won't manage to see them a second time, since the guys in the band are so old. It's true we're not that old yet, but all the same, we prefer to play the songs people want to hear.

I don't know if that's also true of the song we're playing now to end the concert. This is "Pussy." This song is the only one of ours that made it to number one on the charts in Germany. The song is a bit poppier than our other songs, which is to say, it's not as heavy. Which confirms my theory that the softer songs are the more successful ones. But then again, maybe Germans just like the word *pussy*. Or they like that the lyrics are half in English. Or that they're about sex tourism?

For this song I grab a small, handheld keyboard and go up to the front of the stage. The cable gets stuck on a corner and I have to tug at it a little bit. Sometimes the jack gets pulled out of the keyboard and when I start playing no sound comes out. Now, though, I can hear myself—phew—and I look out at the crowd to see who all is out there tonight. Some of the people I even recognize. They must have a whole lot of free time if they can come to so many concerts. But I'm sure it's fun. I'm happy to get to see so many different cities myself. After all, you don't have to be a musician to travel. You can just as easily be part of the crew or a fan.

A lot of people are singing along excitedly. Do they know what the song's about? And do they know that it's the last song? Now here comes the bridge—how many times do I have to keep saying that? But it is the last song, of course, and this time there's no fire for once. Instead Till throws the microphone away after he's pulled it out of the microphone stand. Then he takes the microphone stand and twists it into a kind of pretzel, seemingly effortlessly. He stuffs the result into a box, which promptly explodes. I always hope that the people in the crowd are seeing it for the first time and are surprised. Just what must they think of us? All these stunts are totally absurd. What must someone think who has seen this whole production more than once? To put on a show like this every night is even more absurd.

If I see a band in concert, I try to completely forget the fact that they played the day before and will also perform again the next day. I want to feel like I'm present for a unique occurrence. And as a musician, I also try to make sure that the people who see our concerts feel this way. For us it isn't so simple, especially because our show is supposed to give the impression that we're spontaneously reacting to one another. Or that Till really is beside himself with anger. Of course, no one seriously believes that Till wants to cook and eat me during "*Mein Teil.*" Or maybe they do? I mean, there are days when I believe it myself. And so to make sure that the effects really land, I try to get myself so worked up for all of it so that I'm not just acting as if I were completely surprised. Like I said, sometimes I believe it myself. And I can honestly say it makes me really happy every time we pull off some wild stunt on stage.

Here we go again on "Pussy." Till climbs up onto a giant foam cannon with a real saddle attached to it. Like a saddle for a horse. Naturally the cannon is supposed to represent a penis; there really aren't many other ways to interpret it. Already the foam is being shot out of the cannon. Some nights there's more, some nights less. It depends on several factors. The less foam comes out, the worse mood Till is in after the show. Whoever is responsible for the kink in the pressure hose or a similar malfunction makes himself scarce. And now suddenly, really much too soon, the concert is over.

I used to want to play really long concerts, since I thought people should get to hear a lot of songs for their money. Then Paul came back with the counterargument that Brötzmann only ever played for forty-five minutes. We all liked Caspar Brötzmann's music and his live shows, so we couldn't really argue with that. Now, though, it occurs to me that no one made the effort to verify Paul's assertion.

Marilyn Manson once played for only forty minutes in Berlin and he was booed—the crowd was pissed. But today the crowd seems to have had enough. I mean, it really takes it out of you, shouting and dancing the whole time. I think the people are more exhausted than we are. Even the ones who were just sitting in the back had to hold their phones up for hours to film the concert. Those people's arms have to be sore by now. If one of them ever has to go pee, his girlfriend holds the phone up for him. But then most of the time she doesn't pay close enough attention and ends up filming the back of somebody's head for a couple of minutes. But of course that doesn't matter, since no one is ever going to see this video. I guess it's none of my business, but I think it's sad, because a lot of times these people don't pay attention to the actual concert—they figure they're getting it all on film.

Now they aren't calling out for an encore anymore; they know from all the other fans on the internet who have made recordings in the past few days that we're not going to play anymore. If we did, then that would really be something special. Of course, if we did want to play another encore, then we would have had to let the crew know by noon of the day of the concert, so that no parts of the stage would be in the way and the lighting could be programmed for the song. Otherwise, the crew would already have started to pack everything up and load it onto the trucks. You wouldn't believe how quickly everything gets packed away. All of which is to say that if the mood is extremely good one night, we don't do the extra encore until the next night. But by then of course we're in a completely different city.

Today it really is *Feierabend* after "Pussy." I love the word *Feierabend*. In America I kept wanting to say it. I looked for a translation, but I never could find one. "Quitting time" doesn't really cover it; it just sounds like you want to quit smoking. *Feierabend*, though, is a really special word, since somehow it contains not only the plain sense of it being quitting time, but also the sense of joy you feel when the work day is over. I would say of a friend who died, *It's Feierabend for him now*. By that I would mean something positive. I'd mean basically: rest in peace. Just a bit more comfortable. With slippers on. I would even say it for people who spent their whole lives in a frenzy.

To make sure that everybody realizes this is the end, I play a few chords that are supposed to sound heroic. The band goes up to the front of the stage and takes a bow together. We started doing that a few years ago, and everybody gave us these funny looks, since people had only ever seen it done at the theater. By now I've seen a lot of bands do it. I would go out front to take a bow myself, but then who would play the background music? I might be happy about that, though, since I don't like doing something only because everybody else is doing it. Plus I don't think the crowd would get anything out of it if I were to go out to the front of the stage and take a bow. The people would be much happier if we played another song instead of congratulating ourselves. And anyway, Till has already said thank you.

I still have my sunglasses on and it's now dark, so I can't see anything at all. I feel my way down the stairs and off the stage.

III

I'M THE LAST OFF stage, and I hurry through the halls to catch up with the others. I hear them laughing up ahead and walk faster. Finally I catch up to them. Our security guy walks up ahead to get the people who are standing in the hallways to move aside.

They wave at us and call out something that sounds like "Great show." We smile and wave back. In the hallway, there's a table with a pitcher full of juice. The kitchen people put it there for us—they figure a few vitamins couldn't hurt us. And so we stop here for a moment and drink our cups of juice. Olli asks if anyone wants to go swimming tomorrow. He's got a nerve. How am I supposed to know that now?

Then we're back in our dressing rooms, and the door falls shut behind us. We sit down, humming contentedly. Till puts some music on. He's put together a special playlist for the time right after the concert. This is actually the best moment of the night. Because now I get undressed one article of clothing at a time. First I take my sunglasses off. It's really very bright here in the dressing room. Then I take off my neckband and my earbuds. Now I can breathe properly again. The fuck shorts are, of course, soaking wet. It makes sense, given that Till was spurting on them for so long. They didn't even dry out during the rotisserie. But then again, the shorts are made of a strange material that's slow to dry. I think they might even be made of leather. I can still remember from when I was young what it felt like to get rained on while wearing my Thälmann jacket—that is, a leather jacket like the kind the famous communist Ernst Thälmann used to wear. It stayed wet for days afterward and smelled ripe. I could barely lift it, it was so heavy. Still I kept wearing it. Thankfully my wife finally threw it out. Otherwise I would still be running around in it, looking ridiculous. Though I'd probably feel young and edgy.

Now I take off my boots. They smell like dead dog. The socks are so gross that I just feel like throwing them away. But that's not how things work around here. Here comes Paulo to collect the stage clothes. He uses a kind of pole with a grabber on it like the people who pick up trash in the park. I don't have my suit with me. I already took it off backstage. Later, someone will hang it up in the dresser in the foolish hope that it'll be dry by tomorrow.

I go to take a shower. Olli is already in there. How does he manage to get there before me every night? He stands in front of the mirror and washes the makeup off his face with a makeup remover towelette. I do the same. Earlier I would try to just wash my face with soap, but this way is much faster. Still, I can never get all the makeup off, especially in the spots I can't reach as easily, like inside my ears. There I'm usually still white the next day. So long as we're still on tour, it doesn't matter; in theory I don't need to take my makeup off at all, then I'd even save myself the step of putting the makeup on every night. Unfortunately, though, the makeup is rather prone to smudging, so I'd probably ruin all my clothes. Besides that, the band always yells at me on the plane if one of them notices that I'm still all white. And so I feverishly rub the towelette over my face and hope that all the showers aren't taken by the time I'm finished.

This worry turns out to have been unjustified—because we're playing in a sports arena today, there are enough showers for everyone. It isn't so easy to figure out how the shower head works—there are always ways of turning the hot water on that you never quite suspect. I look to see how the others do it. Now the hot water starts to flow. The gel on my head is rock hard by now, but with the shampoo it comes right out. I've thought about leaving the gel in till the next concert, but the one time I actually tried it, my hair was so hard I was scared it would break off. All it would have taken was for me to pull a sweater over my head. Or to rest my heavy head on my hair at night. In Africa, there's supposed to be a tribe of people who hold their heads up at night so the ants won't get in their ears. But that's something you'd have to learn as a child. I sometimes practice during my afternoon nap.

Suddenly the water gets boiling hot. I jump back. Someone turned the cold water on to refresh themselves, something we all tend to do at the end of a shower. As a result my water got suddenly very hot. Whoever did it could have given a heads up beforehand. I feel like a crab. Or I look like one at least. I start cursing under my breath, but still think about giving a heads up myself when I turn the cold water on. But of course there's nobody left in the showers; they're probably washing their makeup off or soaping up. I dry off and am happy to see my favorite deodorant in the makeup box. It's called Brut, and there are only a few places left in the world where you can find the stuff, probably because it's so hazardous to your health. The first time I bought it, I couldn't believe it was supposed to be a deodorant. I thought the salesperson hadn't heard me correctly when I asked for deodorant. The store I was in was very dark and crowded. When I screwed off the top, it didn't smell like deodorant, but good, in its own way—I would recognize the smell right away among a hundred others.

When I've sprayed myself with it—those in the trade say "spritzed"—I feel invincible. Then I brush my teeth—I still have to talk to a bunch of people, and because the music is always so loud, everybody always gets really close to me. For those who don't have time to brush their teeth, there's also a pack of gum here. We call it "social gum," because we use it to help us take the plunge into the maelstrom, i.e., social life. There's cologne here too, but I'd better not use any of that today since I've already used such a generous amount of deodorant. With a towel around my waist, I step lightly back to the dressing room.

A whole bunch of new people have arrived in addition to all the people who were here before the concert. Why do I get the impression that the people who congregate in our dressing room tend to be drawn from the criminal elite of whichever city we're in? Are these the only people who are into our music? Do we make music for criminal elements? That's what they were called in East Germany. Or is it because the people who bring drugs and women with them have a much easier time getting backstage than the ones who want to talk to us about books and social assistance programs? The latter kind probably don't have any interest in hanging around a dressing room. Meanwhile, those who have managed to make it in here are having a splendid time. Since the concert was so loud, they're still screaming. In response, Till turns the music up.

I look around and try to see who all is here. You usually don't recognize the famous people, because they look completely different from what they look like in the movies or in your own imagination. Robert De Niro, for example, is very short. I haven't been able to confirm that for myself, since I've never seen him, but literally every person says so whenever this subject comes up. Today there's no one I recognize—even though I picture the short people as being taller—so I guess I can just go get dressed.

I scan the wall with my eye. Right, there's a plastic bag hanging up with my name on it. Or rather, the name is on the gaffer's tape with which the bag is stuck to the wall. I carefully peel it off, since I'll need it later. I pull out the clean, albeit very faded, underwear and socks from the bag and put them on. With every wash they get a little smaller and a little more worn. All the same it feels refreshing to put on these clean clothes. Thankfully I've hidden my clean T-shirts and pants under a chair. In all the commotion, no one pays any attention to me anyway, so I can go ahead and take my time getting dressed.

Now I'm starting to get hungry. There are still a few nuts left. Somebody has already ashed in the nut bowl, if "ashed" is a word. Most of our visitors, especially the ones who were here beforehand, are very drunk and screaming their heads off; the others look really lost, like they're wondering what they're doing here. Some of the women might have wandered in on account of Till, but he can't concern himself with them now. And so they try to call attention to themselves by laughing loudly and squealing. Others quietly exhibit their physical assets. They keep running back to the bathroom to check how they look.

When I pop back into the bathroom myself to comb my hair, my freshly washed clothes already smell like cigarette smoke. So I give the clothes a couple of sprays of cologne after all. Back in the dressing room, I figure I can go ahead and smoke a cigarette myself. I've barely sat down and am looking for my lighter when a woman comes and asks if she can have the chair. I don't feel like arguing about who gets to sit in the chair, and I slowly get up. Out of politeness, she asks me where I'm from. Do I also like Rammstein's music? Truthfully I answer that I'm from Berlin and that yes, I do like Rammstein's music. But she's long since turned away and resumed talking to a friend of hers.

I wander a bit aimlessly through the dressing room and think about where I could go to smoke a cigarette. My bandmates don't smoke, so I don't want to go to their dressing rooms and smoke up the place. At the door to the hallway, I'm recognized, and a few enthusiastic young men quickly hand me their CDs with the urgent request that I listen to them.

Since I neither want to lie to them nor to disappoint them, I just nod my head. I rarely feel like listening to the CDs people give me. Even if I were to like the music, I wouldn't know how to help these young people. I figure if I think the music is good, then other people will like it too, and so the band will find success one way or another. But I'm probably deluding myself a little bit. Really my taste isn't very broad, but this too should reassure the bands, since it means that if I don't like the music, they still have a good chance of being successful. But the easiest thing to do of course would be to just not give me the CDs in the first place—that way there's no chance of a misunderstanding.

I take them all the same and put them in my underwear bag. I can always listen to them after the tour when I'm out driving. I grab a new crime novel from my dresser drawer and put it with the CDs. Now everybody in the dressing room starts taking photos again, and I escape into the hallway.

Will the whole picture-taking thing eventually go out of fashion? Could it be that soon no one will be taking selfies anymore? After all, almost nobody asks for autographs anymore. And when I tell people that we actually used to get bags and bags of fan letters sent to the record company's office, and that the letters were all opened and read, they just shake their heads, like who is this grandpa and why does he keep digging up stories from the postwar years? But there are so many things that we took for granted, that we didn't even think about, and now they don't exist anymore. And on the other hand, things that didn't use to exist are now commonplace.

There used to be a comic about that in *Atze*, a children's magazine in the GDR. The center spread in every issue was a comic that told some historical story in which a modern object was hidden. Usually it was something like a wristwatch. If you found the object, you could write to the magazine and win something. I think a subscription to the magazine. Not many people must have written in, since the magazine wasn't very well liked. Though it did cost just ten cents.

Other than *Mosaik*, it was the only magazine with comics—though the term *comic* didn't exist in the GDR; we called them *Bildergeschichten*, or *picture stories*. But the other kids' magazines also had illustrations, of course.

There was *Bummi*, for example. The magazine was meant for children of kindergarten age and was about how the bears Bummi, Maxl, and Mischka played with kids from the Soviet Union and wanted more than anything to join the National People's Army so they could drive tanks. The only problem was that the kids these stories were written for couldn't read yet, and what adult was going to read such drivel to them?

The kids who could read tended to go for the *ABC-Zeitung*. It mainly talked about the Pioneers. That didn't do much for us, since we had all been more or less forced to be in the Pioneers since the first grade. So our being Pioneers didn't make any difference. The only thing in this magazine that I had any use for was the crafts page, where they taught you how to build your own fire truck or garbage truck. But I usually wasn't able to pull it off; I just didn't get how you were supposed to score the sticky folds before you folded them. That's what glue was for. With glue and some toilet paper I once tried to make papier-mâché, but after I'd boiled the mixture in water for a while, stirring the whole time, I had to spend the same amount of time vomiting and in pain from all the fumes I'd inhaled. I did still manage to slap together a small boat. That's how it was in those days if we wanted a new toy.

—

Now that our second record had gotten a bit more attention than the first and we had played songs from the first two records everywhere we possibly could, we almost automatically began thinking up songs for a third record.

It gradually became clear to us that the work of a musician consists primarily of thinking up songs, recording them, and then playing them live. As a kid, that wasn't something I was really aware of. I just thought it was one big party—every week you buy yourself a Rolls-Royce, then you drive it into a swimming pool. In reality we sat around in the practice space, gasping for air and wondering where we should eat lunch. And then getting tired. It all dragged on quite a bit.

At this point, we began to fall prey to the habit of holding meetings all the time so that we wouldn't have to go back to the practice space. We could always find something to discuss; worst-case scenario, we sat around in the office drinking coffee. In the little office kitchenette, there was a coffee machine, and the time passed so slowly that we drank endless cups of coffee and got really hopped up. We were used to drinking the kind of coffee where you just pour the water right over the coffee grounds. After a minute, you bang the coffee cup hard on the table so that the dregs sink to the bottom. The record company executives from Hamburg had a theory that this was the reason we East Germans had such brown teeth. But that's just the kind of coffee I like best.

We quickly learned, however, that a meeting was much more taxing than band practice. Sometimes one of us brought a CD that he liked, but most of the time we argued over unimportant things that none of us really had a clue about anyway. I soon started to sweat from all the coffee and excitement, and then I got headaches. When I got back home, I wouldn't want to say another word, since I'd already been yelling angrily the whole time at the office.

We were desperately trying to come up with an idea for what the cover art for *Mutter* should look like. We had just heard about "corporate identity" for the first time—that means that the record, the stage set, the T-shirts, and the tickets all fit the same general theme. So that way people can see that everything is related. Up to that point, we had just done whatever occurred to us in the moment. None of us would have imagined that we ourselves could dictate how the tickets were supposed to look. The tickets used to just come on a roll, and each would get torn off along the serrated edge.

One day, one of us brought along a magazine called *Max*, which at the time had really original articles in it. The magazine isn't around anymore. In this particular issue, there was an article about the married photographer duo Geo and Daniel Fuchs, who specialized in photos of medical specimens. That is, photos of animals or body parts preserved in alcohol or formalin. The animals were dead, of course. There were also deformities pictured in their photographs. We really liked these photos, especially the one of the three preserved polar bear embryos. Our manager got a copy of their photo book and got in touch with them. Just like that, we had a new reason to hold a meeting.

Luckily the two photographers were very nice. The idea that came out of the meeting was for them to photograph us as specimens. They were over the moon at the prospect of finally getting to photograph something living for once, and we were happy because all we had to do was pretend we were dead and not try to look strong or dangerous.

In attempting to realize the idea, a few problems emerged. For one, there wasn't an aquarium available anywhere that was big enough and that you could light from all sides. Finally a Plexiglas tank was built in a Hamburg film studio—this after the first tank we tried to use couldn't withstand the water pressure and burst. So in we climbed, one after another. We were supposed to be completely submerged in the water—which of course was meant to be preservative fluid—so we were forced to hold our breath. We hooked our feat around weights placed at the bottom of the tank, and for the portrait photos we also put on a lead belt. Each one of us was in the water for about four hours straight, for at least two of which we had to hold our breath. When we were all finished, the photographers realized that the water had gotten progressively murkier and that the photos differed too greatly from each other. And so two of us had to go back in the murky broth, which thankfully had warmed up a bit. These two had gone in the water first specifically because they wanted to get it over with quicker.

Finally we took the group photos, which was pretty difficult since we couldn't hear directions very well underwater, and one of us always had to go back to the surface to breathe at the decisive moment. A further aggravation was that it stank barbarically whenever anybody farted, since the gas stayed in the tank for so long—this, though, was a cause of great merriment. We also had a lot of fun wandering around the studio in bathrobes all day like pensioners.

In the end, the photos really were used as the artwork for our third record, which was called *Mutter*. On the cover was a photo of a baby. This, of course, was also taken by the two photographers. Thus, little by little, we came to develop our corporate identity. The stage for our coming tour was also supposed to fit the theme. And so we were able to arrange a whole lot more meetings. I don't know when we started using that ungodly word, *meeting*. We simply had no need for it earlier, since we decided everything important at band practice. But there was a positive side to it as well. Now everything really did start to fit together.

The stage was meant to look like an operating room, and real surgical lamps hung from the ceiling. We had taken them from an old clinic. But since they were pretty massive and made of iron, we later replaced them with lamps made of plywood, if I'm not mistaken. I played keyboard on a modified dentist's chair. That is, not directly on the chair—which we've still got lying around somewhere—but rather on the work surface where dentists keep their drills and lamps and stuff. They've also got a kind of tray on a moveable arm, and that's where my keyboard was. I was also dressed like a doctor. It almost seemed logical for people to address me as *Herr Doktor*.

Once, much earlier, I'd given myself the title by accident when we were supposed to submit our names for our GEMA membership. GEMA handles performance and licensing rights for songwriters; it's kind of like ASCAP or BMI. Anyway, I thought you had to come up with something original. Ever since, all our records have my name listed as Doktor Lorenz or something like that. If only I'd just put my real name down. Now everybody wants to know why I call myself doctor. It is true that as a kid I wanted to be a surgeon for a while. But I also wanted to be a fireman, pilot, inventor, or musician. Or at least what I imagined a musician to be.

—

LOUD MUSIC ASSAILS ME. It's coming from the so-called party room. Inside there's a DJ who is blasting a few helpless fans with music at earsplitting volume. They've just made it through a concert that wasn't exactly quiet, and now here it comes again at full strength. There's no one from the band in sight. I am just standing in the doorway. Nevertheless, I'm discovered, and immediately the phones start straining toward me like hungry little insects. It's much too dark here anyway; you wouldn't be able to see a thing on the photos. I promise to come right back and disappear down the hallway.

Did I always use to lie so much? I guess it wasn't necessarily a lie—once I've had something to eat, I really can take a few photos. I don't have to think about whether anyone will ever see the photos or what else people are going to do with them. After all, it's not my phone they're taking them with. There's already a bunch of junk on mine. Sometimes I erase a few of my own photos before anyone else has even seen them. Sometimes even before I myself have seen them. But maybe the people wouldn't dare erase photos of someone in the band. That's a bit like you're killing the person. When a friend of mine died, I waited a very long time before deleting his number from my phone. When I finally did, he was that much more gone.

The cooks from the catering company are also gone. Maybe not forever, but for today. I look around for leftovers, but everything has been cleared out. They had plenty of time to leave, really the whole concert. Maybe I'll check in my bandmates' dressing rooms to see if I can find anything. I don't feel like passing by the party room again, so I look for a way through the arena. I don't even recognize it. The crowd is completely gone, and the stage too has already been dismantled. The cleaners are almost finished sweeping the floor. A few of our crates are still there. Their number is rapidly diminishing; the local crew are pushing them toward the trucks. Every crate has a set place. The stage manager planned it all out, down to the last detail, before the tour began. Now he keeps watch like Argus to make sure no crate gets put in the wrong truck. He had everything color-coded for the purpose: yellow for lighting, red for sound, orange for the stage, or something like that. I have no idea who Argus was.

I once knew a dog named Argos—maybe the two names are related. This Argos played Hitler's dog in the movie *Downfall*. That's that movie with Bruno Ganz. The real dog was apparently named Blondi. Once shooting for the film had wrapped up, they didn't need the dog anymore—it was fairly unlikely that they would ever make a sequel to *Downfall*. Unless somebody came up with the crazy idea that Hitler didn't really kill himself, that he was actually still among us. Here he is again—surprise! But even in this very unlikely scenario, you'd still need a new dog, since Blondi would have died of old age by then.

At any rate, nobody had any use for Argos anymore, and he was supposed to be put to sleep. And so a certain young man said he would take the dog. As fate would have it, this man was a chef. One of his friends happened to be friends with us, and we were about to go off to a house on the Baltic Sea to write the songs for our third album in peace and seclusion. Since we were so deeply immersed in our music, we needed someone to take care of our physical well-being during this time. Or, well, that's a nice way of putting it, but it's only half the truth. We were simply too lazy to cook our own food and do the dishes afterward. Or to buy groceries. But mainly it was the dishes. And so we were joined by the chef and Hitler's dog. And he went out and procured delicacies like cod liver and fresh herring from the fishmonger. I mean, I always look forward to meals, but when we had this chef, it was even more extreme. I couldn't think of anything else. And in the morning, after I'd eaten a breakfast consisting of the aforementioned cod liver, fresh bread, three fried eggs, mozzarella salad, a matie or fried herring, and a piece of pastry after that, I was so full that I could have gone right back to bed. Heavy music and a good cook don't really go well together.

I can look up Argos and Argus the next time I'm on the internet.

But I'll have to be back in the hotel and not staring off into the empty arena. So off I go, then, back to Paul and Olli's dressing room. Not much has changed in here. The same very relaxed music is still playing, and the boys are taking their time getting ready for the party. I take a quick look to see what kind of food they've got. Bananas are always good. There are also a few nuts left—it doesn't seem like anyone really likes them. With the bananas in my hand, I walk over to the next dressing room. Here, too, there is music playing, if a bit louder. And here there's a bowl of candy; I take a few candy bars with me. The commercials tell you that they contain a bunch of vitamins and actually no sugar at all.

Then I peek back into the Sackhaus office and ask for something to eat. I get an old sandwich and return with my booty to my dressing room. There I pack everything, along with the last water bottle that I find under the table, into my underwear bag. Unfortunately I can't get the tape with my name on it off, but this way at least everybody can see who I am and won't have to go to the trouble of asking when they want to talk to me.

In our dressing room, our visitors have already moved from talking to screaming. Maybe Till should turn the music down a little. But then again, maybe I've just become old and oversensitive. It could well be the case. I don't want to always be shifting the blame onto other people. And so I decide to go back to the hotel. I head back to the dressing room next door to ask if anybody would want to come with if the shuttle went back to the hotel.

It occurs to me that I'm doing a lot of running back and forth. Sometimes waitresses will talk about the improbably large distances they end up covering in a day. Twenty kilometers or something like that. It could be I'm thinking of nurses. You wouldn't believe it, since they work in such small spaces, but it's true. They've proven it with a step counter. I bought one of those myself once. At first I couldn't believe it was working properly, and then after taking a walk I was really disappointed at how short a distance I'd gone. I was completely exhausted and I thought I had walked much farther. Besides that, the gadget just showed the number of steps, and I couldn't convert that to meters, since I couldn't find any path that was exactly one hundred meters long. Then one day I lost the thing, and I never found it again.

Now I have to keep on walking, because there's nobody in the dressing room. I carefully saunter over to the party room. The other band members have now arrived and are taking pictures with everybody. Since they probably won't want to leave the room before they're finished, much less head back with me, I can just as well join in. I'm now wearing glasses, just like I do on stage, but what with the other guys being here, hardly anybody recognizes me, so there's not much for me to do. But there really are a few very good-looking women here. That I can't deny. Why weren't they around before, when we were all running around horny as hell? When we weren't getting any, as the saying goes. When we so longed to be noticed by the female sex. Where were all of them then? The truth is, they weren't even born yet.

We used to wheedle our way into the dressing rooms of the bands who let us open for them just to try and lure away some of their women. We laid all dignity aside. All in vain—nothing worked. And now, when the women are actually here, we're spoken for, or at least some of us are.

When I've worked my way to my bandmates, I ask them if they want to come with me to the hotel. Just as I thought, they don't. All right, then, I'll stay here a while too, since otherwise the shuttle won't be there when my bandmates want to go to bed. But since the so-called party differs in no respect from the parties that took place yesterday and the day before, I'm assuming I won't have to wait long until the others also want to leave.

And so I head back to the Sackhaus office with my bags. They're packing up the shower stuff and the shampoo, the brushes and combs. I also see disinfectant, cigarettes by the carton, piles of various adapters—everywhere you go in the world, there are different plugs and sockets—plus radios, computers, and all sorts of other stuff. We've set aside an assortment of T-shirts especially for the border guards. We just have to hope that the customs officials are fans. Sometimes they go through the bus and grab drinks for themselves. You get thirsty doing that kind of work, I guess. So long as they let us go afterward, it's fine. We drink too much anyway. The guys are already finished packing everything up.

After the concert, everybody in the crew works really fast so they can still make it to the party room before the guests are gone. And of course they want to have showered by then too. Now there are towels lying around everywhere. But they too are gathered up and counted. We've only borrowed them for this one night. I throw my cigarette in a plastic cup. It's already got a few butts swimming in brown water inside. Everybody is smoking openly now. At this point, nobody seems to care about the fire code. The general mood seems very carefree. The people from the crew are proudly showing each other the things they bought in the city. Various technical items are apparently cheaper here than in Germany.

I want to head into town tomorrow to see if I can find any Brut. When I say "head into town," it makes me sound like I'm from the sticks. I'm from Berlin, but even there I say that I'm heading into town whenever I'm walking toward the city center. In Budapest, we're staying right near the Széchenyi Chain Bridge. So actually right in the middle of the city.

Thirty years ago, with Feeling B, I spent the night a hundred meters from the hotel where we're now staying. Back then we were sleeping in our modified delivery truck. Since we got into town at four in the morning, we thought this spot was an idyllic location. No sooner had we gone to bed than the first tram went by, two feet from my ear. I thought the world was ending. I hadn't seen the tracks and had no idea what the noise was. Then more and more cars started driving past, not only next to us but also above us, cars and buses driving constantly over the bridge.

When day came, countless ships went past. We could hear long-winded recountings of the city's history in several languages over several loudspeakers. It was so busy there during the day that we couldn't even pee in peace. Between our truck and our current hotel—which of course was there at the time, but which we didn't notice, since we didn't dare go in—was a small lawn with a few little bushes where we could pee so long as no one was walking past. That's also where we got water to drink and cook with. Though we could only get it when the sprinkler was running. We crept alongside them in a circle with our canisters so we wouldn't get wet. Then we daringly leapt forward, held the sprinkler in place, and popped the canister over it. The water pressure was so high that most of the water spurted right out again. Once the canister was a quarter of the way full, we ran off, and at that point we got wet, if we weren't wet already. We didn't realize that the water was just pumped up out of the Danube.

After two days, we were all suffering from horrible diarrhea, which was all the worse because there wasn't a toilet far and wide that we could use. So early in the morning we would run off in a panic to find a café where we could use the bathroom. Then we'd also have to buy something to eat there. And it was shamelessly expensive. Besides that, we didn't have any appetite—quite the opposite, in fact. There was a public toilet somewhere, but I could never find it when I needed it. Even if I had found the toilet, though, it probably would have been too far away—to be honest, I didn't even make it out of my sleeping bag. The rest of the tour I covered myself up at night with the old blanket that we'd brought to lie on when we had to crawl under the truck to fix the latest thing that had broken. I threw the sleeping bag off the bridge into the Danube one night, because even when it was lying outside behind the bus, we could still smell it.

Now I'm looking forward to my hotel room. Even if I don't show it. I learned this from Oliver Kahn. On the outside, I look like a sad old man who's staring at an ugly wall. That's not my opinion—that's what our sound guy tells me. He's just now walking toward me in the hall.

He asks me what condoms and keyboard players have in common. Naturally I don't know. "Simple," he says. "It's safer with them, but without them it's more fun!"

This is so dumb that I have to laugh, but I don't get what's supposed to be so safe about having a keyboard player. Maybe it comes from the days when dance bands wanted to cover international hits. They probably needed an organ sometimes, but I've never felt that my presence in the band confers a sense of safety.

I don't want to break off the pleasant conversation we're having, so I try to tell the joke about the blind musician who asks his drummer on stage: "Are the people dancing today?" And the drummer says: "Why, are we playing already?" He was deaf or something. No, then he wouldn't have been able to hear the question. Unfortunately I can't ever remember jokes. Shame, it was so funny, but there was some other way you had to tell it.

Since we've been traveling together for weeks—or actually, more than thirty years all told—it's not always easy to find new topics of conversation. The sound guy just nods, and together, spirits high, we stroll to the party room.

—

IT WAS HOT. IT was very hot. But actually it was just right. I simply wasn't cold anymore. In the seventies, when I used to tiptoe into our ice-cold bathroom on winter mornings, I could never have imagined that such a pleasant state could even exist. Nor could I have on the windy, cold days of our vacations on the Baltic Sea. But now I was warm; I was even sweating a little bit. It was very pleasant. I felt like there was no separation between my body and the air—it was just as warm outside as it was within. I could have taken all my clothes off. No, that I couldn't have done, since I was already naked. I was sitting at a table, normal as can be, and trying to put together a puzzle. I pronounce it "poozle," since that's what I learned as a kid. In my memory it was also spelled *pussel*, which I thought was fitting. The puzzle was supposed to depict a map of the world, with pretty pictures of fun little things peculiar to each country.

I had found the puzzle box on the street two days earlier. The picture was on the top, and I felt like putting it together. I didn't, however, feel like counting to see if all the parts were in the box. I just took it with me. And so now here I sat at the table in a hotel room in Sydney, searching desperately for the other half of Iceland. But how did I even get to Sydney in the first place?

Our third CD was recorded and mixed, the single picked out, and there wasn't much else for us to do other than wait for the CD to come out. If we had gone out and toured our new songs in Germany, no one would have been able to sing along since, logically enough, no one knew the songs yet. And we didn't dare go out and play in Germany again with our old set. So the request that we take part in the Big Day Out Tour came at just the right time. This was a touring festival with a whole bunch of bands that took place every year in Australia. We longed for the sun; we had spent the winter in Stockholm.

Before we could leave for sunny Australia, we still had to film the video for the song "*Sonne*." This was to be the single for our new album. All we were missing was a good idea for the video.

Then I remembered this one night when we watched an opera by Mozart in a cabin in the Czech Republic. Because something was wrong with the TV, we heard a different piece of classical music while still seeing the Mozart opera. Since I didn't know either piece, I didn't notice the mistake, but I really liked the program. I thought I was experiencing a revolutionary new kind of filmmaking, which gave the music an incredibly exciting quality. Only when the orchestra on screen was finished, the news began, and the music was still playing did I realize my mistake.

We tried to make use of this extraordinary effect ourselves by playing our songs along with different movies that happened to be on television. In new contexts, the songs took on a completely different meaning and in some cases were even better than before. And then Olli played "*Sonne*" along to the old movie about Snow White on his computer. We were so thrilled with it that we asked our director to make a video with us playing the Seven Dwarves.

It didn't bother us that there were only six of us; we thought—rightly, as it turned out—that nobody would notice, and proudly dubbed ourselves the Sex Dwarves.

In the studio, two identical huts were built: a big one for us, so that we would look small inside, and a small one for Snow White. As always, the shoot was considerably delayed, and we ended up filming in Babelsberg two days before our flight to Australia. Actually, work was supposed to have ended at 6 p.m. the day before we were set to leave, but of course nothing was finished yet. We didn't even manage to pick up our luggage from home, and sent Tom to our apartments during the shoot in the hope that he would be able to pack more or less the right things.

We worked into the night and then lay down to sleep in the dwarf hut. There were beds in there, after all. We had booze with us. In the night, when I had to pee or throw up—most of the time you don't know which until afterward—I tripped over a strut that was propping up one of the dwarf hut's walls and landed on another strut, breaking a few ribs. The next morning, I couldn't even get dressed properly.

At the airport we met back up with Tom, who had brought our mystery luggage. But it didn't make sense to put on clean clothes. In the video, we had played dwarves who worked in the mine, and for two days great care and expertise had been applied to making us look dirty. They'd even dirtied up our fingernails. To clean ourselves up would have taken hours.

The flight attendants were a bit surprised. They had probably never had such dirty passengers. The headrests turned completely black—our hair, too, was supposed to look like we'd been in the mine. They were understanding once they found out the reason, though—the flight attendants, I mean. We changed flights in Los Angeles and continued on with an American airline to whose staff we couldn't offer such a clear explanation for our filth. They asked us indignantly just what it was we'd been doing in America and how we'd gotten so dirty, whereupon I truthfully replied that I'd only used the bathroom there. And then we arrived in Brisbane, still dirty, with the temperature around 110 degrees.

The whole tour in Australia was amazing. There were at least twenty bands playing in giant stadiums on different stages. It was impossible to see them all. PJ Harvey and Placebo played right before us; after us was Limp Bizkit, who we knew of course from the US and who were a bit surprised that we were still playing our old set. They had put out two more albums by then. They were the headliner on this tour, and when they were on stage, people went crazy. When they danced, they kicked up the red Australian earth. We'd all be standing in a big red cloud, unable to see a thing. Another band we played with was Coldplay. They were four very nice young guys who all looked like college students.

I felt at ease in Australia right from the start. It had all the greatness of the US but without all the bad sides. And there were actually kangaroos. On just the second day we were there, I saw one sitting on the side of the road as we drove to the hotel. The next kangaroos we saw were also on the side of the road, but they were dead. It seemed like running them over was a kind of national pastime in Australia. The closer we got to the coast, the more dead koala bears we saw. Even run over, they looked really cute. Before I'd thought they only existed in fairy tales. And on those jackets the environmentalists wear. Or are those panda bears?

We did want to see all these animals while they were still living, so we went to a wildlife preserve. There I was actually able to cuddle up in between two pretty big kangaroos that were just hanging out in a field. The ostriches or emus or whatever were even bigger than we were. I had never seen such animals close up. We pushed our way through the crowd to feed the crocodiles. The sound of bones crunching still haunts me today. And the main attraction was an enclosure with aborigines inside. I couldn't believe it. There were actually people in a cage, dancing and making fire. Naturally they were also playing didgeridoo. I knew that Indians had also been exhibited as an attraction in Berlin once. And they died within a short span of time because it was too cold for them in Germany. But even in warm countries, it's not a good idea to lock people up in the zoo. Of course I was hoping the aborigines were allowed to leave at closing time. Wasn't all of Australia once used as a penal colony? We considered it to be more of a vacation spot. Though really we weren't there as tourists, we were supposed to be playing concerts.

The tour was accompanied by several party planners who were there for the sole purpose of keeping the bands in the best mood possible. After every show, they threw a giant party with free alcohol, as much as you wanted. Actually even more than that. I got progressively less lucid. Then I fell in love with PJ Harvey, or her guitarist, or the lead singer of Placebo, I can't really remember anymore.

To me the most fun band on the tour was the Happy Mondays. Whenever we were about to fly to the next concert, they'd drink a few bottles of vodka and several liters of beer before takeoff. They smelled like death. Throughout their whole set, the singer would sit on the drum riser and read his lyrics off an ancient computer, with his wife helping to scroll. Sometimes his wife wouldn't go back there, and then the singer just didn't sing. The guitarist would drop his pick and bend down to pick it up. Then he would catch sight of his beer bottle and take a drink. When he stood up again and tried to keep playing, he would again realize he didn't have his pick and bend back down. Then he'd see that his beer was almost empty and ask for another. Then, to make things easier, he'd just sit down on the floor and stay there.

Once, at an afterparty, I poured a half liter of beer in his mouth while he slept. I wasn't entirely sober myself at that point. The next morning, he was sitting in the row ahead of me on the plane and he kept glancing back at me. He was trying to remember where he knew me from, but it just wouldn't come to him. Then one time I ran through the whole plane holding a video camera while everyone threw beer bottles and trash at me. But I lost the video and never found it again.

The organizers also had the brilliant idea of building a swimming pool behind every stage so that after their set the musicians could dive right in. We even left our stage clothes on. It was hot, we were young, and we felt unbelievably good.

In Melbourne, when we had a day off, we bought two bicycles for thirty dollars at a flea market. We wanted to explore the city. When we stopped outside a café on these pieces of junk, we felt just like locals. That night we rode our bicycles into the hotel lobby to leave them with the hotel concierge. The receptionist called us every half hour and asked what she was supposed to do with the bikes. I put the receiver under the pillow. A trick I learned from television.

At night I always went swimming. It seemed strange to me that this marvelous beach I'd found was so empty. Naturally I hadn't looked to see whether any flags were raised or a basket was hoisted up, and I definitely didn't read anything. Thus I was completely unaware that the beach was closed not only due to shark attacks, but also due to poisonous jellyfish.

On a different day, we went snorkeling on the rocky coast. A tiny bit of jellyfish grazed my arm, and I was amazed that something so small could hurt so damn much. Later I was even more amazed because all throughout the tour the pain never got better.

—

HERE AT THE PARTY, people have started pairing off, but some of the guests have already left, most of them because they didn't want to leave their friends who weren't allowed in waiting too long. As the DJ is himself trying to talk to a woman, he's turned the music down a little.

My bandmates aren't here either, so I head back toward the dressing rooms. Our dressing room is locked, and the others are empty. Am I such a schmuck that I missed the shuttle leaving? I run out to the parking lot with my bag. Luckily the minibus is still there. Here come the guys from the production office. Now it's really time to go.

The driver wants to show us how cool he is, so he drives through all the security gates. The security people yell and try to stop us, but the driver just keeps going. This phenomenon can be observed with every shuttle driver. In the brief time they have with us, they want to leave as lasting an impression as possible. For some of them this has meant putting us in life-threatening situations.

One driver stopped in the middle of the highway, and through the back window we could see the cars speeding toward us. I don't even know why he stopped. I think he didn't know where he was going and wanted to wait for the car with our luggage. We cried out in terror, and he slowly started driving again. By some miracle, the cars behind us managed to stop in time.

In Mexico, we had a driver who rapidly alternated between the gas and brake pedal. We called him the paddler. His driving made us all queasy, and I wanted to get out. But under no circumstances did the driver want to let me out in the middle of Mexico City. He felt it was too dangerous. I guess he felt responsible for us, though you wouldn't have noticed it from the way he drove. When we were stopped at an intersection and he wasn't paying attention, three of us got out and started making our way on foot, relieved. We quickly realized that we really didn't know where we were or how to get where we were going. When, three blocks later, a group of rough-looking teenagers started following us, we started to understand what the driver had been talking about. We walked faster and faster, while trying not to seem like it, but the teenagers had no trouble catching up to us. They didn't have any nefarious intentions, though. They just handed me a dirty tissue and a pencil. They really only wanted our autographs.

Our driver today just wants to drive fast. Whenever policemen try to stop us, he unleashes a torrent of rapid-fire Hungarian at them until they let us drive off. The only word we understand is "Rammstein."

It's about time for everybody to get out their sandwiches. I get mine out too. We sit there chewing contentedly. Budapest at night is mostly just dark. Nevertheless, at every street corner and even in the smallest details, you can see what a beautiful city it is. Maybe even because it's so dark. Darkness is something I associate above all with coziness. If you want to make a city ugly, all you need are some big bright office buildings with nobody in them, the kind of buildings where nobody even knows what they're there for. Here, on the other hand, you can almost smell the past. You can see the influence of the Romans and the Turks. The thick stone walls of the buildings still give off the warmth of the day. Of course, the walls in uglier or more Western cities would also do this, but then again maybe not, since they're seldom built of such thick stone. These quiet streets are especially cozy, and I can't help thinking of my childhood. Of the endless-seeming summer holidays when I would wander through Berlin with my brother and keep discovering new, unexpectedly beautiful spaces.

In Berlin-Mitte at that time, there were still big gaps between buildings where there'd either be weeds and chamomile growing or the remnants of the old foundations. There was also the pleasant heat that lingered between the bare stone walls of the buildings. When we walked past the large open doors of certain buildings, we would feel a waft of cool air with a faint smell of cabbage and potatoes stored in the cellar. I liked this smell a lot. There are a lot of smells I find appealing that others might find unpleasant. When they're repaving a street and laying out the hot asphalt, I could stand there for hours. Probably only because I recognize it from my childhood. I immediately start thinking of hot summer days on Greifswalder Straße. I'll also never forget the smell of Kittifix. That was a kind of glue that we used as kids to paste together the tents for our little Indians, and later on, pirate ships. I would have liked to wear the glue behind my ears as perfume, but then I'd probably have ended up gluing my earlobes to my skin. That wouldn't have been so bad, though, since I was often teased as a kid on account of how much my ears stuck out.

Once when I got in an accident and was almost run over, the doctors at the hospital wanted to pin back my ears, since I was already there and all. I was only just able to stop it from happening. In any event, the glue smelled really good. Maybe that's why I always used to breathe it in. When I went to Budapest for the first time as a kid, there was an especially enticing smell coming out of all the subway tunnels. I went out of my way to walk by as many subway entrances as possible.

It was years before I rediscovered this smell. I had my first car from the West. For some reason, I thought the car was out of differential fluid, and so I crawled under the car to fill it up. As soon as I'd opened the bottle of oil, suddenly there was this lovely Hungary smell again. I've often thought about making perfumes out of smells that I like, but it's difficult because in some cases I don't know what the raw materials are that produce the smell. For example, the Indian dolls from the West, the ones you could take apart—they smelled great. But I can't dab an Indian doll behind my ear. I did, however, find a grass-scented lamp oil that came pretty close to approximating the doll's smell. But unfortunately I can't make a direct comparison since they stopped making the Indian dolls.

A lot of the good things that were part of why we wanted access to the West don't exist anymore. Meanwhile, nothing from the East exists anymore.

A short while back, I tried to buy matte white paint at the hardware store, and they simply didn't have it. There was just an empty spot on the shelf where it was supposed to be. It was the same the next time I went. And here I thought they always had everything in the West. I was kind of happy; it felt like the old days. I took a few futile trips to the store back then as well. It made it all the nicer when you actually found what you were looking for. And I met the most interesting people while waiting in line. So you can find pleasant aspects to a lot of things. Except for urgent material needs.

Which reminds me: I have to pee again. There's really always something. When am I ever going to reach the state where truly everything is good? This state probably doesn't exist, since if you're wondering whether everything is perfect or not, you can't be completely enjoying the moment anymore. Or could it be that you actually need these little worries and cares in order to lead a happy and exciting life? I think you might. Why do I have to think about these things right now? Is it really true that you get to feeling a bit funny after a concert? I never know what certain musicians mean when they say that, after a show, it's like they fall into a deep hole. Others have to drink a whole lot of alcohol before they come down again. I don't think I need that; I probably never rise up there in the first place.

Of course, I, too, used to drink loads of alcohol after our concerts. But I would have drunk without the concerts, too. The alcohol was supposed to give me the courage to ask girls if they would sleep with me. As far as the asking went, this worked really well, but the answers, as you can imagine, were usually negative. How was I supposed to appear both brave and attractive? That was a very fine line to walk. If ever a woman unexpectedly said yes, then it was in large part due to the fact that she was even drunker than I was— which, I think, is far better than when one of the two is sober. If ever I really did manage to have sex, it meant that all the drinking over the last few days had paid off, so to speak. But otherwise I had no reason to drink after the concert. It didn't matter to me in the least if I was alone or with people.

By now what I want most after a concert is to go home. And when we're playing near Berlin, that's not a problem. Although it's hard to determine what the cutoff is. Dresden is close to Berlin; Munich not so much, but compared to Moscow, it's right around the corner. I can easily manage to get back to my pad, as I used to call it, in four hours. Supposedly there are musicians who stay at a hotel after a concert even in their hometown—it makes them feel more comfortable. They don't want to burden their families with the emptiness they feel after a concert. That's what they say, at least. But maybe it's that when the concert is over and all the people are gone, you really start to reflect on things. I mean by that point everything you're famous for is gone, just like that. At that point, you're just a little person. By "little" I of course don't mean physical size, but rather a person's unimportance among the mass of other people. All the same, after a tour I think every person I see on the street is one of our crew members, and then I get really sad when I realize my mistake. And so I guess I also feel a bit naked or at least alone without the whole band around me. I mean, that's the great part about being in a band: you always belong somewhere, and there's always other people there with you who somehow have the same goals and the same cares.

—

WE HAD JUST PLAYED a concert in Vienna, and I was sitting in my hotel room watching television. I wanted to just watch a movie and then fall asleep, but I couldn't concentrate. And so I flipped through the channels to find something a little less demanding. Maybe a talk show. But then I heard really mean music. And I saw gloomy images to go with it. A few clearly deranged dudes were beating each other up in the mud. Then they crawled through the street like dogs. It all looked sick. Only then did I recognize the music. It was "*Mein Teil*"! Our song. I had just played it on stage, but here it sounded completely different—much, much meaner. Like it was by a really mean band. I was excited. I would never have thought MTV would play that video. It was the video for the first single on our new record, and we had only just made it a short while ago.

After the *Mutter* album came out, we had toured for a long time and then taken so much time to make our next record that it was now three years later, and a few fans were afraid we'd broken up.

When I went to buy a cable at the music store, all the salespeople would ask me what I needed it for. Meanwhile we had been working like madmen and put a whole bunch of energy into the new songs until they were finally finished.

Now they were going to come out on a record with the wonderful name *Reise, Reise*. We wanted to come back with a real banger—though I'm sure nobody says that anymore. Except maybe discount stores when they talk about doorbangers. Or, wait, maybe it's doorbusters. At any rate, our banger was supposed to be "*Mein Teil*." We owed the basic musical idea to Paul, and at first we had some placeholder lyrics that were about the world ending and no one surviving, and I thought the song sounded too forced, like it was trying too hard to be mean. I made fun of it and complained about it again and again. In our band, you have to say something very often and very loudly if you want to be paid attention to. Mercifully, Till brought us some lyrics about the alleged cannibal of Rotenburg, told from the victim's perspective. Everyone was excited. All we needed was the video.

There was one idea we thought was really funny, where we're all castaways who land on an island and get cooked by the natives in a big pot, with Till as the chief. This is where the pot we use on stage when we play the song live comes from. But then the band would have been split up again, and we had had a bad experience with that during the "*Engel*" video.

The director wanted to have aliens land on our desert island, shoot all the people, and then abduct us, like in the movie *Mars Attacks!* The computer animation this required would have cost an incredible amount of money. As an alternative, we proposed a creepy movie in a butcher shop, where a fat butcher keeps chopping sausages and then it turns out that all the survivors are tortured and turned into sausages one by one. Kind of a tribute to the movie *Delicatessen*. But then we decided this was too conventional.

We spoke with another director. He wanted to have us riding on a bus through the countryside. We would get in an accident and then meet a group of Japanese schoolchildren. First they would ask for our autographs, but then they'd bite our fingers off and finally they'd eat us up. Naturally there would also be sex involved. That wasn't bad, we thought, but we would have had to fly to Thailand, and somehow we just couldn't make it work.

At that time, I was listening to the White Stripes a lot and I would catch myself dancing to the music alone in my apartment without realizing it. It's really a very private thing, and I imagined how interesting a video would be in which someone who didn't think he was being watched started dancing to a song, without any choreography, just in a way that was really honest and unselfconscious. It would be interesting because it would be real somehow.

When I suggested it at the next meeting, the band wasn't against it, especially since you could make the video without a set and for practically no money. That's what we thought at least. The director was happy to go along with it. He ended up making the bus video with a different band, I think Die Fantastischen Vier. Just having us all dance struck him as too boring, but we all liked the idea that every band member would do something without the others knowing what it was, and also that none of us could be around when the others were doing it. Each of us was supposed to come up with whatever it was he wanted to do and only speak about it with the director.

We all thought of something good, but the best idea came from Schneider, who played a naughty woman eating pralines. Nevertheless, the director was still concerned that these scenes weren't powerful enough, and so he wove in a fight in the rain and mud. The costs rose astronomically. Especially because of the mud and the rain. I mean, the water had to run off somewhere. That's why you rarely see a stage show with real water. But whatever. We got down to work. Oh, right, we were also supposed to be led through the streets like dogs. The hair and makeup on that alone was really funny—when else were you ever going to be made up like a dog?

The shoot began. Immediately we noticed that it wouldn't be possible to achieve the private atmosphere we'd wanted for the dance scenes. Everybody and their grandmother was always walking around on set. We got all worked up about it, but the mud fight let off the tension and everything was okay again. Unfortunately they used coarse potting soil to make the mud, and I scratched my knees up so much that I had a really hard time crawling like a dog the next day.

Schneider took us out for a walk in front of the Deutsche Oper in Berlin. He was dressed as a woman, and we were made up like dogs. He led us around on a leash. On all fours, of course. It was a lot of fun. The people on the street didn't know what was going on. A dog owner, a woman—she and Schneider looked a lot alike—started swapping dog stories with him. The cars almost ran us over because we couldn't cross the street fast enough. Afterward I went to a bar without taking my makeup off, and I wondered why the waitress was so grossed out. I had forgotten that my teeth had been made up to look like brown stumps. Though they didn't need too much makeup to do the job.

And now that I was seeing the video on television for the first time in the hotel in Vienna, I was shouting with excitement. And the record was also doing well. It was still just like a fairy tale, and sometimes I was scared that I would wake up and find out I'd just dreamed it all. Or we would be exposed as imposters, wouldn't be allowed to make music anymore, and would have to go work in a factory.

—

AND ALREADY WE'RE BACK at the hotel. There are a few pensioners standing around in the lobby. Of course I don't know whether they're actually pensioners, or for that matter whether you can only call people pensioners who actually get a pension, but in any case the people are old.

Once we got to be a little more successful, our management started booking us in more expensive hotels. It's a fallacy to think that the more expensive hotels are also the more comfortable hotels. A lot of times, the more expensive hotels are just more expensive. And it can be the case that the guests are more unpleasant, because the kind of people who are able to lay out so much for a hotel aren't necessarily the nicest. That probably applies to us as well. In any case, most of the guests are a bit older, since of course they first had to make all that superfluous wealth, and that takes time. Again, this also applies to us. Some people consider it a luxury to go out and spend a lot of money on something that isn't at all worth the amount they pay. No Ferrari, Bentley, or Lambo—I don't know how to spell the rest of it—can justify its shameless price tag. At least not in my eyes. Same goes for all the different wristwatches. And yet people still buy them. Our hotel rooms are a similar case.

Now we have so-called suites, which means we have an additional large room with a desk and a sofa. I don't actually need it, since all I'm going to do here is sleep. Meanwhile, the bedroom is really tiny. So I lie down on the living room couch. In a cheap hotel, things would have been easier.

One time I even had to sleep with the lights on because all the remote controls and touch sensors were programmed in such a complicated way that I couldn't figure them out. And that was in Frankfurt, where I understood the language.

Fortunately, our hotel here in Budapest is very old. There are still actual keys for each room. It's nice and old-fashioned. Like my jokes. I prefer to take the key with me when I leave, because it could be there's no one here when I get back so late, or that I have to show my ID. Besides that, I can't always remember my room number, and then the people at reception get suspicious.

I ride the elevator up to my room and open the door. I've left the window open so that there will be lots of fresh air, and I've also left the little standing lamp on so I don't come stomping into a dark room and fall over. I mean, it could be that I get back and have to run to the bathroom. Ecologically speaking, that's a poor choice on my part, and I'm immediately punished for it, because the light has attracted flies, which are now waiting for me. Thanks to the band, my carbon footprint is already bigger than Godzilla's anyway. Was that the ape with the woman in his hand who was shot off the Empire State Building? Or was that King Kong? Whichever it was, mine's bigger.

Leading the life of a musician must have affected my brain, otherwise I wouldn't make such dumb jokes. I take off my shoes and sit down on the bed. Should I turn on the television? Better not. Growing up, I didn't have a television, so I never learned how to engage with the medium in a sensible way.

Once I've turned it on, I watch whatever it is I'm watching till the end. The people have put so much effort into all these movies and shows that

I wouldn't be comfortable just turning it off in the middle. If I'm unlucky, then I end up watching *Lanz*—a boring talk show—or something like that. If I'm really unlucky, the channel never goes off the air, and I just keep watching. With a little luck, on the other hand, an old show will come on. For me it's new, since I wasn't able to watch it back then. Shows like *Bonanza, Lassie, Magnum PI*, or *Riptide*. Or was that a movie? *Sledge Hammer!* and *MacGyver*, on the other hand, I did get to watch—apparently after the wall fell, they ran them again just for us East Germans. And of course at that time I wasn't working; I just sat around on the couch at my friend's place, drank booze, and watched television. Still, I wasn't able to keep track of everything that happened on the shows, so now I could actually watch all of them again. Meanwhile, the fall of the Berlin wall and reunification just happened yesterday. Or, well, twenty or so years ago. Sometimes it feels like all the time that has passed since then has just been washed away. What can you do to stop life from rushing past you?

A friend who was in prison for a long time once told me that time flew by while he was in there because he experienced the same thing every day, and so now I try to collect a bunch of different impressions in order to kind of stretch time out a bit. Unfortunately there's a monotony to this constant variation. As a musician, too, the routes you travel are fairly uniform. And if you're in a different city every night, that might sound like variety, but it isn't, since you're constantly flying into each new city and sleeping in a hotel. After a tour like this, where we play thirty concerts back to back, I can't remember a single one individually unless something unforeseen happens, and even then I only remember this particular occurrence and not the whole concert. Nor do I know why I try so hard to make my life seem longer. When I die, it won't matter one bit whether the time before my death seemed long or short; I won't notice anything anymore. And it definitely won't matter as far as eternity is concerned. I could just as well have died right after I'd been born. The meaning of life might end up being to serve your time as quickly as possible. So you can be reincarnated, or something like that.

I'm fifty now, and I don't know if my life up to this point has been short or long, since I don't have anything to compare it to. If I were to ask someone, their way of measuring time would be different. Besides, I can't remember everything I've experienced in life all at once; rather, individual things will suddenly occur to me, for example, when I find myself in a similar situation. Thus at Christmas I think of earlier Christmas celebrations, and then I don't think of them for the whole rest of the year. Is life just a series of Christmas celebrations?

All this thinking feels like work. Or at least, after doing all this thinking, I don't feel relaxed, more like unsettled. I should probably just turn the TV on after all so I don't have to think anymore. TV is perfect for that. But I don't want to risk staying awake till late at night again and only ending up watching something on NTV about American nuclear tests. Or U-boats in World War I. And so I grab one of the many books I've lugged along with me, only to realize that I can't remember where I last left off reading. Before I've found the page, I'm already asleep.

IV

WHAT'S THAT NOISE? WHERE am I? Ah, in a bed. Right, I'm on the road with the band. A glance at the clock—it's half past six. We don't leave for the airport till ten. I soon fall back to sleep. As usual I dream a whole bunch of things in the early morning hours that would definitely be of great interest to a psychiatrist. For the rest of humanity, there's probably nothing more boring than other people's dreams. I once bought Jack Kerouac's *Book of Dreams* and was amazed at how little it engaged me. I couldn't even finish it. A person would do better to keep his dreams to himself; he definitely shouldn't write them down.

I actually don't have to write that I got out of bed, since that could be deduced from the fact that I'm now going down to the breakfast room. We used to say that a rock 'n' roll breakfast consisted of a cola and a Karo. A Karo was a really strong cigarette with no filter. A lot of blues and rock fans used to smoke them in the GDR. But very few people in the GDR had cola in the house, and so the rock 'n' roll breakfast became coffee and a Karo. The Karo was the more important component anyway.

The basic idea wasn't bad, since a Karo most definitely won't make you fat, and what rock 'n' roller wants to stand up on stage with a big gut? On the other hand, a breakfast consisting of coffee and a cigarette doesn't promise a very high life expectancy. But even that is no problem for musicians. Some kill themselves, of course, possibly so that they don't have to experience their own slow decline. If you become famous at a very young age, the many uneventful years of your life after that can be very difficult.

As a young man I wasn't famous at all, and only now is my life really starting to be fun, so I'd like to live just a little while longer, and for that reason I'm not lighting up a Karo, but rather pouring myself some granola. Just like a granola cruncher. Do people even use that term anymore? Are granola crunchers still granola crunchers?

Back in the day, anybody with long hair was a granola cruncher, unless they were a delinquent. But even in the granola crunchers' time, nobody used the term "delinquent" anymore. Nor does anyone today think, when they hear the word granola, of the smell of buckwheat groats or sweaty women in threadbare sweaters. The granola crunchers were the ones who always wanted to sit down and quietly discuss everything. They were so understanding. They loved all the animals and plants, but also showed understanding for us punks. We punks of course nurtured a deep loathing of these people, not suspecting that pretty soon we would be exactly like them. The granola crunchers might themselves once have hated what they would later become, namely politicians. Even if it's only with the Green Party. I still don't like using the word granola, but what else am I supposed to call my breakfast?

In case anybody's interested, I'll try and describe it. I pour a handful of oats into a bowl and pour cold milk or hot water over them, depending on what's available. Then I add flax seeds, grains, and dried fruit, like dried plums or apricots. Maybe a few walnuts, because for whatever reason I'm not allergic to them. Then I plop a few spoonfuls of yogurt on top of that. And then a small dollop of jam. But it shouldn't be too sweet, so that I don't stimulate my pancreas and develop even more of a craving for sweet things. Recipes are almost more boring than other people's dreams. And cooking is the old man's sex.

And so I have breakfast and then go into town for a bit. I want to buy cigarettes and keep an eye out for Brut. That's my favorite deodorant, I can't say it enough. For whatever reason, they only carry this brand in very cheap drug stores. These are of course the only stores in which you can still find things that actually reflect the country you're in; in expensive fragrance stores nowadays, you can't tell where you are. Besides that, the salespeople always come running up to me and asking me what I want. If only I knew!

That is, I do know, but I've never found a salesperson in a fancy fragrance store who knew of Brut. The stuff smells so good that I even wanted to name my son Brut. But I guess my son didn't want that and so he ended up being a daughter. That only leaves Bruta, which sounds like *Bruder*, which is German for brother, which just makes things confusing.

I'm excited to be back in Budapest's beautiful city center. I always try to keep going in a particular direction so that I can find my way back to the hotel if I just circle back. So long as I run into the Danube on the way back, nothing can go wrong. I just have to pay attention to what direction the water is flowing in. When I walk around in foreign cities, I try to look into the apartment windows and imagine what it would be like to live here. I could easily imagine living in Budapest. Here they have giant apartment buildings with bare stone façades. But there aren't as many people on the streets as there used to be. I especially miss the old people.

I can clearly remember the old women in their apron dresses who used to sit around talking as I walked around the hot city, full of curiosity. Even if the change didn't come so quickly here after the wall fell as it did in East German cities, it's apparent that capitalism has moved in.

I actually think fewer architectural crimes were committed in the GDR than in the time since reunification. The age of plastic windows. Budapest, however, still looks quite good. Sometimes there's a positive side to not having that much money available for development. I see a few small galleries and alternative cafés. Here there's even a drugstore with Hungarian products. Down on the bottom shelf are the really dusty old packages. And behind them is the Brut. I start quivering with joy. They don't just have the green deodorant, but gold too, and also, now this is really crazy, blue! I buy two of every kind. The saleswoman is a bit surprised by my selection and says something that I don't understand. Hungarian is one of the most difficult languages in the world.

It occurs to me that I once had all my Brut taken away from me at the airport in London. I had found it in San Francisco after much searching. Naturally I wasn't allowed to take it in my hand luggage. I just hadn't thought of that. Someone once told me that the luggage compartment isn't pressurized and any container you put in there will burst. But that could have been decades ago. Don't large dogs fly in the luggage compartment? Or do they have their own special cabin? I'm very glad that I'm not a dog.

In interviews, I'm sometimes asked what kind of animal I am. Or would like to be. I have to think about it for so long that the interview is practically over by the time I answer. Now, to be safe, I think about it when I'm not being interviewed so it won't take so long if I ever get asked again. But I've never come up with an answer. I could be clever and say that, biologically speaking, humans are also animals, and so therefore I'd like to be a human. Unfortunately that's not so much clever as smart-alecky. I definitely do not want to be a snake, because then if I had an itch I couldn't scratch myself. Maybe a bird instead? Then I could scratch myself with my beak, and on top of that I could fly without having to wait in line forever at the Air Berlin ticket counter. But who comes up with such stupid questions anyway?

Interviews in general are difficult for me. If I could answer all the questions I get asked, I wouldn't need to make music to express myself. Sometimes they ask me what cities or countries I most like being in. Or which place has the best fans. I end up insulting every country I don't name. I mean, I can't list off the whole world, and if I say that I like playing everywhere equally, I sound phony and a little bit sleazy. The smartest thing you can do is to always keep your mouth shut, but in an interview that's no good. It makes you seem arrogant. That's why I try to avoid interviews. Sometimes I'm pushed to do them anyway, usually with the argument that this or that interview is really important, but I have never seen anything positive come from doing an interview. I mean, people tend to go to shows because they like the music, not because the band has an interview in *Rolling Stone*. Who even reads magazines anymore? Who even reads, period?

Of course, I could also give television interviews, but sadly I'm just not capable. As soon as a camera is pointed at me, I start acting combative, and I immediately feel ashamed of myself. Then I see the interview, and that's when it gets really bad. Doesn't everyone notice that I'm completely nuts? Why did I do that again? For me as a viewer, an interview like that would tend to scare me off. I still don't understand how everyone else can be so good at it. Interviews with K.I.Z. or Kraftklub are really captivating. Even Tokio Hotel were able to speak competently and fluidly from the get-go. Some people have probably mastered this art before they even pick up an instrument.

I've met people who were practically born to be stars. They radiate such intense self-confidence that they immediately win the audience over. They also accept all the little favors people do for them so naturally and so graciously that everyone around them feels a little bit important themselves. Hotel suites were probably built for just such people. For them the world is in perfect order. I, on the other hand, am always worrying about something all the time. Is everybody like this?

Once I took a yoga class where I was supposed to lie down on the floor and not think of anything. So first I had to think about how to not think about anything. Then I thought about how I was paying a lot of money simply to not think. And about whether maybe I'd be better off becoming a yoga teacher myself. But of course I wasn't supposed to be thinking. What happens in the time when I'm not thinking about anything, though? It's like I'm already dead. And anybody who wants to tell me he doesn't think about anything during sex is probably lying. Either that or it really is just me. I'm always being assailed with new impressions, and I have to process them somehow. For example, the car exhaust here smells different than it does in Germany. What's different about Russian gasoline? Why does it smell so sweet? Is there more lead in it? Or are the engines just ancient?

Kurt Vonnegut once said that man's biggest defects were bad teeth and an excessively large brain that allows him to think useless thoughts. I feel that to be true in my case. I need to focus on some kind of pursuit so I don't think so much. But what should I do? Am I not interested in anything at all anymore? Am I just some philistine who only cares about his family and his car? Could I have become my own worst enemy? No, that can't be—I'm still invested in life. And not just in mine. Plus, it's not like I was doing anything sensible before now anyway.

Some things that are now so simple required more commitment back then. If I wanted to hear certain music, I had to sit by the radio at night or go visit my friends, hoping they had this or that recording and would let me dupe it. That was fun, and nothing compared to the feeling of holding a record from the West in your hands. Even if it was just for a brief moment. Or simply to hear a new song by a band you liked. Now I just have to turn on my computer and I can listen to almost any song that pops into my head. Even the songs I can't remember anymore—my computer recommends them to me. Apparently by this point it knows me better than I know myself. Of course, if I can listen to any song any time I want, then I can just as well do it tomorrow, too. Or some other time.

Back at the hotel. I just have ten minutes left, and I have to go to the bathroom. You might wonder why I'm always making such a big fuss about going to the bathroom. It's due to the fact we're on the go a lot. Using the bathroom on the tour bus is strictly prohibited because it stinks so horribly for a long time afterward. On the plane, it's almost impossible. It's so small that the toilet is located under one of the seats, so whoever happens to be sitting there has to move, and then the cushions get folded up. Very rarely have I seen anyone in the band use this toilet. Really only in an emergency. That said, at this point, there's really nothing one of us would be embarrassed about doing in front of the others. In the minibuses that take us to the airport and the hotel, there's no toilet. At the airport itself, I never know what to do with my luggage while I'm in the bathroom. And so it's important to remember to take care of everything at the hotel. And now I won't say anything more about it. I'll just walk faster.

THREE MINUTES BEFORE THE shuttle is set to leave, I'm down in the lobby. I'm the last to get here. Everyone is sitting on the bus waiting on me. The others did have more time than me since they weren't running around town. I think it's a good thing that we're all so punctual. It means I can plan on it and never have to wait. Getting somewhere on time isn't difficult. You just have to think about it. And thinking of other people is a good thing in general. Even if I did have to wait on one of the other band members, the time wouldn't necessarily be wasted since I could talk to the ones who were already here. A few of us are seeing each other again for the first time since the party. If one of the guys had a good night last night, and maybe even brought a nice woman back to the hotel with him, you can tell just looking at him. Even if he's tired and hungover, he'll have a special grin on his face. The others are eager to hear every last detail from the night before. As of late, cell phone pictures have also come into play. As proof, so to speak. The other bandmates ask targeted questions, trying to find out all they can. It's like *Tatort*. Even though we've known each other for so long, it's rare that any of us manages to resist. Eventually the one being grilled dishes on everything.

The mood on the bus is fantastic. It's a bit like we're on a field trip, and the teacher is on a different bus and can't hear us. After a twenty-minute ride, we arrive at the Budapest airport. As if by magic, a sliding gate opens and we drive right up to the plane. I feel like I'm in a spy movie. Our pilots are already here waiting and they help us stow our luggage. On our plane, there's not much more cargo room than in the trunk of a car.

A little red carpet has been lovingly laid out over the folding stairs leading into the plane. It's really more like a doormat. I climb on board and am so happy that I'm not afraid of flying anymore. A phobia like that can spoil your whole life, and as I've said already, it won't stop you from crashing. I mostly sit in the same spot, up front on the couch. It faces perpendicular to the flight path, if that's the right way to put it. The other seats face each other so that some of us have to fly backward, but that way we can talk better. It's not at all bad sitting backward. I would have thought I'd get sick, but it hasn't happened yet. Once it was believed that the high speeds of the first railroads would make people crazy. But there's really so much that people can withstand. You notice this here on the plane, too.

One of the guys once put the pilots up to executing a few daring maneuvers, probably in order to mess with me. For a brief moment, I felt like gravity had been lifted. Afterward I was pressed into the couch with a force like I'd never experienced before and couldn't move—and I didn't even have my seatbelt on. I figured I'd die either way. If something happens during the flight, I'd rather at least be sitting comfortably up until then. Though I wouldn't exactly call it comfortable when the pilot started flying in a tight spiral. I could feel the plane groaning under the strain being put on it. Afterward the pilots assured us that they had left a little room to play with before the plane would really have been overtaxed. It's astonishing, but after this incident I had even more confidence in the plane and in the pilots.

Since I'm sitting up front, I pour the coffee for everyone. It's just instant coffee, but it still tastes really good, probably because it's so cozy on the plane. In the back there's a giant wicker bowl full of candy. I take it up front and eat as much as I can, even though I know how bad it is for me. There's real food too, of course. Some of the guys slept in and haven't had breakfast yet. If I eat a lot now, I won't need to eat anything for the rest of the day, and then I won't spend any money either. Of course I haven't thought that through all the way, since the food at the venue is already paid for and thus practically goes to waste if I'm too full to eat it. As is usually the case, there's a happy medium somewhere. But no one can take from me what I've already eaten. When we don't have much time between concerts, we have to hurry a bit. To be on the safe side we always hurry, and sometimes we'll have already gotten a whole bunch done before we even get started.

In the air, I mean at high altitudes, the stomach must expand—I don't know of any other explanation for why it smells so horrible in the plane all of a sudden. It could also be due to the fact that we're all so fond of eating ground beef. An unbridled joy has set in. At no other point in the day do you see your bandmates laugh this much. Every now and again they bite a cushion to keep from throwing up. The pilots, unfazed, put their oxygen masks on. Then the copilot stands up and walks through the cabin with a bottle of aerosol spray. It's not like we can open a window. The spray doesn't help, though. Those who are responsible for the stench look very proud of themselves. I'm more inclined to think of it as a threat to flight safety, but when I voice this objection, the level of merriment grows even more.

This was the case even when we didn't have a chartered plane. I always liked flying with the band back then, too. Most of the time one of us would keep the whole plane entertained by sharing all the new discoveries he'd made. We especially liked to expound on the advantages and disadvantages of the latest technological advances, like cell phones or computers. We were able to glean the requisite knowledge from the many magazines spread across our knees. We always bought up just about everything at the airport newsstand, but as often as we flew, it was hard to find issues we hadn't already read.

One of our guitarists wasn't that interested in magazines, but he did like to take a big guitar with him as his hand luggage. All the flight attendants would have to struggle to find room for it. They came to the conclusion that there must be a famous guitarist on board. And they were even right. Richard is the one real rock star among us. Only he can pull off those long trench coats he walks around in.

Till was a different story. The flight attendants used to make him show them his boarding pass several times—they just couldn't imagine that such a creature could have bought a business-class ticket on board their pretty airplane. Till would then mumble something mean at them, drop down in his seat, and instantly fall asleep. Or he would have luggage with him—gifts for folks back home—that just wouldn't fit in the overhead bins. Once a flight attendant tried to step in when a piece of the overhead bin splintered off, but one look from Till's bloodshot eyes backed her off.

Sometimes he would be in a good mood on the plane. Then he would sing in his gravedigger's voice or throw slices of sausage around. We politely threw them back. I was then able to forget my fear of flying for a while. The rest of the flight, I would sit all tensed up in my seat and try to read something. I usually didn't get past the first two pages. I tried everything I could to avoid a flight and would usually end up sitting on some bus for days. Olli, who wasn't wild about flying himself, once had the idea to go on tour in his camper. But eventually all the work I was doing to get out of flying got to be too much of a hassle, and I slowly got used to it. Sometimes it can even be really great, watching the clouds go by or looking out ahead through the cockpit. But most of the time I just read. The other guys too, actually. Except when it really stinks—then, like I said, everybody's happy.

Now our weariness is forgotten, and thankfully all the lurid details from last night are brought out into the open. We're not the noblest of fellows. But we are really funny, at least as we see it.

Today we land in Zagreb. After landing we have to wait in the plane for a little while until a car comes and two nice women get out to greet us. They'd like a photo with us, and we're happy to oblige. The fact is, we take pictures with people at every airport.

Then we're driven to a waiting room on an airport bus. I try to be funny and let myself fall into the seat, but I overlook the armrest, which catches me right between the legs. When the bus gets to the terminal, I have to limp slowly and painfully after the others, who are quickly running off to the bathroom.

We all drank a senseless amount of coffee on the plane, and since we can't all wait for a stall to open up, we all pee in one toilet at the same time. We call that Wilkinson, because it's like several blades crossing—look it up. Then we wait for something else. During this time, all the airport employees want to get a photo with us. Naturally we also sign the CDs they've brought with them. It's amazing how many people knew we were coming. The flight attendants who happen to stop by all get tickets to the concert. But most of the fans are baggage handlers or security personnel.

Outside the airport, a lot more fans are waiting, and we sign more autographs and pose for photos. It doesn't bother me that some people only get autographs from us in order to sell them. It's not like I have to buy them. Of course, someone could respond to that by saying that I don't have to listen to my music either, so by that logic I don't have to put so much effort into it, but that's a whole different thing. I do like listening to our music; I like it a lot. I even know the songs by heart. I don't even need to listen to them, because I have them all in my head, but I still listen sometimes all the same.

And now I start thinking about which of our songs I would have played at my funeral. I feel like people would expect there to be a Rammstein song. We've been told that our music has been played at a lot of funerals. Mostly "*Ohne dich*"—"Without You"—but I wouldn't want that, since it would mean I was the one who people would be without. Someone on the radio once asked for "*Heirate mich*"—"Marry Me"—which is also one of our songs, and he wanted to hear it, he said, because his dog had just died. From then on I heard the lyrics in a completely different way. Even in Feeling B we made a funeral song. It was just an instrumental; we played things safe and dispensed with lyrics altogether. It was called "*Sonnenaufgang 1*"—"Sunrise 1."

But I'm trying to find a Rammstein song for my funeral. It's hard to choose. We've written more than seventy songs at this point, and you only get one funeral. It's not like you can try a song out to see if it fits. And the thing about dying is that a lot of times it happens more quickly than you expect. Let the people I leave behind pick out a song. Something they like listening to. It could be Modern Talking, far as I'm concerned. "Brother Louie."

Now, trusting as ever, we climb back onto the shuttle bus that's waiting for us. The driver wants to explain something, and we nod excitedly. Though of course we don't understand a word he says. That's not the fault of the driver, who speaks perfect and rapid English, but rather ours—we simply can't understand him. Simple words like *yes* or *no* I can understand, but that's not enough for a conversation. It's lucky that the word for sex is the same in so many languages. And there's body language too, of course. Who knows what my body is currently saying to the shuttle driver?

—

AND THE ECHO FOR *Best National Alternative Rock Group goes to*—long pause—*Rammstein!*

I was sweating. A big camera on a long arm swooped toward us. I looked left and right to see what my bandmates were doing. They weren't doing anything. And so I grinned stupidly, but at the same time tried to look like I was given an award like this every day.

We weren't surprised. We'd known for a few days that we'd be getting the award. Everyone who got an award knew beforehand. First because you got seats that would allow you to get to the stage quickly, and second because you had to know what to do after they announced it. Unless you just happened to bring a piece of paper with you that listed all the names of the people you wanted to thank—otherwise, you might forget someone. Most of the bands who didn't win an award didn't even go to the ceremony. They just went to the party afterward.

The first time we were nominated for an Echo, however, we didn't know all that. Back then we were mostly just surprised to have been nominated, since we'd only just put out our first album. And it hadn't exactly been a success. To tell the truth, no one had taken any notice of the record, and we were still completely unknown.

The category we were nominated for at the time was called Alternative. What the hell is alternative? Alternative to what? If you're alternative, doesn't that mean you're trying to be different from successful normal music? Wouldn't that also mean you have no business at a commercial event like the Echo Awards? I guess alternative probably just means bands that nobody really knows what to make of. In any case, we were excitedly informed by the record company that we had been nominated. And so we went to Hamburg.

Beforehand we had long conversations about what we should wear. We definitely wanted to all wear the same thing so that people would see we were a single entity. Since this was the first time we'd been invited, we got there on time. On time meant two hours too early.

When we walked down the red carpet, there was of course not the slightest reaction from the audience, which wasn't bad, however. The only person who recognized us was the security guard for Die Toten Hosen, who were also nominated and of course actually received an award. We attached ourselves to Nena's manager, whom we knew from the industry tour. We stood around in the lobby with him for hours and were horribly thirsty. Then the ceremony finally started and we thought it was all very exciting.

Otto Waalkes was sitting in front of us. I stared at the back of his head the whole time. I thought back to how, when I was a kid, I would go over to our neighbors' place just to watch the *Otto Show*. Every single gag got rehashed all over school the next day, and I didn't want to be left out. And now I could practically touch him. I was so excited my palms were sweating.

All the nominees were introduced with a short film. When they finally showed our film, there was absolutely no applause since of course no one knew who we were. There was only bored silence.

I think Aerosmith got the prize. We realized that we'd gotten all dressed up for nothing and felt appropriately foolish. Thankfully, though, there was a giant afterparty. We hadn't known about that either. There we could eat and drink as much as we wanted and didn't have to pay. We weren't the only ones who got exorbitantly drunk; those who were still there at four stayed till six. Moses Pelham broke Stefan Raab's nose. The next day, a bunch of zombies stood freezing on the train platform, waiting for the train with their Echos in their hands. Or not, in our case.

Then two years later, we got the award. We stood there on stage like six bumps on a log and didn't know what to say. Under no circumstances did we want to toss out an embarrassing litany of thank yous. When it was my turn at the mic, I just talked about my vacation in Sri Lanka—I'd just gotten back two days earlier and was still overflowing with impressions. Plus, while the boring ceremony was going on, Ben Becker had been teaching us that drinking vodka mixed with tonic water was very refreshing.

The trophy they handed us was I guess supposed to represent a sound wave—I mean, I don't know what an echo looks like, technically speaking— and it was pretty heavy. It was an unwieldy thing to have to hold onto at the party afterward, so I just left it sitting around somewhere.

All told, I didn't bring many of my Echos back home with me, even though for years we went to the ceremony and always ended up getting one award or another. The categories kept changing, though. At some point I guess we stopped being alternative, so we got the Echo for best video or something like that.

Sometimes they also came up with a special category for us. We never got the award for best band or best album. But in the end, that didn't matter to us at all. We just looked forward to the parties, which were always an experience. I saw the Bloodhound Gang hoisting a pair of familiar-looking underwear on the end of a broomstick and carrying it across the dance floor like a trophy. Where could they have gotten them? No idea—I think probably the bathroom.

I saw Ben Becker step onto the DJ riser to put on his new CD and then start dancing to it—by himself. The song, by the way, was ten minutes long. I saw myself hugging Campino from Die Toten Hosen. The awards show itself interested us less and less. Sometimes it really had all the charm of a company retreat in Luckenwalde. We preferred going to the Comet Awards. That was the award show the Viva channel put on.

Even better, of course, was their competitor, the MTV Awards. There, for the first and only time, we met real stars like Madonna, Robbie Williams, U2, REM, and so on. Boris Becker was there too, but I can't remember anymore why. Once Mikhail Gorbachev was even in attendance, but that was no use to me, of course, since we didn't say a word to each other. Actually, we didn't meet at all. But still, I did see him in real life. Harald Schmidt even sat at the table next to us. I didn't go and talk to him, but it wasn't easy—I would have liked to tell him that I thought his show was really good. But I assume he didn't need my opinion to know his show was good. It was a late-night show on television; with a little luck, I could catch it in my hotel room after our concerts. The young people out there won't know who I'm talking about.

We were also given an award by the teen magazine *Bravo*. Until it happened, I didn't know that *Bravo* gave out awards for bands. Our award is the Silberne Otto—the Silver Otto. It looks like a little cartoon Indian.

Some of the people who worked at *Bravo* thought we were really good, and they tried to make us appealing to teenagers. That didn't work so well, despite the fun article on us that appeared in the magazine. They even wrote a caption under a concert photo explaining that the photo showed Till flying six feet over the stage with rocket packs attached to his shoes.

If the teenagers believed this claim, they must have been disappointed when they saw us on stage in real life. There were no rocket packs. Incidentally, it was Robbie Williams who got the Golden Otto. I'd love to know if he ever found out.

In any case, I was happy to get the award, maybe in the same way that I was happy to get my fire safety badge in third grade, but these music awards are most definitely not the reason I play music.

It wasn't just the awards that made the award shows exciting. It was also that we got to perform. Strangely enough, the stress we had to deal with when we were only playing one song was much greater than at our normal concerts. I mean, we weren't a television band—we didn't have any experience with brief appearances. The stage had to be specially built, and the whole thing was meant to be broadcast live. In order to make this happen, the song had to be rehearsed several times the day before. See, the camera people had to know what to film. They would be running around on stage with us. I was really worked up the whole time. I mean, we only had three minutes to present ourselves in the best possible light, and of those three minutes I was only on screen for a few seconds. Plus we were playing with a lot of other bands, and under no circumstances did we want to embarrass ourselves in front of them. But amazingly enough, these appearances had a really broad impact. In the days after the song was broadcast, people would recognize us on the street and say hello.

—

THESE DAYS I KNOW MY way around here pretty well in Zagreb, so when I go for a walk I know where I'm going. That's not always the case. The geography of some cities is a little harder to grasp, and if I'm somewhere for the first time, I sometimes end up walking right into the industrial sector.

A friend once came to meet me in Istanbul, and we ended up in a very boring neighborhood with nothing pretty around. We wanted to see the Bosporus or the old city, and so we finally took a taxi. The taxi driver spoke neither German nor English, which is no wonder, since of course we were in Turkey. Meanwhile I unfortunately do not speak Turkish. And so we tried to explain to the taxi driver that we wanted to go to the city center. And maybe where there was a little market where we could shop for something nice.

Off the taxi went, and we were quickly on the highway. Now we saw for the first time how big the city was. From afar we saw beautiful temples, the river, and parks. We tried to point them out to let the driver know that that's where we wanted to go, but he heedlessly kept on driving. The speedometer hit eighty-five miles per hour. Things got really dangerous, but the driver did a good job weaving his way between cars. Finally, after what felt like an eternity, when the city was no longer even visible, he got off the highway and drove us into a commercial district and right up to the doors of an Ikea. The driver, putting together our requests for somewhere to shop and the city center, had come up with shopping center, and that's where he'd taken us. Before we realized where we were, he was already gone, and there was no taxi to be seen far and wide. And so we spent a nice day in the Istanbul Ikea. If I'd just walked a hundred meters in the opposite direction from the hotel, I would have found myself in the prettiest part of Istanbul. So much for my sense of direction. Luckily, today we're in Zagreb.

The hotel is right by the train station and is old and beautiful. It looks like something from an old postcard. They even have old postcards of the hotel in the lobby. I should buy one, take a pen, and write an X on my window to mark where my room is. The window looks out on the train tracks. Old diesel locomotives are parked there; their engines take a long time to warm up. I thought only steam locomotives did that. It smells like my childhood, only a bit worse.

I decide to walk out into the city. As I zoom out of the entrance to the hotel, I'm almost run over by a tram. They're blue here. In German *to be blue* can mean to be drunk. I'm not drunk, but I still wasn't paying attention. The city is bordered by a few hills. This means that I can walk through the woods on top of one hill and end up walking around half the city. I meet a lot of dog owners along the way. Sometimes I pretend like I myself have a dog and it's off frolicking through the underbrush. I keep loudly calling out a name that my dog could potentially have.

I once had to look after a dog that, stupidly enough, was named Stalin. The dog weighed about twice as much as I did and had no trouble running away from me in the woods. He wouldn't have had any trouble if he'd been smaller either, I guess. So anyway, I walked around the woods for hours, loudly yelling "Stalin," while said Stalin was actually already back at his master's house, waiting patiently outside the door. He must have hitched a ride from the parking lot or something like that. In any case, he could get around Berlin faster than I could, even though I'd taken my car and tried to hurry once I noticed the dog wasn't going to come back to me.

As a musician, it would be really difficult for me to have a pet. I'm too rarely at home. Some American bands take their dogs on tour with them, so there's always a big commotion whenever the bus door opens. It already stinks inside most bands' tour buses anyway, so that in itself isn't an obstacle. But I do just fine without a dog. I walk briskly through streets that seem very familiar to me. Many of the buildings are still unrenovated, and it smells like the old days too. That's partly because they still use coal for heating here, and also because, at least in this neighborhood, there aren't any perfumed fashion boutiques. And no teashops.

When the first teashop opened in our part of Berlin after the wall fell, the whole block smelled like vanilla or rooibos or whatever the flavor was; in any case, it made me feel ill, and I don't even know anyone who drinks this stinky tea. They probably had incense sticks there too. Like the incense they have in churches, the stick kind was probably originally supposed to disinfect places of worship so that churchgoers or Indian pilgrims or whoever didn't all contract diseases at their big gatherings and die. Given the alternative, people were happy to put up with the stench. But if this smoke is capable of killing bacteria, it can't be especially beneficial to human health. I doubt that all the people who buy incense are trying to disinfect their apartments; maybe they're just happy to be able to show other people how worldly they are because they practice old Indian customs. Or they got the incense sticks as gifts. Or they really do like the smell.

Thinking about these things helps me to distract myself from the fact that I'm so anxious. In a few hours, I'll be back on stage. Will everything go well today? It's a mystery to me why so many more things don't go wrong during our set. Whenever I think about it, I really start to worry.

Not long ago, when George W. Bush was still in office, I used to imagine that while I was out walking a helicopter would crash right in front of me with the president of the United States inside. I'd pull him out of the wreckage and save his life. He would of course be infinitely grateful. Then I'd think about what kind of policy requests I would make of him. I could list off all the things he's done that I thought were stupid, and he wouldn't be able to lock me up because I'd saved his life.

But now that I've seen *House of Cards*, I don't put it past politicians to pull any kind of dirty trick they want to. I mean, I don't think I can ever watch another movie with Kevin Spacey in it, even though I know he's only playing a part. Anyone who can so convincingly portray someone who lies, cheats, and murders probably has a dark side himself. And yet still, maybe for that very reason, actors are always so eager to play the bad guy. It's probably because they get to do or at least say things that they would never dare to otherwise.

I guess I do the same thing with the band. I put on all this makeup and act all mean, and then I'm surprised when we get called shock rockers. The band would only be truly authentic if I really were as nasty a guy as I play on stage. When I really commit to the role, it affects people's perception of me. And of course that's not what I want. But on the other hand, I think we as a band have a good approach to things. I think it's a good thing when you don't try to flatter the audience. People should come to the show because they like the music and they can get something out of the concert, and not because we tell them how great they are and that we play only for them. Nobody would believe us anyway. Even though most of the time it's actually true. We prefer to say nothing at all and instead just play our songs as well as we can. If I were in the crowd, I'd also appreciate that.

Now I realize that I'm falling into the trap again, because for listeners like me, our behavior actually does end up being a form of ingratiation. Or am I an exception as a fan? Just because I love so objectively? I like bands that don't try to get me to clap along. If I ever do want to clap along, which is rarely the case, since like I said I want to actually listen to the music—even if, as I myself now realize, this makes me sound like an old man—then I don't need anyone to tell me when to clap.

Besides that, the whole clapping along thing always reminds me a little of *Ein Kessel Buntes*. That was a variety show in East Germany, and even though, knowing me, you might not expect this, I thought it was awful. It's really not true that I think everything in East Germany was good. A lot of people just think that about me because I always speak up when I hear how East Germans are portrayed in hindsight. Like they were these gullible idiots who just dully parroted whatever the party told them. I've even been asked if we in East Germany also celebrated Christmas. Some people can't seem to imagine that Christmas can be nice even without all this consumerist terror and media insanity. That there wasn't such a high value placed on material things is, for example, one of the things I really liked about East Germany. And that friendship carried a different weight than it does now. The cultural offerings I certainly didn't like. Although, then again, actually I did. In every play, we waited excitedly for the smallest allusions. You could find us at every art opening. It made no difference what we were doing, we regularly tested the limits of tolerance—that of the audience and that of the state authorities. Even the science lectures at the Urania were always packed. And there were presentations on Janis Joplin's music at the city library, where everyone sat in reverent silence while the record was played and then there was a discussion afterward. But best of all were the actual concerts.

I can still remember the Billy Bragg concert—we soaked up every single word. Or all the other great concerts by Hard Pop, Freygang, Bayon, Die Art, DEKAdance, Ornament und Verbrechen; even Kevin Coyne, Tom Petty, and Bob Dylan played in Berlin. We felt like every song was addressed directly to us.

But this wasn't the case with *Ein Kessel Buntes*, which was kind of the flagship for state entertainment in the GDR. For starters, even the crowd looked bad. And they clapped over-enthusiastically along to everything, even the worst pop songs. The people were probably just happy that they'd managed to get tickets. It must have been really difficult; in my whole life, I have yet to meet someone who was really there. Even stars from the West made appearances.

I don't really know how you'd define a "star." My understanding was always that stars shine for the people just like the stars up in the sky. And like the actual stars high up in the sky, fans look up to them. But who knows how many people have to look up to you before you're considered a star? If I think somebody is really damn good and I look up to him, then for me he is a star and would be justified in calling himself one.

I'm starting to get hungry from all this running around. Earlier that was the whole point—I didn't run around before or after our shows because there was something I wanted to see, but because I still felt so bad from the night before or whenever else it was that I couldn't stand being cooped up indoors. So then I would just walk around near the club and try to breathe a lot and hope all that walking would get my blood flowing. Sometimes I got it flowing so well that I immediately had to go throw up behind a bush. I would set a goal for myself, say the next street corner, and I'd have to get there without throwing up. And then maybe I could smoke a cigarette. No, that was more of a long-term goal. But not unattainable, because with every step I took, I felt a little better. Amazingly, this method always worked, no matter if it was warm or cold out, if I was in a newly built suburb or a beautiful forest. It also didn't matter how much I'd had to drink or how many hours I'd slept the night before. Unfortunately with every step I also got a bit of my memory back. Then I'd start to feel all hot, and I'd walk even faster. Why the hell was I so awful when I drank? Everyone else was just fun; they did crazy things and then went to bed with a beautiful woman, but I on the other hand preferred to douse women in beer and do other embarrassing things. And then I would insult people who had done absolutely nothing to me. I was just like the annoying drunks in movies. So I would go around whining—if I didn't know myself better, I wouldn't want to have anything to do with me. I was literally trying to run away from myself. And for a while it worked, too; at least I managed for a short time not to think about the night before. And then the moment would come when I could turn around and go back and sit in the dressing room. And this was also usually the only time of day when I could eat something.

Today I'm not hungover, but I could eat something right now. I only have the courage to go to self-serve places, since there I don't have to worry about having to talk to a waiter. The implementation of the euro works very much to my advantage when it comes to food. There probably wasn't anyone happier about the euro than us bands. I can remember times when we would exchange money like madmen, and then every time we ordered a coffee we would have to spend all this time and effort calculating how much it cost. Then we would forget to exchange the money back into Deutschmarks. I still have all of it in various drawers. No one remembers anymore what all the different currencies were. Whenever we saw something nice and wanted to take it home with us as a gift for someone, or wanted it for ourselves, we couldn't buy it, because we didn't have the right currency on hand. Often we didn't have enough time in a given country. Who knew if it would be worth it to exchange money for the one hour you would spend in that city?

Then, lucky for us, the euro came. Even to really remote countries. Now I can see at first glance if something is expensive. But that's only of some use to me—with a lot of things, I generally don't know how much they cost. Who knows what a jacket is supposed to cost? And if I feel like having a coffee, I buy one, no matter if it's one euro or two. Even if it costs three euros, since the only alternative would be not to drink any coffee, which would be ridiculous if what you want is to drink some coffee. Unless, that is, you derive profound satisfaction from saving money. I know people like that. For them, it's been a good day if they've spent less than ten euros total. Some people say happiness lies in doing without. That's kind of my opinion too, but I could even do without doing without.

Not too long ago, I got a lot of joy out of buying things simply for the pleasure of owning them. Or well, not just anything—strictly speaking, I mean cheap old cars. I'm reminded of it now because I'm walking by an old Zastava. I cross the street to take a closer look. Which is completely pointless, of course, since it's not like I can figure out any specs; I'm no better informed than before. I don't even know what I should be looking for—I actually don't know anything about cars. I just see that this car looks cool. It's bright yellow. No one would paint their car such a color today. I like the color, though; it reminds me of the matchbox cars I had as a kid.

The classic cars I used to buy also looked really good, but of course cars aren't for looking at, they're for driving. And here the drawbacks to having an old car were quickly revealed. Some had no seatbelts, so the kids couldn't ride with me. In others, the heat didn't work, not even the defroster, so the windows would fog up and I wouldn't be able to see anything. The light was also really weak, and let's not even talk about the brakes. In spite of it all, though, I loved those cars.

I think people will feel the same about our band. We've been around for more than twenty years now. A lot of people found out about us through their parents—either the parents listened to us or they told their kids who we were. The music we're making now does still sound like Rammstein, but it isn't new or fashionable anymore. I don't know if today a young person could discover our music for him or herself. It's like with the cars. Successful young soccer players like Özil or whoever buy themselves a new Mercedes SLS. They wouldn't go out and get a classic car because they want the newest and the best. When Netzer had his Ferrari back in the seventies, it was also brand new. Some people, though, some people still buy classic cars. But they don't expect the car to be able to go fast. No one cares if there's any precision technology built into it. With a classic car, everything that's normally important in a car doesn't matter. You're just happy if you see a model that's still around. Is that the reason people come to our concerts now? Are we really that far gone?

I ALWAYS FEEL AN immediate affection for the cities of the former Eastern Bloc, and I walk the old streets as if my being here were the most natural thing in the world. It's not so much the buildings and the shops that remind me of my childhood as the way the people here live. Here they have these great vacant lots that just have no use whatsoever; here the parking spaces between buildings aren't paved and it's dusty as hell in the summer. The sidewalks aren't paved with those linked-together concrete blocks that are so unspeakably ugly. At night too it gets properly dark, and the people don't seem to give a shit what the neighbors think of them. And here there's no trace of this assiduous fake friendliness that so annoys me in every country I go to with a service economy. The people don't act so superior, like they do in some cities in the West. I really feel at home here. Maybe I just think that, as an old East German, I belong.

Only in Moscow was the feeling somehow different. At school, Moscow was trumpeted to us a kind of paradise. Only the most decorated functionaries were assigned posts there. If the descriptions in Russian class or in the newspaper were to be believed, GUM was simply the most amazing department store in the world. And then there was the Kremlin, too. And this unimaginable mausoleum—the name alone was so funny because it sounded like *mouse*. There was meant to be an endlessly long line outside of it because people from the whole Soviet Union—i.e., the whole world—had come to get a fortifying look at—what, exactly? I mean apparently Lenin was in there, Lenin who ranked way higher than God in our conception of things. But he had been dead for decades. I guess he was probably supposed to rise again.

To us, the Soviet Union was at least as mysterious as America. Everything was possible. We were told that the winters there were so cold that people had to leave their car engines running all night long because they wouldn't ever start up again otherwise. And that they all drove with only one headlight, to spare the lightbulbs. Naturally I expected everybody there to be walking around with a shapka—a fur hat.

But when the band went to Moscow in 2000, that's not really what we saw. It was just a big, dirty, loud city where it took you three hours to get from the airport to the center. The snow was almost black with filth, and it stank of exhaust. Having grown up in East Germany I would hardly have noticed, but by that time I had gone a bit soft. The Rossiya, supposedly the biggest hotel in Europe or even the world, had just been torn down. The streets were ripped up or completely jammed with traffic; the only cars moving were a few giant off-road vehicles that drove recklessly in the opposite lane with lights flashing. Then they would park in the middle of the sidewalk and all the grandmas would have the hardest time trying to scuttle past them. The clubs were full of girls who were trying at all costs to bag a rich husband.

The concerts were good, though, even if, here too, there were also difficulties. The organizer had sold the best seats right in front of the stage as expensive VIP tickets, which meant there was a fairly large empty section where only a smattering of people sat on big red velvet seats drinking champagne. All the fans had to stand behind them. The whole event was overseen by the army, whose treatment of the young people who'd come to see us wasn't exactly delicate. At the subway station, even before they got to the venue, anyone who couldn't produce a ticket was apparently beaten up and put back on the train. This, of course, made things difficult for the people we had promised to put on the guest list. And the ones who did make it into the building were standing so far away from us. After the first song, we stopped playing and encouraged the people to come forward, but only a few dared to. The guards looked very menacing and pushed the brave few back. I can't even remember how it all ended.

But I can remember one really good concert in Russia. This one we played outside. It was in Samara, a city on the Volga. The Lada used to be built there, a very beloved Russian car. It looks a bit like a Fiat. Shortly before the wall fell, there was also a Lada Samara, but at the time none of us knew that it was named after a city. I thought Samara was a woman. Maybe she was, too, and the city was named after her, who knows?

So anyway, in addition to the Ladas—which were also called Zhiguli, after a nearby mountain range—the Soviet rockets were also built in Samara. I mean the ones that flew to the moon, or rather into space. And a little outside the city, the owner of the Zhiguli brewery had decided to put on a rock concert. In the middle of the steppe. Or on the steppe; in any case, nothing grew there except grass. There also wasn't any fence around the festival grounds—if they'd put up a gate, it would have taken people far too long to get through it. The concert would have been over by the time they did. Entry was free, and the people came from all over. The city and the army had placed twelve thousand buses at the organizers' disposal, but most of the rock fans came on foot in a giant human flood. The closest train station was over thirty kilometers away, but that didn't bother anyone. If you were there, you were there. There was no going forward or back anymore—just an ancient helicopter that kept taking off and landing somewhere behind the stage. It had two rotors and was apparently from 1949. When we asked if we could go for a ride, everyone vehemently refused. The reason was that they needed us all to stay alive till our set that night. And so we just went and sat in the American RV that the organizers had provided to serve as our dressing room and got ready for the concert. Or we walked around a bit to take it all in. The buses the soldiers were sitting in looked like they were from World War II. When we got on stage, I couldn't even begin to see where this sea of people ended. I imagined Woodstock to have been like this. The next day we learned that 700,000 people had been there. They were all waving flags from their hometown or some other symbol to show where they came from.

The atmosphere was indescribably good. It didn't matter if everybody went in their pants because it was impossible to get to a bathroom in such a thickly packed crowd of people. It was summer, and your clothes would dry out on the way to the train station. We were able to observe this on the drive back to Samara as we crept forward at a snail's pace through the crowd of people. The next day, I excitedly wandered around on the trails amidst the new buildings. Nobody paid the least bit of attention to me. In some cities I must look like a local. I'm always being asked for directions. And if I can even help someone, then I'm proud as punch.

HERE IN ZAGREB, REALLY old grandmas stand around on the street selling honey in big Mason jars. I don't know why they're called Mason jars—maybe they used to be made of brick. A few of these must be repurposed soup jars. They still have their old labels on them. A big jar of honey costs only two euros. Now I feel guilty because that's so cheap. All the same I usually take one with me to give as a gift. In the past I've had jars break in my bag. Of course, that was my fault, not the honey's.

This time I also buy a jar, and the grandma is happy. Next to her is a grandpa; he's selling little cartons of different kinds of berries. I don't mean to sound derogatory when I say grandma and grandpa; I don't know if they have grandchildren. Maybe I'd better say an older lady and a gentleman of advanced age. But then you would imagine different people than the ones who are here selling their wares.

By our standards, the berries are a giveaway. For that price, you could hardly find someone to pick them, much less someone to lovingly grow the plants. On my walks, I'm always fascinated when I see people puttering around in their gardens. Every flower is just so. But you don't see the brunt of the work—breaking up the soil, adding fertilizer, and plucking out the weeds one by one. It's like icebergs; you only see the tip. Where do people get the energy?

I've sometimes wondered if it's all people who don't have sex anymore and have turned to such activities as a result. So long as you're still interested in sex, you don't worry about your garden. As musicians of course our performances are pure mating ritual, and we even sing about sex on top of that. Just in terms of the music alone, we're probably trying, if unconsciously, to get people sexually aroused. When I hear certain songs I feel a strange, yearning feeling that comes really close to so-called horniness. I'm not talking about any of our songs in particular; where horniness is concerned, the style of music is of secondary importance. Is it a real feeling, or is it just these stupid pheromones? Do I even have real feelings? All these studies about how hormones work are going to ruin my whole conception of love. I don't think it's because of hormones or my constant drive to reproduce that I love my wife. Although I've also read that a woman will unconsciously pick out a man with whom she can have resilient children and who can then provide for and protect those children. No talk of love there.

I nevertheless believe in love. We could also make a song about it, but none of us has hit upon the right idea yet. Including me, of course. Originally what I wanted to express in my music was more that I thought everything was shit and that I really wanted to break something. As a young man, I could get endlessly worked up about all the horseshit that goes on all over the world and how people act like it's normal. All these comfortable philistines who just care about their own small slice of well-being and their even smaller garden. And pick their little berries. But that was earlier.

I buy another carton of berries. They're moldy on the bottom, which makes me feel even sorrier for the man. Who knows how long he's been standing here with his berries? I quickly walk away; if I don't, I'll end up buying even more. I put on a really standoffish look and furrow my brow with concern so that no one will start talking to me. Like I'm going over an important problem in my head.

That's almost true—I'm worried about the concert. Or rather about myself, about messing up. I put it all on myself. It's bad. I'm my own worst enemy.

When I was young, I once tried to climb up a radio tower on the Baltic. There was a totally normal ladder that led up the side. So in and of itself it was not at all dangerous, but once I was about eighty feet up, I was overcome with the feeling that I just had to let go. In my terror, I clung to the ladder and couldn't climb up any farther. Then I started to cramp up, and it really did become dangerous, even though it's actually impossible to just fall off a ladder like that. It's the same on stage. My vague fear of the unknown is enough for me to get nervous and start to lose focus. Sometimes I even get so sick with fear that I actually feel physically sick. I guess I could also try to avoid this by thinking of something else. I do that the whole time anyway, though what ends up happening is that I just think of other unpleasant things, and then as soon as I stop thinking of them I turn right back to my fears. And so I try to actively reassure myself with realistic thoughts. If I simply do what I do every night, then nothing can go wrong.

And now I've almost gotten myself run over again. Man, that was close. My heart is beating really fast and my face feels hot. The Škoda driver yells something at me, and even though I don't understand the language, I know what he's trying to tell me.

On the other hand, now I finally feel fully awake. I look around. The hotel is right nearby, and there's still enough time for a nap. Now I have to weigh the benefits against the disadvantages. Sleep is a fine thing, and I'm always able to fall asleep quickly, but when I wake up I feel groggy, no matter if I set an alarm of if I wake up on my own. And if I know beforehand that I don't have much time, then I have more trouble falling asleep. Besides that, in this strange time between waking and sleep I start to get crazy notions. I can't pin down my thoughts, I can't follow them. It's like there's an anthill inside my head. Plus I get this feeling like I've had these thoughts a bunch of times before. Probably in one of these in-between states. Sometimes it seems to me as though there were an in-between world to which I always return just before falling asleep. That's what I imagine dementia to be like: I'm lost in a thought and I can't resurface or step back to consider the bigger picture. These notions that pop into my head are not at all related to my life. Maybe this is what it'll be like right before I die. Now I'm even less excited about the prospect. Of dementia too I'm terribly afraid. I don't know what's worse: to know that something is wrong with me or to not even realize it. I don't want to be a vegetable sitting in a hospital. If I don't know who anybody is anymore, then nobody will have much use for me either. Would I even still be me?

Man, what have I become? I used to think about how to get a woman into bed, not getting dementia and dying. It's bad—with this attitude, they really shouldn't let me make cool rock music. But if the German population is aging as rapidly as they say, then actually I fit right in. I'm already looking forward to the punk ravers at the old folks' home. Though even the word "raver" is hopelessly old-fashioned. I can understand the dilemma aging rock bands are in. It can't be easy for Mick Jagger, pushing eighty and singing "Jumpin' Jack Flash" and still having to act like he's almost bursting with horniness. It's fitting for what the song is, but not for a grandpa.

The embarrassing thing, of course, is that you don't notice when it gets embarrassing. Luckily, if you have young children, they tell you again and again how much you embarrass them. But my kids are at the age where they're embarrassed by absolutely everything I do. So I don't know if any given thing is really that bad. And by the time the kids are fifty themselves, they'll have other worries than their embarrassing parents.

When the wall fell, my father was younger than I am now. But to me he seemed unspeakably old. How will I feel when I'm as old as he is currently? At the moment I feel younger than my father seemed to me when he was this age, but will it stay that way? Is seventy the new fifty? Is eighty the old death? Oh, that's all nonsense. Even grammatically speaking.

Finally I'm back at the hotel. I look at my phone. No one has called. Of course I think it's a good thing that I'm not so media dependent and I don't have to keep staring at my phone all the time, but if nobody wants anything from me then that's also something to worry about.

I mean, I could call home. But I don't think I will right now. With all the things I've been thinking about, my voice will probably be all shaky, and I wouldn't want to start whining about things to my family back home. They have enough stress as it is. I don't want to burden them with my anxieties on top of that. My conscience is guilty enough already. One reason being the fact that I travel all over the world in a band while my family sits at home and waits for me to get back. My wife has to take care of everything all day long, and if a kid gets sick or something like that, then things get to be even more of a strain. And here I am strolling around town. It'd be ungrateful of me not to at least be excited. It would be whining of the lowest sort.

Of course I do think that touring and living the life of a musician are wonderful, I just can't quite get a handle on myself. Or rather, on all my various anxieties. And even if I were to do something different than, for example, playing music, things still wouldn't be any different for me, because of course it would still be me who was doing that other thing. Even if I were someplace completely different. It doesn't actually matter at all, not any of it— so I might as well start looking forward to the show tonight. To the comforting monotony of the preparations beforehand. To seeing my bandmates. Or my *Kollegen*, as I call them—my colleagues. I don't know who started using the term "colleague" in a band context, but I think it comes from the GDR days, when it was meant ironically. None of us wanted ever in his life to go get a normal job and have colleagues. But actually it's a nice word, because it means that we're a collective, we belong together, and for me at least that's something worth striving for. To be part of a group of people who are there for each other.

I decide to put a quick end to my walk. I also scrap the nap idea. I want to get to the concert. And the surest way is for me to head to the venue now.

—

WHEN I TRY TO REMEMBER the best moments with Rammstein, strangely enough the first things that occur to me are small episodes that have nothing to do with music.

We were once sitting on the edge of a swimming pool somewhere in the US, just lazing about and talking. It was hot and we'd all been swimming. Till tried to swim a few laps as fast as he could; it looked like a motorboat was plowing through the water, but there were too many people in the pool so he could never get much momentum going. We didn't have to play until that night and we had some free time that afternoon. When we got hungry, we put our dirty shirts back on and waited outside for our bus.

Out on the street was this great sports car with a faded, dark red, almost brown finish. We had a lot of fun taking pictures of one another doing different poses in front of this car. We'd bought several disposable cameras at a newsstand so we could take pictures while we were in America. They were these little cardboard boxes with a lens in the front and a roll of film inside. We were in such a good mood that we also ate the little unripe apples off a tree right there on the street. When we went to pick up the photos after getting them developed, the guy working at the photo lab was really taken with them—he had studied them all very closely. He was probably even allowed to do it, since to him we probably looked like we might be terrorists.

Another time, in Spain, first thing in the morning—after waking up in the bus outside the venue—we drove straight to the beach to go surfing. That is, the others wanted to surf, and I used the time to walk up and down the rocky coast. When I came back after a few hours, exhausted, they were all sitting outside a little café and drinking coffee. I sat down with them, and every now and then one of us would get up and get something else to eat or drink. We looked out at the ocean, absolutely at peace, and felt very connected to each other without doing anything.

If I'd been there without the band, all it would have been was boring. It's almost magical somehow to be on tour with a band. I feel more important than a tourist, since everywhere we go in the world I really have something to do. And I feel a bit like a kid who's got the house to himself for once. Just really uninhibited. Like there's no adult watching me and telling me what I should do. Or rather what I am allowed to do. Quite the opposite. I mean, when you're a musician they almost expect you to get into trouble. This even though musicians aren't any more exalted or crazy than people in other professions. You don't need to be especially inventive or have a huge intellect to throw stuff out of a hotel window; often all it takes is to be so drunk that you forget that the next day you'll just end up having to pay for the TV.

In any case, I've gone to places with the band that I didn't even know existed. We once flew to America to make a record. Whenever one of us was recording his parts in the studio, everyone else had the day off. And so as often as I could, I grabbed a bandmate and the rental car and went off exploring. It was really exciting. We came across mountain lakes where people were testing out the speedboats they'd built themselves. We came across abandoned farms that looked just like we'd imagined the Wild West when we were kids. At sunset we sat silent on a mountain as darkness fell. I smoked a filterless cigarette, though I had to be careful not to start a wildfire in the bone-dry terrain we were in. If a car came up the mountain, we could follow it for minutes until it reached us. Then the coyotes started howling. Before then, I could never have imagined that these animals actually existed in real life and not just in the stories I'd read as a kid—or that there were so many of them.

Making a record was always exciting for me, because wherever we went, I got to discover the place for myself. In Spain, where we recorded the album *Reise, Reise*, the landscape was even more beautiful than in America. Our house was about four miles from the coast, and when I went walking around it I wouldn't see another person all day long, just a few dogs who kept me company as I walked over the mountains. And in the South of France, I got completely lost among the cliffs. Often I wouldn't come back until nightfall. In my hands I carried giant fossils of shells and snails. They were just lying among the rocks that the rain had washed over the path. I was a little concerned about the many metal signs in the forest that I couldn't decipher and that clearly prohibited something, but they probably just said that only people with permits were allowed to hunt there. Judging by the noise, there were rather a lot of them. So I figured I'd better stick to the road and rode my bike a half hour down the mountain. I used the coaster brake so constantly that the bracket was glowing—it was that hot. That takes some doing!

Down in the valley was a little village where I would drink a little coffee outside a shop by the creek. Life couldn't have been more beautiful. Going back, I just had to push the bike up the hill. That way I worked up an appetite for dinner. It seems like to a great extent my life revolves around food. That's because, probably thanks to my thyroid, I was able to eat as much as I wanted without being punished by putting on weight. I ate ungodly amounts. Other people envied me; this was really something that not many people could do. It all just tasted so good to me.

I only need think of certain dishes, and then all the circumstances surrounding my encountering them, like place and time, come flooding back to me. From our first trips to Poland, my head is still full of the names of all the really delicious dishes we ate there, like zapiekanki, gofry, rurki, bigos, and fasolka. Meanwhile, I don't remember the names of the towns we went to. I feel like all I did the whole time was eat. Actually, I feel that about my whole life. But suddenly, out of the blue one day, I noticed that I'd gotten really fat and couldn't keep packing it in anymore. This was a shame, but as I said before, happiness lies in doing without. I think everybody tells themselves that—everybody, that is, who has to do without something.

—

By this point, there are a few fans waiting outside the hotel. Getting past fans going into the hotel isn't so bad. But when I'm leaving the hotel, they sometimes follow me all over town. I'll look back and there will be fewer and fewer fans—most of them aren't used to such long walks. Plus a lot of them turn back, figuring that in the time they would spend following me around, the other guys in the band could have come out of the hotel. And they're easier to catch, since usually they don't want to walk too far.

I stop and give people a few autographs and take pictures with them. But I can't stray too far from the hotel, or else they'll call their buddies and they'll start showing up. And then I'll still be standing here an hour later when everybody else is finished with their breakfast.

Sometimes it helps if I act like I'm on the phone, but even that doesn't stop most fans from asking for a photo. Or from just running up beside me and snapping a photo of the two of us. In the latter case, I can just keep on talking and continue my phone conversation. Or at least pretend that's what I'm doing.

Today, though, like I said, there are only a few young people outside the door. They look friendly, so I don't try and slip past them. It's a joy to experience how happy a short conversation and a few autographs can make them. Otherwise I sometimes hide behind a couple or a jogger and then hop through the door and into the hotel.

The sincere enthusiasm of our fans is another thing I could never in my life have predicted. I could never have predicted that people would tell me after a concert that this was the best day of their life or something like that. There have been ninety-year-old grandmas who wept with joy at our concerts. Others tell us that we kept them from committing suicide. Of course, we can't make too much of that, since we lack the means to compare—we don't know how many people we haven't kept from suicide. And it's hard to ask them, since they don't come to the concerts anymore. But that's not to say that everyone who has stopped coming to our concerts has necessarily committed suicide. Some people stay away for other reasons. They've simply grown up. Or our music is too aggressive for them. Apparently our music has been used to bring coma patients back to consciousness. I imagine it was probably more a matter of volume. But then again, for a lot of other people our music has become too soft. Or too poppy, whatever that means. In any case, not hard enough. But it's also difficult to come up with hard new music as a fifty-year-old half-grandpa. Maybe we're better off playing the old songs. That way people get to complain that we can't come up with anything new. I've never found the recipe for how you do it right. And so I just keep doing it and hope that no one notices.

Now I'm sitting in the shuttle, and we're stuck in traffic. When so many people try to make their way through an old city whose planners never accounted for rock concerts, things tend to take a little bit longer. I make another attempt to talk to the driver. Maybe he can tell me something interesting about the country and its people. Or he can tell me if he's ever driven anybody famous who's done something crazy.

Thankfully the air conditioning is off. The drivers can never understand that we don't share their excitement about their fancy air conditioning. Meanwhile, for American bands, it can't be cold enough. And they also need giant tubs of ice to keep their drinks in on their buses. I don't want to know how much money Americans pay for cooling. I'm happy if my apartment is halfway warm in the winter, but that's completely different.

On tour, your sense of the seasons gets a little blurry. In Spain it's so warm in late October that you can sit outside in a T-shirt and even go swimming. For the Spaniards, though, it's already winter; they've got their thick jackets on. A tour usually lasts from October through Christmas. Or at least the fall tour does. Every day I go to a different Christmas market. I've developed a technique for quickly threading my way through big crowds of people. If I don't move quickly, my feet get cold. It's true that with my athletic gait I don't get to take in much of my surroundings, but the Christmas markets are all so alike that I don't miss anything. It doesn't even matter what country I happen to be in. Even the food is the same. Definitely the music is. You might be getting the impression that I find it monotonous, but that's not true. Actually I find it soothing.

I once knew someone who celebrated Christmas all year long. All he ate was cookies and gingerbread. Every night in his apartment, the electric candles shone bright on the Christmas tree. He just liked the Christmas atmosphere. I like Christmas, too. And I love being on the go. So Christmas markets are perfect for me. Now, though, it's summer, and that's good too. It means I don't have to do as much dressing and undressing. And even if I'm just sitting around on a bus almost every day, I feel really good.

I think I feel like just about everything in my life is generally pretty super—although, thanks to Heidi Klum, I'm trying not to use the word *super* anymore. I don't even know when, or why, I watched that Top Model show. I was probably seized by a perverse fascination with idiocy. In any case, I heard the word *super* enough to last me a lifetime.

Life is pointless, the world full of suffering, and in the end everybody has to die. How come I can't ever think of something funny instead of stuff like this? What is wrong with me? It feels like I've got a tape loop of strange thoughts running inside my head. I once had an endless tape loop cassette.

It was just two minutes long, which I realize contradicts the idea of it being endless. I tried to dub a song by Bob Marley onto the cassette, but I had to make sure I stopped the recording right after two minutes so I wouldn't erase the beginning. The song was two minutes and forty seconds long. By the time I realized that, I had lost my interest in tape loop cassettes. I think that happened to a lot of people, because they stopped making them soon afterward. But I did still like the song.

When I got my first flip phone and started exploring all the different functions on it, I saw that I could download the song as my ringtone. I just had to push "Accept" twice. I did get the song as my ringtone, but every month I got hit with an absurdly high fee. I simply could not figure out how to cancel it; still today, I'm paying the fee every month. So then I decided I at least wanted to get my money's worth, and I downloaded a long, drawn-out vomiting sound. Now every time someone called me, that's what you heard. The band grew increasingly annoyed. If they had known what would come after that, they probably wouldn't have said anything. Because then I hit upon the idea of having my ringtone be the sound of a baby crying. Our producer was aghast. He asked me if it was my kid crying. It was unimaginable to him that a musician would willingly choose to hear such an annoying sound. Then I switched to neighing. That way I could always think of my horse, out in his stable in the country. Now I could at least feel like I was visiting more often.

When I got a new phone, I couldn't download any more sounds, unfortunately, but there was a ringtone that sounded like birdsong. On tour in America, I kept pulling my phone out because I thought it was ringing. There was a kind of bird that lived there whose call sounded just like my cell phone. I changed my ringtone, but the chirping was stuck in my head, and I still jump every time I hear a bird. And now the thought of it is stuck in my head and I can't get it out.

Why am I doing all of this anyway?

"If you'd paid attention in school, you wouldn't be in this mess," as Till likes to say in these situations. But of course that's not true—first of all, I did pay attention in school, and I always got good grades, too, until I told them I didn't want to go into the army; and second of all, I like being here. I wouldn't call it a mess at all. Plus I don't have to work. That was my express goal when I was a kid. And not just mine—half my class, just the boys of course, when asked what career we would choose, gave "paid vacationer" as our answer.

Well, I didn't really say that—I didn't have the nerve—but that's exactly what I've become.

As a result, I have a lot of time to make music. I can even live off music. Doubtless I could also live without music. I've read interviews in which artists claim they just couldn't do without their art. They just have to express themselves all the time. It sounds a bit gross. I mean, there are some people who think they can't live without their phone. Take it away, though, and somehow they manage. But that's not what I was trying to get at. Shouldn't I be reflecting on why I always wanted to make music? Did I even want to? And why, actually?

Sometimes I think it's like riding a bike. As a kid, I never thought for a second about whether I wanted to learn how or not—I just jumped on my brother's bike the first chance I got.

"Pedal, just keep pedaling and don't stop!" the neighbor yelled after me, leaning over the garden fence. Those were the only words he ever said to me before he hanged himself, but they were very helpful. Just don't stop. I was so happy about my newly acquired skill that I completely stopped thinking about the strain and the false starts.

Before learning to ride a bike, I pushed my cousin's tricycle with great effort up the hill in my grandma's garden, and whenever I think about it—those few triumphant seconds of zooming down the hill—it's still so present in my mind that it's like it just happened. I don't think I've ever felt such an adrenaline rush since then. Does every person have a need somewhere within them to simply let go for a second and lose control of themselves? Why else would there be so many roller coasters? But of course I wasn't even trying to lose control—the pedals knocked my feet away, and there was nothing I could do except fall over.

A short time later, all I wanted was to learn to play piano. It took a bit longer for me to start to have success, but it was all the more amazing when I was actually able to play my first pieces. It would have been stupid of me to have stopped then. And so I just kept playing. Only in my imagination did I play in front of other people; in reality, I was much too shy.

I can't remember if, when I was a kid, I ever thought of trying to impress someone with my playing. I definitely wasn't thinking about girls at that age, especially since the few girls I knew—because they lived in the same building or went to school with my brother—weren't interested in music or musicians.

More like Barbies and horses. You can see right there how little I know about girls, since there weren't any Barbies in the East; I myself never knew about them till I was twenty-five years old, and the only horses I saw were the ones hauling bulk garbage down the street. These horses weren't suited for riding, and they definitely weren't suited to serve as the inspiration for little girls' dreams. Meanwhile the girls hung around in a little group on the sidewalk and played jump rope. I, on the other hand, sat with my parents in the living room, listening to the radio and taking note of the new, very intense feeling that music gave me. This of course isn't sufficient cause to become a musician. I could also have spent my whole life listening to strange music. One life isn't enough to hear all the good songs even once. One of my friends was renowned for always taping the best music off the radio and being really in the know, and among us he enjoyed a reputation just as lofty as the musicians themselves.

When I sometimes claim that I just want to make music for music's sake, my bandmates laugh at me. Their thinking is that nobody gets up on stage if he doesn't want to be seen and admired. It's not so important to me that I be seen, more that a few people think I'm good. But in order to think that, they have to notice me first. And so I get up on stage, and I'm also happy if our records are on the shelf at Saturn or wherever. Who wouldn't feel that way? Who doesn't want to be loved? Isn't that the root of all endeavor? Why else would anyone toil away trying to come up with something cool? Just so they alone could see how great they are?

No, or rather yes—I probably make music because I want to be loved. I can love other people or animals just as well on my own. But being loved is hard to do by yourself. You really need other people to do it. Which means you actually need other people. And I guess I want to reach those other people with music. But as I have learned over many years, the music that I make doesn't always help me in that regard. It tends to make it more difficult, since it's so aggressive that the listeners don't immediately think of love; instead, they give vent to all their stored-up hatred.

Musicians in and of themselves aren't necessarily lovable either. They're often complicated, egotistical, and unreliable beings who aren't capable of intelligibly expressing themselves, and thus escape into music.

All the same, I became a musician in the same way that I was born a boy—it was inevitable; there was no choice on my part. I think that's good. All the time, no matter if I'm playing music right then or not. That I'm now actually playing in a real band is, for me, and probably for other people who know me, hard to imagine.

We fly in an airplane to all our concerts and everyone acts as though it were normal. But really, even flying itself isn't normal for people. We sell actual tickets and a whole lot of actual people come to these giant arenas to see us. I can't believe it. Nor can I say when or how it came to be—I couldn't believe it in the mid-eighties, when Feeling B opened for Freygang in the small-town auditoriums of East Germany and got to play in front of three hundred drunken blues fans. The time we drove together as a band in a salvaged Barkas van to a concert at Die Scheune in Dresden, I thought that life just couldn't get any better. And the first time we were played on the radio, I couldn't sleep for days afterward. That's how excited I was. And it was just a few seconds during the program's closing remarks.

It's still a wonderful feeling for me, since we basically never get played on the radio. It always takes a while before I recognize the song, because I listen to the radio with different ears. I'm listening on my own time and am not expecting to hear any of our music. But to hear our band mentioned in conversation, or to see a car with our bumper sticker on it almost every day—I mean, it's just about every day that I'm driving outside of Berlin—is no longer particularly unusual. And I haven't done anything to help us get to this point—in fact, it's quite the opposite.

If it had been up to me back then, I wouldn't be sitting on this bus right now. Not because I wouldn't have wanted it, but because I lacked the imagination to envision all the things we could do. I would have tried to keep my old band together for as long as possible. I would have stuck with our first manager, who refused to speak English, and under his management would only have played in East Germany. I would definitely not have gone with the band to America, since my experiences there with Feeling B weren't so encouraging and I start to panic when I can no longer see the Berlin TV Tower. I probably also would have signed with the first record company that ever condescended to listen to our tape.

When I was ten years old, I bought my first record. It was in a small town in Thuringia that we passed through by chance when my grandma took me and my brother on vacation. Polish vendors were there selling rock 'n' roll records of Polish bands playing songs by Chuck Berry. I didn't know who Chuck Berry was, I also didn't know that rock 'n' roll wasn't normally associated with Poland, but it was clear to me that rock music would contain an important message for me. On the cover was a picture of a leather jacket, which I guess was what a rocker was meant to wear. The zipper was crooked. I had never seen anything like it. I would have liked to have a jacket like that myself. The face of the person wearing the jacket wasn't in the frame. That was how the Poles got around any copyright difficulties from using the image. When I listened to the songs, I couldn't tell they were being played by Polish musicians. I just thought they were good. There was also a piano on some of the songs. At least I thought I could hear one when we listened to the record at night. *That's what I want to be*, I told my grandma. *The piano player in a band.* Even back then I didn't want to be a singer and have to bear that responsibility. Just to sit in the back and play piano. It's like the Olympics. Being there is everything.

We've now arrived at the venue. At the gate, our security guy comes to meet me and takes me to our dressing room. I could have found the way myself, since they've got signs taped to all the walls here too. On the table there's a bowl of nuts. The tablecloth is clean.

I wonder whether I've traveled back in time to yesterday. Again I grab a handful of nuts without thinking and take in the room. It all looks nice and cozy. A mild scent of decay wafts over from the dresser. I feel like I've arrived.

Where might my bandmates be? I look in their dressing rooms. Nobody there. Then I see a technician I've known for a long time coming down the hallway. We grin at each other even though nothing funny has happened. We're just stupidly happy at how far we've come since the early days. And we both know that it definitely has nothing to do with whatever talents I possess. He goes on tour with other bands when we're not playing, but I couldn't do that. What would I do? I'm happy just to have my band.

He asks me, "You know what's really rough? When you're bleeding all over the place and you don't know where the blood's coming from or why you're bleeding." He tells me that earlier he sat down on a plastic bottle full of fake blood without realizing. Later, when he touched his pants, he was completely shocked since he didn't feel any pain.

I ask him if he's seen any of my bandmates. He says they all just went to yoga.

There aren't many things that I associate less with our music than yoga. Not that I have anything against yoga. I myself am stiff as a board, totally inflexible—and I breathe wrong. I eat the wrong things and I digest wrong. I drink too much sometimes, and sometimes too little. Most of the day I sit in a chair, which apparently is pretty much the worst thing I could do for my back. Even the doctor keeps telling me that at least once a day I should do the Sun Salute—not to be confused with the Hitler Salute. How come I never manage to do it?

Some people who do a lot of yoga make such a fuss about it. Unprompted, I hear about asanas and chakras; I get an overdose of -*a*'s and completely forget that it's just a couple of back exercises. When people get to be such missionaries about something, I don't want any part of it. Things that are good don't need to be advertised. All that aside, I can't be sure if the band is actually going to yoga for health reasons or on account of the well-built yoga teacher. So now I don't feel so guilty for not doing more for my body.

I could, of course, do something healthy that has nothing to do with yoga. Sadly, though, I don't. Quite the opposite. I think I'm trying to ruin my body on purpose, given how I act and what I eat. Although nuts are good. But I mean, I also eat pork. Which sounds bad, I know, but frikadeller made from beef just don't taste as good to me. I've tried them. And pork knuckle is pork knuckle. It's an aspect of our culture, in a way; it's part of our identity.

Once when I was in Egypt and explained that I was from Germany, the people got excited and yelled things after me like *Beckenbauer* and *sauerkraut*. Pork knuckle fits in there as well. But it's not just food. Playing music is anything but healthy. Noise is almost the leading cause of heart attacks. And then there's all the excitement. I don't remember the last time I got to bed before midnight. They also say that on planes you're exposed to radiation because you're so close to the sun. And given the lower amount of pressure in the atmosphere, your brain expands and hits the wall of your skull. At least that's what it feels like to me. But the worst thing is the alcohol.

"Do you remember the slammer?" I ask the technician. Apparently he can, because he winces.

"Five bottles of tequila at the bc-Club," he answers. The bc-Club was a club for students at Ilmenau University and was deep in the basement of a new building. I also have to mention that shortly after reunification, the only kind of tequila available in Thuringia was Sierra Tequila, and it really wasn't fit for drinking. But to do a slammer you need tequila.

"The bc-Club was a real pain—it had those narrow doors," says the technician. He sees all the clubs from a different perspective than us musicians; he naturally places greater importance on being able to get things in and out easily. No question he has a list in his head of all the clubs with long or especially narrow staircases.

From this standpoint, the worst spot in East Berlin was the OKK Club. I don't know what OKK stood for; I don't think I ever knew. Maybe it had something to do with the Oktoberclub, though I don't know what that referred to either. The club was above the Kino International movie theater on Karl-Marx-Allee, assuming the street is still called that. Four flights of stairs up. For architectural reasons, there wasn't a single window, and lots of narrow, winding hallways. Naturally, smoking was allowed everywhere, so you couldn't see more than five feet in front of you. And this was a club we really liked to play, because the atmosphere was so heated, and not just temperature-wise. At one concert, I got the idea to not stand up on stage but rather with the technicians at the mixing board. This way I could finally see the band. Without me, of course. It was really strange because it seemed like I simply wasn't in the band anymore. It wasn't just me who felt this way, but the crowd too; no one noticed that I hadn't stopped playing, no one guessed that I was standing by the wall behind everybody. My new spot was right next to the sound guy, so I could watch what he did all throughout the concert. He was busier than I was. And I believe that's still the case.

In any case, the technicians start working a few hours before we do. Some of them use the time between doors and when the show starts for a little nap. And after the concert there's time for a beer or two.

When we all still rode in the same bus, we would stay up so late drinking together that we'd see it start to get light out again. "Smells like busted liver," one of the technicians said once when the bus pulled over so we could pee in the bushes. I can still smell it.

Once I tried to imagine the sum total of all the drinks I'd ever drunk and I saw before my eyes several tanker trucks full of alcohol. I started to feel really sick. And that I'm now whining about it is even worse—I mean, I didn't have to drink it all. Self-pity is the worst!

That's why I don't want to start complaining about sitting in this ugly dressing room, in the so-called backstage area. I'm even getting paid for it. Who wouldn't want to trade places with me?

But when I really think about it—and of course I think about it—it occurs to me that this area is only interesting for the people who don't work here. In America, the backstage area is considered a kind of paradise. *No ass, no pass*, as the old rockers say. They're only talking about women, of course. Men have no business here no matter what, unless they're in the band or the crew. For people like us, though, there's nothing mysterious about these rooms. Whereas for others they might be the object of all their dreams. Is it something to do with sex again? Do I even still have dreams?

In my case, I guess they've all come true. Though most of them I never dreamed in the first place. No more than I ever thought of going to the moon. I'm sure a rocket would take me there. There's always something happening that I never expected. I never used to think that one day I'd become a real family man. I definitely didn't plan on it. I'm surprised I even grew up in the first place. I mean, it's unbelievable! And I didn't have to do anything other than wait and maybe survive. Now people even say "Sir" and "Mister" to me. Except for the cashiers in the East. Recently one of them addressed me as *young lady*. That's when I finally went and got my long hair cut. I immediately looked much younger. Ha, now I just have to laugh. And I can't stop, now that I see myself here, a so-called adult sitting in an athletes' dressing room deep underground in Zagreb.

The door opens and Tom sticks his head in. He sees me sitting on the couch, laughing. Humming contentedly, he turns and leaves.